REACHING THE UNSEEN CHILDREN

C000162108

Reaching the Unseen Children p｜   ｜rce for schools working to close the ａ   ...ｕｉsauvantaged pupils, with particular emphasis on white children from low-income backgrounds.

This group – especially boys – consistently on average underperform in the education system, and the effects of COVID-19 will only have widened the gap. Drawing on her long experience of working with disadvantaged and left-behind communities, Jean Gross describes the path that many children take, from early language delays to persistent literacy and numeracy difficulties, which lead to progressive disengagement from learning. She argues that progress will only be made through early intervention and building pupils' sense of capability, and sets out low-cost, low-effort ways in which teachers can transform outcomes for their students – through the everyday language they use, the expectations they convey, and the relationships they build with pupils and their parents.

Providing practical, evidence-based strategies and case studies of schools with outstanding practice, this is an essential guide for anyone working in education who is seeking equity for all their pupils.

Jean Gross, CBE, is a best-selling author and expert on children's issues. Formerly the government's Communication Champion for children, she has led many national initiatives to improve life chances for those who struggle to succeed in our education system. Her previous books published with Routledge include *Time to Talk* (2018) and *Beating Bureaucracy in Special Educational Needs* (2015).

'An extraordinary book. It makes those "Unseen Children" visible to us all with incisive arguments, an array of evidence, along with compelling personal stories. It offers anyone with an interest in education a comprehensive account of the challenges faced by so many children in our education system. And yet, it manages to remain hopeful and practical. It is both a call to arms and a helping hand to everyone in education who wants to address the disadvantage gap and make "Unseen Children" seen, heard and supported to thrive.'

– **Alex Quigley,** *the Education Endowment Foundation, and author of* Closing the Reading Gap

REACHING THE UNSEEN CHILDREN

Practical Strategies for Closing Stubborn Attainment Gaps in Disadvantaged Groups

Jean Gross

Routledge
Taylor & Francis Group

LONDON AND NEW YORK

First published 2022
by Routledge
2 Park Square, Milton Park, Abingdon, Oxon OX14 4RN

and by Routledge
605 Third Avenue, New York, NY 10158

Routledge is an imprint of the Taylor & Francis Group, an informa business

British Library Cataloguing-in-Publication Data
A catalogue record for this book is available from the British Library

Library of Congress Cataloging-in-Publication Data
Names: Gross, Jean, author.
Title: Reaching the unseen children : practical strategies for closing stubborn attainment gaps in disadvantaged groups / Jean Gross.
Description: Abingdon, Oxon ; New York, NY : Routledge, 2022. |
    Includes bibliographical references and index.
Identifiers: LCCN 2021020199 | ISBN 9781032009315 (hardback) |
    ISBN 9781032009322 (paperback) | ISBN 9781003176442 (ebook)
Subjects: LCSH: Children with social disabilities–Education. | Poor children,
    White–Education. | Educational equalization. | Academic achievement.
Classification: LCC LC4065 .G76 2022 | DDC 371.826/94–dc23
LC record available at https://lccn.loc.gov/2021020199

ISBN: 9781032009315 (hbk)
ISBN: 9781032009322 (pbk)
ISBN: 9781003176442 (ebk)

DOI: 10.4324/9781003176442

Typeset in Interstate
by Apex CoVantage, LLC

Access the Support Material: www.routledge.com/9781032009322

CONTENTS

TABLES

FIGURES

ACKNOWLEDGEMENTS

I am grateful to the headteachers and leaders who gave their time to speak to me about their good practice for this book: Broken Cross Primary, St Mary's C of E Primary, Haytor View Primary, Scalby School, Great Torrington School and St Ives School.

My sincere thanks go to Alex Quigley, Marc Rowland, Megan Dixon and Di Hatchett for their very helpful advice.

I am also grateful to Kerry Clegg and Catherine Worton for their descriptions of work in North Tyneside, to Sharon Gray OBE for sharing the inspirational work she led at Netherfield Primary, to Daniel Sobel for permission to draw on his stories of inclusion and to Ben Pollard for allowing me to quote from his writing.

The poem 'Cos I Ain't Got a Pencil' on page 165 is reproduced with kind permission from Josh Dickerson, the author.

I am grateful to Widgit Symbols for permission to reproduce the symbols on page 95.

Figure 5.1, Scarborough's 'Reading Rope,' is reproduced with permission from Guilford Publications.

Excerpts from Ian Gilbert (2018), *The Working Class: Poverty, Education and Alternative Voices* (Carmarthen: Independent Thinking Press) on pages 33, 146, 147 and 214 are used with kind permission from Crown Publishing Ltd.

An extract from 'Teaching children how to use language to solve maths problems' (2006), by Neil Mercer and Claire Sams, *Language and Education*, 20:6, pp. 22-23 is reproduced on page 113, with kind permission from Routledge.

Quotes from Ofsted and parliamentary publications used in this book have been approved under an Open Government License.

Introduction

This is a book about closing the attainment gap for socio-economically dis-advantaged children – boys, girls, children from all ethnic backgrounds. The model it presents and the strategies it suggests will be relevant for all those groups. Nevertheless, the book often focuses on one group in particular: those who have been called 'the unseen children' – white boys eligible for free school meals.

These children became the subject of a media furore at the end of 2019, when two leading private schools rejected a philanthropist's offer of scholar-ships for poor white boys, on the grounds that it was discriminatory. But the issue is not new for those who work in and with schools in the state sector. As long ago as 2008, Ofsted flagged this group as persistently underachiev-ing and published a survey report (Ofsted, 2008) that highlighted common features in schools that had been successful in improving the educational experiences and achievements of white boys from low income backgrounds. There was another Ofsted report in 2013 on the same theme five years later (Ofsted, 2013). The parliamentary Education Committee published a report on the issue in 2014 and in 2021; the latter titled as 'The forgotten: how White working-class pupils have been let down, and how to change it' (House of Commons Education Committee, 2021).

Is it in fact discriminatory to analyse the specific attainment issues for disadvantaged white boys and suggest ways of closing the gap between them and their peers? I would argue that it is more discriminatory to ignore the problem. This book makes no judgements about these boys. It makes no assumptions about their underlying abilities. It is based on hard data, but recognises that the data represent overall averages. Not all white boys who live in families experiencing poverty do poorly in our education system, and we have as much to learn from those who do well against the odds as we have from those who struggle and fail.

DOI: 10.4324/9781003176442-1

Writing about one group does not mean that other underachieving pupils from different ethnic groups – for example some pupils from black and minority ethnic (BAME) backgrounds, or disadvantaged white girls – are not also important. Every underachieving child matters and it is the aim that many of the strategies suggested in the book will be useful across the board.

Focusing on one group who fare particularly poorly when at school does not mean we should not focus on issues that affect other groups once they leave school. It matters that women are hugely under-represented in top jobs, and that the gender pay gap has hardly narrowed since 2012. It matters that just over one in 20 chief executives of FTSE 100 companies are women, and none are women of colour.

We should be outraged by the fact that students from BAME backgrounds are much less likely than white pupils to gain a place at a Russell Group university, and less likely to leave university with a first or upper second class degree. We must never forget figures showing that Black Caribbean children are more than twice as likely to be permanently excluded than the school population as a whole, or that Black people were in 2018 twice as likely to be unemployed as white people. Nor should we forget that Asian offenders of all ages are much more likely to be given a custodial sentence than other ethnic groups, or that people from some BAME backgrounds were many times more likely to die in the COVID-19 pandemic than those from white backgrounds. It is completely unacceptable that for every £1 that white households in this country have in wealth, Black Caribbean households have 20p, and Black African and Bangladeshi households just 10p.

All of these issues matter, but we should not lump them together. Each is wrong. Each needs its own forensic analysis to establish causes and remedies.

We can and should apply that forensic analysis to understand the issues facing disadvantaged white boys at school. Yet efforts to address their underachievement by differentially allocating scholarships to a top school were not seen as appropriate by a section of the media. Could it be that establishments weighted towards white people are embarrassed to be seen promoting better lives for people of their own colour?

Or could it be that middle class commentators do not want to be seen to be looking down on the working class? The whole issue of class is contentious. I am sure this book will be criticised as 'classist'. But it is not a book about class, nor a sociological study. That does not mean that class does not matter, or that sociological perspectives are not important. They are. But this is unashamedly a book written by an educationalist. It is largely about what happens in classrooms.

Nor is this book directly about issues of curriculum relevance, vocational versus traditional 'academic' qualifications, or what happens to pupils when they leave school and enter the jobs market. These too are very important, but not within the scope of a book that deliberately focuses on factors that stop many children ever getting to the starting gate of access to qualifications.

Finally, the book does not pretend that tackling wider societal issues is not important in closing the disadvantage gap. Poverty of itself damages lives and leads to underachievement. There are many things that poor children need and often do not have in our society, whatever their ethnicity. They need shoes, a washing machine that works, a table to do homework on, the bus fare to travel beyond the estate where they live to see the wider world. Unless we address poverty directly, we will never wholly close the gap. These issues are difficult for schools to address, however, although many – including the ones described in this book for their outstanding work with parents – try very hard. But the author has chosen to focus on the issues schools can more easily address themselves, and makes no apology for that.

A note on terminology

Where I use the term 'disadvantage' in this book I am referring to socio-economic disadvantage. The focus is on underachieving disadvantaged children, but for brevity I have often left out the 'underachieving'. Many disadvantaged pupils of course do well academically. Similarly, for brevity I have used 'parent' as a shorthand for the wider group of adults who may care for and about a child.

1 We need to talk about Jason

I first met Jason when I was a young educational psychologist. He was referred because he was six and showing no signs of learning to read. Jason's small village school, which sat in the shadow of a spoil heap, served a former mining area on the Somerset coalfields.

Jason's parents, both out of work, were suspicious of school but were persuaded to meet me. They were not sure why he was struggling but did tell me he was very late talking. I also learned that Jason's dad had not learned to read when he was at school.

Jason had started school full of excitement, like most four-year-olds. All had gone reasonably well in Reception, though he didn't always do as he was told and found it hard to share. When I met him at the end of Year 1, however, he had begun to notice that other children could read and he couldn't. He sat next to a little girl with neat handwriting and could see the difference between her work and his big messy writing, with lots of rubbings-out and torn pages.

When I talked to Jason I was struck by his limited vocabulary and lack of life experience. He had never been to the seaside, nor even played in a park. His horizons stretched not much further than the small council estate where he lived, the village shop and the school.

I gave the school some advice about how to teach him phonics and went away. He was placed in a small group made up of other children the teacher described as 'low ability', and had help in class from a teaching assistant (TA) allocated to the group.

A year later he had made little progress in literacy and was now well behind in maths. When the teacher asked a question, he was still

DOI: 10.4324/9781003176442-2

struggling to process it while other children had their hands up. Again, he noticed that he wasn't doing well. I felt that by now he had concluded that trying hard didn't help – nothing he did seemed to make a difference.

At some point in KS2 the school referred him again, in the hope of obtaining what was then called a Statement of Special Educational Needs. He still couldn't read. By now he had begun to have friendship and behaviour problems, increasing as he moved into Y6. He had a few fixed term exclusions, but his very caring school managed him well and generally contained his behaviour.

I next caught up with him in secondary school. He had a Statement by now, for TA support in lessons. It made little difference. He still struggled with reading and at this point had begun to truant. When he was in school he often got into fights. He was permanently excluded while we were reviewing his Statement to try to get him into a special school. After months out of education he went to a very good Pupil Referral Unit. But it was too late for him to catch up academically and he left with no qualifications.

The saddest thing was not just that he now had almost no chance of getting a job and a high probability of getting into crime, but that if he followed a pattern I had seen many times in his community he would before long get into serial relationships, and in all likelihood have several children who would follow a similar path when they went to school. The cycle of disadvantage would repeat itself.

Jason's story is one of waste. His failure is also my failure, and his story is in a sense my story too. Later in my career, motivated by what I saw happen to Jason, and to so many boys who lived on the huge council estates of South Bristol – another area of high unemployment, where people used to work in the tobacco factories that have now closed, and hope is in short supply – I searched out the best evidence about what worked in tackling early reading failure and early social and emotional needs. As Head of Children's Services I was able to access funds from the Council's sale of its airport to introduce Reading Recovery to the city, along with the Incredible Years parenting programme, family learning on early language devised by speech and language therapists, and a universal social and emotional learning curriculum. I saw schools making a real difference as a result of these initiatives; I became even more convinced that we need not have failed Jason and others like him. It is these experiences that have led me to write this book.

Jason is just one child. There is of course no one stereotypical disadvantaged white boy, nor one life history. Every child is different, and labels can be dangerous and lead to self-fulfilling prophesies. Nevertheless, there are aspects of Jason's story that I met repeatedly in the children I worked with. We can learn, I think, from these commonalities.

The barriers to learning that these children shared were:

- Limited oral language skills
- A sense of powerlessness
- Difficulties in regulating emotions
- Early educational failure, particularly in reading, leading to low academic self-concept, disengagement from learning, truancy and exclusion

In the chapters that follow I will explore each of these barriers and the strategies we can use to overcome them. But as a school you will need to consider each individual child in turn, and ask 'Is *this* a barrier for *this* child?' And if so, what can we do about it? The generalities I present are no substitute for knowing each child and understanding their unique needs. Those needs should be assessed in partnership with the child and their family, with evidence gathered through diagnostic assessment, conversations with the pupil and their parents, information from teachers and a deep understanding of the community. And in all cases we should be looking for strengths as well the challenges faced by the child and their family.

We also may need to reflect on whether, with the best of intentions, we might be falling into the same bear traps I saw in Jason's case:

- Over-supporting children in class, inadvertently reducing their sense of capability and independence
- Further reducing their sense of control by using only external reward systems to manage behaviour, rather than teaching them strategies to self-regulate
- Identifying them as having special educational needs, and in so doing placing them outside their teachers' perceived spheres of responsibility and control

Who are the underachieving children?

Jason was not alone in his struggles at school. As we will see in Chapter 2, white boys eligible for free school meals tend to perform poorly in the Early Years Foundation Stage Profile at age five, in the phonics check at six, in KS2 SATs and in GCSEs – with attainment well behind that of all other ethnic groups except for the very much smaller group of pupils of Gypsy Roma and Traveller heritage.

Only pupils of White Irish, Gypsy Roma and Traveller heritage make less progress over their years in secondary school than do disadvantaged white boys. These boys make up a high proportion of the 'forgotten third' (Blatchford, 2020): the pupils who reach the age of 16 without any meaningful qualifications. The gap for them starts early – in spoken language, as early as 18 months – and widens over time.

The challenges faced by boys

A question posed by the data is why boys seem particularly vulnerable to the effects of disadvantage. It is not that disadvantaged white girls do not also underachieve; as a group, they do. But the extent of their underachievement is less.

The reason may be that being born female is a protective factor against many of life's early vicissitudes. Girls, whether rich or poor, are simply less vulnerable to all sorts of developmental difficulties than boys, and particularly those that impact on school achievement.

Boys are:

- At higher risk than girls of prematurity, birth complications and perinatal brain damage (Kraemer, 2000).
- More affected by maternal pre- and post-natal depression and anxiety than girls, the effect extending into nursery school years, long after the depression has lifted (Sinclair and Murray, 1998; Braithwaite *et al.*, 2020). One of the most notable effects is inattentiveness and hyperactivity, especially in boys from disadvantaged backgrounds.
- At greater risk of a whole range of developmental disorders in childhood, including specific reading delay, hyperactivity, clumsiness and articulation problems (Kraemer, 2000).
- More likely than girls to show disadvantage-linked weaknesses in 'executive functions' such as concentration, working memory and self-control (Ellefson *et al.*, 2020).

The gender differences in language and literacy are particularly striking. Boys make up more than 70% of late talkers and just 30% of early talkers (Adani and Cepanec, 2019). At five they are nearly twice as likely as girls to be behind in early language and communication (Moss and Washbrook, 2016), and the differences in verbal performance persist right through the school years (Etchell *et al.*, 2018).

Boys are more likely than girls to experience reading difficulties – overall around 1.83 times more likely than females, but with the ratio varying according to the age of the pupils and the type of reading skill assessed (Wheldall and Limbrick, 2010; Quinn and Wagner, 2013). The gender imbalance is particularly pronounced amongst children with the most severe reading difficulty (Hawke *et al.*, 2007).

Even if they succeed in learning to read, boys are less likely to read for pleasure than girls, and this compounds their relative educational disadvantage (National Literacy Trust, 2020).

Finally, boys are later than girls to develop the fine motor skills they need for handwriting (Kokštejn *et al.*, 2017), and this can have lasting effects on their willingness to put pen to paper.

Starting early

Another question posed by Jason's story, and that of others like him, is whether we have tended to pitch interventions to close the disadvantage gap too late in pupils' school careers. Whilst giving glancing acknowledgement to the importance of early years, commentators almost uniformly give most airtime to events and experiences in pupils' secondary years and the transition to post-16 education or employment. The 2014 House of Commons report on disadvantaged white pupils, for example, devotes just 182 words to its early years section, compared to 652 for vocational education and work-related learning.

Disengagement from learning, disaffection and truancy are what observers, researchers and teachers often see in disadvantaged white boys of secondary age. This can lead to an assumption that these are the prime causes of low attainment for this group of pupils. Jason's story, however, suggests a model in which disaffection is a consequence of much earlier events.

Perhaps because they remember their secondary years rather better than what went before, policy makers often fail to recognise this. There is remarkably little recognition of the statistics which show how hard it is to enable disadvantaged pupils to catch up once they reach secondary school. In 2019, only 1.9% of pupils with low prior attainment at the end of KS2 (below the former Level 4 age-related expectation) achieved a strong pass in English and maths results at GCSE (DfE, 2020).

But even the later years of primary school can be too late to intervene. The die may be cast much earlier. Fewer than one in six children from low-income families who have fallen behind by the age of seven will go on to achieve five good GCSEs, including English and maths (Save the Children, 2013). If we really want to close the gap, we need to start before the end of KS1.

The very earliest years, before children are four or indeed two, are of course where we should be putting the greatest effort and investment, as any primary headteacher will tell you. But that's another book, not this one. This one is about what schools can do, given the disparities that already exist in their intake. It suggests we need to base our strategies on an understanding of the trail of early oral language gaps leading to severe early reading difficulties (and to a lesser extent maths difficulties) which progressively deny the child access to learning, and increasingly lead to disaffection – particularly in the secondary years, when to be unable to read is to be unable to participate.

This argument implies that we should weight our efforts to close some disadvantage gaps towards children under seven. This is not impossible, but it does mean looking differently at budgets, capitalising on the trend towards all-through schools and multi-academy trusts that span both primary and secondary schools, to devise innovative plans that respond to evidence and children's needs, rather than arbitrary divisions based on historical structures.

Communities

Finally, when we consider the lessons from Jason's story we need to think about his community. He grew up in a former mining area where the pits have long closed. It is similar to other communities where a dominant industry has died out, whether it be the shipyard or the factory. Experts write about the poor attainment of white working class children, but in many areas where unemployment is high, the working class has become the non-working class. At best, people who live in these areas are often only able to find zero hours contracts without status or certainty. There is no security and no steady money. Disadvantage is passed from one generation to another, and individuals feel stuck.

What this does to communities, I think, is to take away a collective sense of self-efficacy – the belief that people there can exercise choice and control. The adults can become undemanding, as noted by David Miliband, former MP for South Shields, who found it worrying that his constituents spent so little time letter-writing and complaining: 'they took what they were given, even if it wasn't much' (quoted in Aaronovitch, 2020, p. 28).

Another loss in communities like these has been a strong sense of identity and culture. Journalist Sean Coughlan (2014) has described this well, noting that the institutions which once supported vibrant white working class communities (trade unions, social clubs, churches) have been marginalised, while 'local high streets are filled with pay-day lenders, pawnshops and poundshops.'

Differences in the strength of cultural identity for different ethnic groups have been observed by researchers. In one study (Demie and Lewis, 2010), a headteacher commented that

> 'In the Caribbean community there is an ethos of hard work, with Church and music providing a strong focal point for families. Whereas the white British probably have nothing but the pub . . . there is no pride in the white community, no strong sense of a cultural identity.'

Former industrial areas are not the only 'hotspots' for low attainment amongst white disadvantaged children. Remote rural and coastal areas are also affected, perhaps again because of a lack of perceived choices and sense of agency. Young people who grow up there more often expect to stay than those who live in cities. Researchers (King and Welch, 2012) found that of the teenagers they interviewed, those from urban areas were much more likely to picture their future as somewhere out of their current environment than those from more rural or coastal areas. Similarly, while those from the urban centres who had expressed a desire to aim for a particular career were willing to travel to fulfil their ambition, those from the more rural/coastal areas were not.

Demie and Lewis report similar issues in the schools they studied:

Twenty years ago half the school population was white British – now most of them have disappeared. Many have moved out to Kent or Essex or Croydon. Twenty years ago there was also a culture of someone bringing in some money. Those that are left in the area have no social mobility and no way of getting out. Many of them were born and brought up in the immediate area. Other groups change and move on and out. This group is stuck.

Member of staff in a Lambeth school

Can anything be done to address the issues facing these communities? Many are societal and require government action. Nevertheless, I have seen initiatives that have restored the sense of pride and agency in local people.

I remember a project in the Knowle West estate in South Bristol, where local mothers became angry about what drugs were doing to their children and formed an action group, going into schools to tell the story of how drugs affected their family. I remember how these mothers changed and grew in confidence. Many went on to travel the country, meet other groups, make speeches, meet politicians. They had developed a new sense of control and direction in their lives.

Another example is Blackpool's Lottery-funded Better Start project, which is seeking to improve outcomes for under-fives in the town's most disadvantaged wards. Here, every development is planned with local parents, who sit on powerful steering groups. Local residents are employed as Community Connectors, whose role is to reduce social isolation and parenting stress by linking families to each other and the services they need. There is a Volunteer Academy, providing training and support to get more people into volunteering, as a step towards employment. Groups of fathers have transformed parks and play spaces, and organised events specifically for dads. A community-led panel allocates funding for ideas that come from local parents, such as a Baby Clothing Bank.

Again, the impact is significant, but here it goes beyond individuals. A new sense of community agency and pride is growing. It can be done – and as we will see in Chapter 10, schools can play a key part.

Key take-aways

- Many disadvantaged white children, boys in particular, follow a path from early language delays to reading problems (and to a lesser extent maths problems), which lead to progressive disengagement from learning.
- We need to start early – preferably before children are seven – to tackle barriers to learning, and avoid common 'bear traps' that reduce children's sense of capability and independence.
- Schools that are most effective in closing disadvantage gaps understand the need to engineer transformational change in communities, as well as for individual children and families.

2 Understanding the gaps
Data, theories and research

In this chapter we probe data that sheds light on attainment gaps in relation to poverty, ethnicity and gender. We then explore theories that have been put forward to explain the undeniable and long-standing underachievement of white disadvantaged pupils, and research that can help us understand what is going on for these children and young people.

What do we know about the attainment gaps?

The attainment of white British pupils is polarised by social class to a greater extent than many other ethnic groups. In 2019, the effect of socio-economic status (SES) on GCSE attainment in England varied between ethnic subgroups by a factor of almost three (DfE, 2020). White British, and mixed White and Asian groups, each had an SES gap equivalent to 3.4 years of education, whilst Bangladeshi, Pakistani, and Black African students had SES gaps of 1.1–1.3 years of education.

The underperformance of *all* disadvantaged pupils is an enduring blot on the education landscape, and one that has become even more concerning following the school closures forced by the pandemic. The underperformance of disadvantaged white pupils is of particular significance because, in the words of Sir Michael Wilshaw in his evidence to parliament (House of Commons Education Committee, 2014) 'they make up the majority – two thirds – of such pupils. So the lowest-performing group of poor children is also the largest. If we don't crack the problem of low achievement by poor white British boys and girls, then we won't solve the problem overall.'

The early years

In the Early Years Foundation Stage Profile, white British children eligible for Free School Meals (FSM) are the lowest achieving of any ethnic group

DOI: 10.4324/9781003176442-3

except Gypsy Roma, Irish Traveller and White Irish pupils, where pupil numbers are small. In 2019, only 53% of disadvantaged white British children aged four to five met the expected standard of development, compared to 76% of white British children not eligible for FSM. The particular issues for boys appear starkly at this age: only 45% of white British boys eligible for FSM achieved a good level of development, compared to 62% of white British FSM-eligible girls.

Key take-away

By age five we can see that disadvantaged white children are a group whose development and progress gives cause for concern, with boys in this group doing less well than girls.

Primary school

In 2018, 30% of children eligible for FSM failed to meet the expected standard on the national phonics test at age six, compared to 16% of all other children. Thirty-eight per cent of white FSM-eligible boys failed to reach the expected standard. At re-sits when they were seven, *one in five* such boys still had not met the expected standard.

Teacher assessments at the end of KS1 show white British boys eligible for FSM are the lowest attaining group apart from children of Traveller or Gypsy Roma heritage, in both English (53% attaining the expected standard compared to 74% of other boys) and maths (57% compared to 79%).

At the end of KS2, an analysis of 2019 data (Nye, 2020) shows that in the combined reading, writing and maths measure, white disadvantaged boys were the lowest attaining of any major group – lower attaining than mixed ethnicity, Black or Asian pupils, for example. It should be noted, of course, that these categories are very broad: the Black pupils group includes those of African-Caribbean heritage, Black Africans and other groups, whose attainment also varies considerably.

Nye's analysis also highlights that within the disadvantaged white pupils, it was non-EAL learners who did worse than EAL learners (Figure 2.1).

Nye's analysis of *progress* data shows a similar picture for reading, with non-EAL white disadvantaged boys making less progress during their primary years than any other group. In maths, however, it is girls who are more likely to be struggling. The figure for girls' progress is half that of boys overall, and

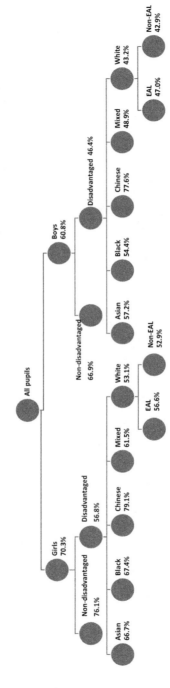

Figure 2.1 Percentage of pupils reaching expected standard in KS2 Reading/Writing/Maths, 2019

Source: Philip Nye's analysis for the FFT Education Datalab. How pupil characteristics interact to influence education outcomes, 1st September 2020

the figure for disadvantaged girls 14 times lower than the figure for disadvantaged boys. White disadvantaged girls, particularly non-EAL learners, are making much less progress in maths in their primary years than their male equivalents.

Amongst disadvantaged boys, the groups with the lowest maths progress score are non-EAL learners not only from white but also Black and mixed ethnicity groups. Amongst disadvantaged girls, the maths progress scores are lowest amongst white non-EAL learners, closely followed by mixed ethnicity non-EAL girls. Non-EAL Black girls do somewhat better, though still worse than Asian pupils.

For girls, but not boys, the maths progress scores of white pupils show greater polarisation linked to poverty than is evident in other ethnic groups.

Key take-away

KS2 data show that in overall attainment and in Reading progress, non-EAL white disadvantaged boys are the group of greatest concern, apart from the smaller group of pupils of Traveller or Gypsy Roma heritage. In Maths, however, progress scores suggest we should be much more concerned about disadvantaged girls than boys, particularly girls who are white and non-EAL, but also those of mixed ethnicity.

Secondary school

At age 16, the overall disadvantage gaps, irrespective of gender and ethnicity, have widened very significantly. Only 22.5% of disadvantaged pupils got a strong pass in English and maths GCSE in 2019, compared to 46.6% of all other pupils.

Again, the gap between rich and poor (the 'poverty penalty') is much greater for white pupils than for pupils from other broad ethnic groups, as shown in Figure 2.2.

White disadvantaged *boys* again fare particularly badly. The DfE's 2018 GCSE performance statistics showed that while the national average Attainment 8 score (a measure of a pupil's performance at the end of Key Stage 4 across eight core subjects, including maths and English) was 46.5, white boys who are eligible for free school meals scored an average of just 28.5.

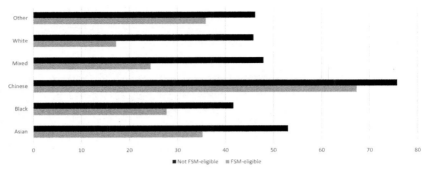

Figure 2.2 Percentage of pupils getting a strong pass in English and maths GCSE, by ethnicity and eligibility for FSM (2018 data)

Similar gaps exist in other headline measures. An analysis of 2019 data on the percentage getting a standard pass or better in English and maths (Nye, 2020) shows that when we unpick the 'white' group as EAL or non-EAL learners, non-EAL white disadvantaged boys fall well behind all other headline ethnic groups (mixed ethnicity, Black, Asian, Chinese), with only 35% getting the standard pass or better, compared to 65% of all pupils.

When we look at Progress 8 (the progress pupils make between 11 and 16, compared with others with similar starting points) white British boys eligible for FSM made the least progress in 2019 apart from pupils of mixed white/ Black Caribbean ethnicity, and White Irish, Traveller and Gypsy/Roma groups (Office for National Statistics [ONS], 2020a).

Finally, the ONS analysis shows that there are some GCSE measures on which disadvantaged white pupils do *not* do worse than other sizeable groups. If the data for Black pupils are broken down further, disadvantaged Black Caribbean pupils do less well than disadvantaged white British pupils in the percentage getting a strong pass (Grade 5 or above) in English and maths. Unpicking again to look at gender, we find that this effect is as a result of particularly low attainment amongst Black Caribbean boys, but not girls. Only 11.2% of disadvantaged Black Caribbean boys got a strong pass in English and maths in 2018, compared to 19.2% of all disadvantaged boys, and 19.4% of disadvantaged white British pupils. Mixed white/Black Caribbean pupils also fared poorly (15.5%)

For girls and strong passes, the picture is different. Overall, disadvantaged girls are more likely to get a strong pass in English and maths than are disadvantaged boys. Amongst these girls, white British pupils are the lowest attaining (19.1%), just behind Black Caribbean girls (19.9%).

> **Key take-away**
>
> GCSE data show that on most measures white disadvantaged boys are lowest-attaining group apart from pupils of Traveller or Gypsy Roma heritage. In the percentage achieving a strong pass in English and maths, however, we should be particularly concerned about Black Caribbean boys.

Access to higher education

DfE figures show that male white British pupils eligible for free school meals are the least likely of all the main ethnic groups to progress to higher education (Barnes, 2021). Across all pupils eligible for FSM 26% went on to university by the age of 19, but for FSM-eligible white pupils the figure was 16% – and only 13% for boys. In comparison, 59% of disadvantaged young people from Black African and 32% from Black Caribbean families went to university.

A study by the Office for Students (Millward, 2021) identified particularly low entry rates in former industrial towns and cities across the north and midlands, and in coastal towns. Those least likely to go to university were concentrated in some areas – such as parts of Nottingham, Great Yarmouth, Barnsley, Sheffield, Stoke and Hull. White students eligible for FSM in London seemed to have bucked the trend, with an entry rate that was pulling away from that in other parts of the country.

Another interesting report (Atherton and Mazhari, 2019) looked at access to different types of universities. Overall, this analysis of admissions found that more than half of England's universities have fewer than 5% poor white students in their intakes – but there was considerable variability. Three per cent of the intake at the University of Oxford came from these backgrounds, compared with 28% at Teesside. The report notes that more support is not only needed to get these disadvantaged white students into university, but to keep them there. Of those boys who are accepted, 8.8% of them drop out before graduating, compared with 6.3% of their peers from better-off families.

> **Key take-away**
>
> White disadvantaged young people are less likely to go to university, particularly a top university, than disadvantaged young people from other main ethnic groups. If they get into university, and are male, they are at greater risk of dropping out than their more advantaged peers.

How can we account for these figures?

Poverty

Poverty alone cannot be the explanation for the poor educational outcomes of disadvantaged white children and young people.

White pupils are not the most socio-economically disadvantaged group in England, by far. In the three-year average ending in 2018, children in Pakistani and Bangladeshi households were the most likely to live in low-income households. Yet their attainment at all stages of education is higher.

Nor are white children more likely to live in *persistent* poverty (in a household that has been recorded as having an income below 60% of the median, before housing costs are taken into account, in at least three out of the last four consecutive years). This level of poverty again affects children in Asian households most.

Ability

It is often assumed that children who do less well in our education system do so because they are less able. This view gained some early traction in government, when Dominic Cummings (Cummings, 2013) in his then role as special adviser to the Education Secretary of State, wrote a report contending that educational inequalities linked to social class are mostly due to differences in cognitive ability, that inequalities are inevitable in a meritocracy, and that they do not need to be addressed by policy makers.

Serious researchers, however, have established that cognitive ability, though not irrelevant, accounts for only just over a third of the parental social class effect on individuals' educational attainment (Betthaeuser, 2020). This analysis was based on the British Cohort Study (BCS) data, using a sample that was predominantly white. Children's cognitive ability was assessed at age ten using subtests from the British Ability Scales intelligence test; the educational attainment measure was based on whether the children in the sample achieved at least two A levels or equivalent. The authors conclude that 'more than 60% of the parental class effect on individuals' educational attainment is *not* accounted for by individuals' cognitive ability.'

Other findings support this conclusion. For example, in his own analysis of the BCS (Feinstein, 2003) Leon Feinstein has shown that many disadvantaged children start with high levels of cognitive ability at 22 months, but end up doing poorly in school, in some cases being overtaken by their initially less able but better-off peers. The Sutton Trust's 'Missing Talent' research (Montacute, 2018) found that over a third of disadvantaged boys (of all ethnicities in this case) who were in the top 10% of pupils in attainment at age 11 were outside the top 25% in their GCSEs; they were very able, but this did not translate into good outcomes later on. And among the cleverest children born in the UK in 1970, 80% of the richest children achieved two A levels or their equivalent, compared with only 40% of the poorest (Bukodi and Goldthorpe, 2020). Something more than 'ability' is at work here.

Aspirations

Commentators have suggested a number of reasons for the stronger link between poverty and attainment in white children than in those from other ethnic groups. Chief among them are greater parental aspirations for their child's future and greater commitment to education as a way of reaching those aspirations, amongst BAME groups. Young people's own aspirations – or lack of them – are also often cited.

Ofsted have been particularly vehement on the issue of aspirations. Former Chief Inspector Michael Wilshaw, for example, said in his evidence to Parliament (House of Commons Education Committee, 2014) that 'The reason why London schools are doing so well, apart from good headteachers and good teachers, is because a lot of the immigrant families care about education, they value education, they support their children. . . . I'm working in parts of England with white British populations where the parents don't care. Less than 50% turn up to parents evening. Now that's outrageous.'

For Ofsted and many other commentators the lack of aspiration in families in some areas is in turn linked to changes in the communities in which disadvantaged white children live, which have borne the full brunt of economic dislocation in recent years and seen the 'bedrock' of traditional industrial and manufacturing jobs broken up, leaving high unemployment and low-wage, fragile employment behind (House of Commons Education Committee, 2014).

Social and cultural capital

Social capital has been defined as 'the pattern and intensity of networks among people and the shared values which arise from those networks' (Office for National Statistics, 2020b). Some commentators suggest that it is lack of such networks, rather than lack of aspirations, that holds disadvantaged children back. Social capital is difficult to measure, however, and there is little hard evidence to support the theory.

Equally hard to prove is the idea, popular in government circles, that what disadvantaged children lack is cultural capital. The term was first used by sociologist Pierre Bourdieu, who defined it as the various assets that people have including the way they speak, their level of education and their hobbies and interests.

In the current Ofsted framework, cultural capital has a rather different definition, linked to the national curriculum introduced by government and setting out 'the essential knowledge pupils need to be educated citizens, introducing them to the best that has been thought and said' (Gove, 2014). Ofsted emphasise the importance of cultural capital for disadvantaged children in particular. Their review of the evidence underpinning the framework (Ofsted, 2019) does not, however, present any evidence to support the importance of cultural capital or cultural literacy, other than its own qualitative study of 23 good or outstanding schools, selected because their leaders were identified as being 'particularly invested in curriculum design.' This study found these leaders used a number of different models for curriculum design, some based on a knowledge-rich curriculum but others based on the acquisition of skills.

Ofsted's definition is based on the work of E. D. Hirsch (2016), who drew on evidence from developmental psychology, cognitive psychology and social science to develop the concept of cultural literacy, and discussed the need for a common base of knowledge in the school curriculum so as to ensure equal opportunities for students of all backgrounds. We will explore this theory further in the next chapter.

What does the research say?

Much of the theorising which we have examined so far is based on opinion. What actual evidence do we have about what might be happening for poor white children? One small but interesting ethnographic study (Demie and Lewis, 2010) involved interviews and focus groups with school staff, governors, parents and pupils in 14 schools in one London local authority. In these schools white British pupils formed a minority. The authors conclude:

> ... one of the main reasons for pupil underachievement is parental low aspirations of their children's education, perpetuated by factors such as low literacy levels, feelings of marginalisation within the community exacerbated by housing allocation.

Teachers reported that white working class parents were less likely to participate in opportunities to become involved in programmes to support parenting, and to send their children to after school clubs. They also often noted children's lack of wide life experiences:

> It is a general thing here that children do not get out of the area . . . there is little understanding of a larger world. Children, whose families came here from another country or have lived in two or three countries, have a wider world to relate to, whilst white pupils don't have this, they do not have a mental map of the world . . . these children never expected to leave the estate; they had never even seen the Thames.

In another study, Gillian Evans (2006) undertook two years of research with working class families in Bermondsey in south London. She highlighted that white working class boys often feel pressured by their sub-culture to uphold a tough 'street' reputation which is linked to their views of masculinity, and which competes with a positive attitude towards education. She notes how this leads to the challenge of a 'chaotic school in which a minority of disruptive boys dominate proceedings, a high-adrenaline environment where both children and staff have to cope constantly with the threat of disruption, intimidation and violence' (p. 96). On peer behaviour, she notes that 'the unobtrusive children, the ones who behave well but struggle to learn, continue to quietly demonstrate the fallacy that good behaviour means effective learning. Their lack of progress highlights the cost to the whole class of the teachers' continuous focus on trying to manage the behaviour of disruptive boys' (p. 92).

Perhaps the most substantial research evidence comes from a study of over 15,000 children by Steve Strand (2014) which looked at the correlations and interactions between educational outcomes at 11, 14 and 16 and a range of variables including ethnicity, gender and the attitudes, expectations and behaviours of students and their families. When the pupils were 14, they and their parents took part in face-to-face interviews in their own homes.

Complex statistical modelling allowed the researchers to find out which factors explained the most variance in attainment at age 16. School factors made relatively little difference, compared to parent and student factors. The higher attainment of non-white pupils compared to similarly disadvantaged white British pupils was linked to:

- Greater parental educational aspirations for their child (expecting that the student would continue in full time education post-16)

- Students' own educational aspirations: only 60% of white British disadvantaged boys aspired to continue in full-time education after 16, compared to 75% of white disadvantaged girls and 95% and above across the socio-economic spectrum for all other minority groups (other than Black Caribbean boys)
- Having a positive academic self-concept
- Higher reported frequency of completing homework
- Lower levels of truancy and exclusion

Parents in many minority ethnic groups were more likely than white British parents to have paid for private tuition, were more involved with their child's school, had higher educational aspirations for their children, were more likely to know where their children were when they were out, were less likely to quarrel with their child and less likely to be single parent households.

Other reports confirm the link between underachievement in disadvantaged white children and truancy; in evidence to the House of Commons Education Committee's 2014 enquiry into the issue, the DfE presented data showing that white British FSM children had the highest total absence of all ethnic groups except children of Traveller/Gypsy Roma heritage. The picture on exclusions was more complicated; while white British children eligible for FSM had a much higher rate of fixed and permanent exclusions than similarly disadvantaged Indian, Pakistani and Bangladeshi children, Black Caribbean and mixed white and Black Caribbean children had an even higher rate.

The links between poor attendance and exclusion and progress in secondary school are very strong. One study (Claymore, 2019) found that 55% of the gap in Progress 8 scores between disadvantaged pupils and their more affluent peers can be explained by the between-group differences in absence, exclusion, and a further factor – pupils' KS4 movement rates during secondary school, at both pupil and cohort level.

Key take-aways

- Neither poverty alone, nor differences in cognitive ability, can explain the low attainment of disadvantaged white pupils.
- Theorists have argued that lack of parental aspiration and reduced social and cultural capital contribute to poorer educational outcomes for this group.
- Research studies involving teenagers provide support for the idea that for secondary students low aspirations are involved, along with peer group pressure, truancy, exclusion and pupil mobility.

Bucking the trend – the pupils

Another way of finding out what might be happening for disadvantaged white children is to study those who 'buck the trend' – that is, are successful in their education and in later life in a way that the majority of such pupils are not. One influential study by economist Jo Blanden (2006) looked at the 18,000 (predominantly white) children in the British Cohort Study and identified those who were brought up in poverty but were themselves not poor at age 30. She found that those who bucked the trend:

- Had better spoken language skills (vocabulary) at age five than those who remained poor as adults
- Had better reading skills at age ten
- Were more likely to have been read to by their parents in the week in which they were surveyed at the age five
- Were more likely at age ten to have parents who took an interest in their schooling, as reported by teachers

There were some significant gender differences. For boys, their father's interest in their education had the largest influence, whereas for girls the mother's interest was most important. Peer group influences were more important for boys than girls. Boys who bucked the trend were more likely to attend a school with a higher number of above average ability students. For males, too, having many skilled manual workers amongst peers' fathers had a positive impact, but not for girls.

> My results show that the level of parental interest is extremely important . . . for boys, the father's interest is very important whereas for girls, the mother's interest dominates. For boys, having a father with little or no interest in their education reduces the chances of bucking the trend by 25 percentage points.
>
> Jo Blanden, 2006, in *Bucking the trend: What enables those who are disadvantaged in childhood to succeed later in life?*

Another study (Pascal and Bertram, 2016) focused on 30 high-achieving young boys from disadvantaged white backgrounds, who were at age five in the top 15% on the Early Years Foundation Stage Profile assessment. Many of the boys had experienced or were living with adversities or risk factors such as family conflict, parental illness, parental unemployment or single parenthood, yet were still doing well. The researchers captured retrospectively the characteristics of these boys' early learning opportunities at home and in early years provision. The protective factors that enabled them to learn successfully included:

- Warm, nurturing, relaxed but 'boundaried' parenting styles, with regular routines, consistent rules and behaviour expectations
- Plenty of parent/child talk and book-sharing
- Protective and close key worker relationships in the nursery
- Individualised parenting support from the setting, that helped parents develop coping skills and respond sensitively to their children
- Stimulating, language-rich early education with a focus on children's social competences, self-regulation skills and sense of agency

In a study focused on older children (King and Welch, 2012) 50 white disadvantaged boys from schools across England were interviewed at length. All had bucked the trend and achieved at least five good GCSEs. The researchers pulled out themes from these interviews, related to friendships, the experience of success, and support from teachers.

These boys had either chosen friends who wanted to work hard at school, or created two distinct groups of friends – work 'colleagues' and friends they could have a laugh with.

My school friends are more like . . . like I work with. My friends around my area, I just hang about with.

They had all experienced early success, not necessarily in schoolwork or at school – it might have been through a hobby or talent. As a result their confidence in their own ability had grown.

Their schools were good at noticing and celebrating success, whether through simple praise or assemblies and awards evenings. They had an ethos in which ambition was encouraged and supported. Often the school provided facilities and places for students to work outside school hours.

> [They told me] I could achieve so much more! Like in Geography I got a D I think, but the geography teacher said I could easily get a B if I put my mind to it.

Interestingly, for these sixth-form boys, what the school did seemed more important than home factors. Some had encouragement at home, but others didn't. What the interviewees' schools had done was make up for any gaps.

> Some came from very supportive, loving backgrounds and needed little more than a detailed pathway to help them to achieve their goals; Others lacked the equipment required to explore their musicality at home, for example, but were able to do so at school; others had very little emotional support at home and the school was required to fulfil even the most basic of familial functions in order to allow the student to blossom.

In another study, Mary-Clare Travers (Travers, 2017a) explored the perceptions of 15 academically successful white working class boys who were at university. The young men had grown up in difficult circumstances but also had compensatory factors in their lives: they all came from families who valued education and they had experienced academic success early. Most of their siblings did not go on to higher education, however, which suggests factors beyond the family, such as support from mentor teachers and these students' own personal characteristics. 'All needed persistence, resilience and sheer determination at various stages in their school and university careers,' notes the author.

One of the obstacles these boys had often had to overcome (Travers, 2017b) was setting in the classroom. One participant commented 'I was in the bottom set for everything, I didn't really do anything I just messed about. . . . No one really taught anyone . . . but I ended up doing all right. I got A-Cs. I could have got higher but you can't really get out (of the bottom set). . . . It's the write-off class, the bottom one.'

Bucking the trend – the schools

A number of studies have looked at features of schools which 'buck the trend', in that attainment data show that on average white disadvantaged pupils are doing well or that their attainment is improving over time. Ofsted (2008), for example, in a thematic report on white disadvantaged boys noted that the common features in such schools included

- Support to develop boys' organisation skills and instil the importance of perseverance
- An ethos that ensured that any anti-school subculture was 'left at the gates'
- Rigorous monitoring systems that tracked individual pupils' performance against expectations
- Realistic but challenging targets
- Tailored, flexible intervention programmes and frequent reviews of performance against targets
- A curriculum that was tightly structured around individual needs and linked to support programmes that sought to raise aspirations
- Creative and flexible strategies to engage parents and carers, make them feel valued, enable them to give greater support to their sons' education and help them make informed decisions about the future
- A strong emphasis on seeking and listening to the views of these pupils
- Genuine engagement of boys in setting individual targets, reviewing progress, shaping curricular and extra-curricular activities and making choices about the future
- Strong partnership with a wide range of agencies to provide social, emotional, educational and practical support for boys and their families in order to raise their aspirations
- A good range of emotional support to help these boys manage anxieties and develop the skills to express their feelings constructively

An important feature of the most successful schools surveyed was the close attention they paid to supporting the emotional development of the boys . . . they made good use of programmes such as 'Social and Emotional Aspects of Learning (SEAL).'

Ofsted, 2008, *White boys from low income-backgrounds: good practice in schools*

Pupils were interviewed to find out what types of teaching and learning worked best for them:

> These included 'active' involvement in the lesson; explicit individual learning targets to aim for; tightly controlled lessons which led to clear improvement and progress; 'well-managed discussions'; and 'approachable teachers who showed they cared'.

Another interview shed interesting light on boys' learning preferences:

> Every month the headteacher provided soft drinks and cakes for students who had achieved well. During the inspection, the headteacher asked the group, predominantly girls, why it was that more boys were not represented. One girl said: 'It's not that boys are not clever. They mostly are but they need quick results. You just have to be showing them the cakes!' The boys present agreed.

Boys' preference for more active forms of learning was also highlighted: 'It was good during "Robin Hood week" because we didn't have to sit in the classroom the whole time' (Y5 boy).

A later Ofsted report (2013) reported on visits to 16 schools where the attainment and/or progress of white British pupils (in this case both boys and girls) from low income backgrounds was higher than the national average for this group, or improving strongly. They concluded from their visits that strong leadership of a flexible, carefully monitored and rigorously evaluated package of interventions was a key factor in these schools' success – that, in the words of one Assistant Principal, the school makes sure that 'the right kids have the right intervention at the right time with the right people.'

A case study from the report illustrates what this means in practice:

> In one school a well-qualified school leader was appointed to reshape the school's intervention programme as part of its drive to raise

achievement and close gaps. Searching self-evaluation had shown that previous interventions had not always been successful because they had been delivered by non-specialists and their timing, at the end of the school day, had failed to reach those pupils who needed the support most. A decision was taken to radically change the way support was delivered, focusing primarily on English and mathematics. Pupils making slow progress are now selected through a rigorous assessment and target-setting-process for one-to-one tuition and mentoring. This programme is delivered by subject specialists during the school day.

The Director of Learning (head of department) designs an individual learning plan for each pupil. This identifies clearly the skills or knowledge the pupil needs to improve. The tutor then plans a series of intensive lessons that address these weaknesses. After each session, the tutor completes a detailed review of the pupil's progress. The school ensures that sessions are scheduled at different times to minimise disruption to other subjects. Parents and carers are kept informed about the purpose of these sessions and their child's progress. Mentors provide additional support for families where the pupil's attitudes or behaviours have presented concerns.

Ofsted, 2013, *Unseen Children*, p. 32

Finally, a study commissioned by the NUT and the former National College for School Leadership (Mongon and Chapman, 2008) examined the common features of leadership in schools where poor white boys were on average more successful at the end of KS2 and 4 than their comparable peers in other schools. The authors draw out what feel like features of good leadership in general:

- There was a strong, shared sense of purpose, goals were specific and well understood, expectations were high for everyone – 'Staff and students knew where they were travelling and what was expected of them.'
- Staff and students were provided with intellectual and emotional stimulation 'in which personalised support rather than criticism was predominant.'
- Lines of authority, responsibility, accountability and autonomy were clear to everyone. Close attention was paid to the appearance of the built environment.

- The leaders were relentless in their pursuit of the highest standards of teaching and learning. Success was invariably celebrated; difficulties for staff or students were never ignored. 'Mistakes were acceptable, under-performance was not.'

More illuminating than the generalisations is the detail of the findings. The report stresses that headteachers had a profound respect for the people and areas they were working in. Several came from low-income backgrounds themselves. They had developed an inclusive curriculum that met the needs of white working class children, drew in appropriate role models, and provided effective targeted support and mentoring.

Key take-aways

From the research on disadvantaged white pupils who struggle to succeed, and from those that succeed against the odds, we can conclude that:

- Disadvantaged white pupils *can* succeed. Closing this particular gap is not a hopeless task.
- At the school level, disadvantaged white pupils do better when the schools seek and listen to pupils' views, notice and celebrate success, pay attention to pupils' social and emotional as well as academic development, help them develop ownership of their learning, target interventions carefully on the basis of detailed assessment, seek to engage parents and understand and respect the communities they serve.
- At the individual level, disadvantaged white students do better when they have developed strong social and emotional skills (persistence, the ability to manage friendships and resist negative peer pressure), experienced early success (not necessarily academic success), have developed a sense of agency, had better spoken language skills in their early years than their less successful disadvantaged peers, and had learned to read successfully.

---

3 Myths and wrong turnings

In this chapter we explore the evidence on what works in raising the attainment of disadvantaged pupils. I will argue that many of the interventions that are popular with schools, and on which they choose to spend their Pupil Premium, are based on myths rather than facts.

The myths about what will work often arise from mis-interpretation of the kind of research we looked at in the last chapter. So, for example, if that research shows that the poor attainment of disadvantaged white boys is linked to (that is, correlates with) lack of parental engagement and low aspirations, we conclude that if we tackle these factors then the result will be improved attainment.

This is not necessarily the case. Correlation does not prove cause. I often use the pot plant analogy to illustrate this point. Suppose that there were to be a correlation between schools' chances of being identified as outstanding by Ofsted and the number of pot plants in the school foyer. Does this mean that if staff in a school in the 'requires improvement' category go out and buy lots of pot plants, this will mean the school becomes outstanding? It doesn't, because the pot plants are not actually a causal factor here. If there is a correlation (as there well might be) the likely explanation is a third factor underlying both pot plants and school quality – probably something to do with the quality of leadership, with high levels of attention to detail.

To demonstrate that the presence of pot plants had a causal effect on attainment, one would need to undertake an experimental study in which one group of schools introduces pot plants while another group doesn't, and children's attainment is measured before and after the change. One would also need to make sure that the two groups were well-matched on every possible underlying factor that might explain any positive effect

DOI: 10.4324/9781003176442-4

found. This can be difficult; hence the gold standard of randomised controlled trials in which schools are randomly allocated to either experimental (pot plant) or control (not pot plant) groups. Given a large enough number of schools taking part, this should make sure that any underlying explanatory factors are present in both experimental and control groups in roughly equal proportions.

So it is studies like this, and to a lesser extent high quality studies which were not randomised but where the experimental and control groups were well matched, to which we should look in order to decide whether potential factors explaining the poor achievement of disadvantaged white children are actually causal – and thus whether any interventions based on those factors are likely to work, or turn out to be wrong turnings.

Aspiration interventions

As we saw in Chapter 2, poverty of aspiration amongst pupils and their parents has been a recurring theme for those seeking to explain the low attainment of disadvantaged children, and for those devising national policies to tackle the issue.

Unfortunately, there is little evidence that school-based interventions to raise aspirations have any effect on attainment (Cummings *et al.*, 2012; Education Endowment Foundation (EEF), 2018). Research summarised in the EEF's Teaching and Learning Toolkit seems to show that most young people (and their parents) already have high aspirations. What many lack, however, is the means to achieve their goals. It makes more sense, therefore, to work directly on pupils' knowledge and skills rather than on their aspirations. In those aspiration programmes which do raise attainment, this kind of extra additional academic support is generally found to be part of the package.

Verdict: myth

Building social and cultural capital

Many schools in poorer areas make it part of their mission to try to bridge the gap in social and cultural capital between their pupils and well-off students, such as those attending independent schools. Ian Bauckham, CEO at Tenax Schools Trust, describes this view (Bauckham, 2020):

> How many pupils from disadvantaged backgrounds will have planned and been on a country walk? How many will have been taught to play rugby or cricket, taken to a match, and given the knowledge to talk confidently about what is going on? How many will have learnt a musical instrument and become familiar with the classical canon? This is all part of the secret social code that needs to be broken for pupils who are not born into advantage, and schools need to be the code crackers.

He also notes, however, that there is almost no research evidence showing that activities to crack the code have a direct impact on attainment. Government evidence for a focus on cultural capital, in the sense of access to knowledge, rests largely on E. D. Hirsch's (1996) analysis of the impact of changes to the national curriculum in France in 1989, which he claims turned the country from one of the highest achieving and equitable countries to one of the most inequitable countries with middling overall performance, in the course of just a few decades. Before 1989, the curriculum in France prescribed hierarchical content in every subject, with new content continuously building on prior learning. When the changes came in, the curriculum focused on skills. Hirsh's view is that the shift has particularly negative effects on disadvantaged students, since the parents of better-off children were more able to supplement school instruction with their own experiences out of the classroom.

This may well be true, but without a control group that did not experience the curriculum change it is not possible to draw any firm conclusions. The case for a knowledge-rich curriculum has been strengthened, however, by evidence that children's reading comprehension is highly dependent on their background knowledge, both about the topic of the text and about the world in general (Coppola, 2014). Since children from more advantaged backgrounds are likely to pick up such knowledge at home, there is a case to be made for increasing the emphasis on developing wide-ranging cultural, current affairs and scientific knowledge in disadvantaged children.

Verdict: mixed evidence

Enrichment

Similar to social and cultural capital, but less focused on high-end experiences, are enrichment activities for those children who rarely leave the immediate area where they live, or access after-school activities organised by their families – children like those described by Paul Dix:

> I have worked with children living two miles from the city centre who had never been there, children who are not allowed out of the tower block, those who won't even leave their postcode, teenagers who live just a few miles from the seaside who have never seen the sea, adult learners who won't take a bus to get a job. Despite the world being available online, reality is limited when you've got no bus fare and no partners to share in the pursuit of the unknown.
>
> Paul Dix, 'Are we going on the tube?' in *The Working Class*, ed. Ian Gilbert, 2018, p. 26

There is some research evidence on the benefits of enrichment. One broad-based initiative evaluated by the EEF and classed as promising is the Children's University (Gorard *et al.*, 2017). This involves after-school clubs, visits to universities and museums and volunteering in the community. It is applicable to both primary and secondary aged pupils.

A systematic review conducted for the EEF found that taking part in enrichment activities in *the creative arts* has some limited impact on academic attainment for both primary and secondary children, with larger effects for younger pupils and, in some cases, for disadvantaged pupils. The evidence supporting the academic impact of learning to play an instrument is particularly promising.

Sports participation has also been found to have some limited impact on attainment, often by acting as an incentive to attend school more often or take part in extra out-of-school English or maths instruction. There is wide variability in the findings from different studies, however, and the EEF Toolkit concludes that the quality of the programme and the extent to which it connects with academic learning may make more difference than the specific type of approach or sporting activities involved.

The strongest evidence in the enrichment field is for *outdoor adventure learning* – courses such as climbing, survival, ropes or assault courses; or outdoor sports, such as orienteering, sailing and canoeing. On average, pupils who take part in well-planned activities like these make approximately four additional months' academic progress. The activities rarely include any formal academic element, so it may be that the effect on attainment is a by-product of increased self-confidence and development of social and emotional skills, through collaborative learning experiences with a high level of physical and emotional challenge.

Secondary students benefit more from outdoor adventure learning than younger pupils, and there is particularly strong impact for more vulnerable students. The most successful courses in terms of impact on school attainment tend to be those that last more than a week.

A single but fascinating recent study (Bijnens *et al.*, 2020) suggests that for city children just the opportunity to spend time outdoors in green space could be associated with improved cognitive functioning. The study used satellite images to measure the level of greenness in neighbourhoods, including parks, gardens and street trees. The analysis of more than 600 children aged 10–15 showed that a 3% increase in the greenness of their neighbourhood raised their IQ score by an average of 2.6 points. The increase in IQ points was particularly significant for those children at the lower end of the spectrum. The effect was seen in both richer and poorer areas, but not in suburban or rural neighbourhoods. The researchers took into account the wealth and education levels of the children's parents, ruling out the explanation that families who are better placed to support children simply have more access to green space. It was also possible to rule out higher levels of air pollution as an explanation.

Instead, the scientists suggested lower noise levels, lower stress – as found in other research on green space benefits – and greater opportunities for physical and social activities may explain the higher cognitive scores.

Verdict: some evidence

Smaller classes

Reducing class size is felt by many teachers to be the holy grail in tackling disadvantage gaps. It is also hugely popular with parents. Unfortunately, like work to raise aspirations, this is another myth. Unless it is possible to reduce class sizes to below 20 or even 15 pupils, research summarised in the EEF Toolkit suggests that spending money on smaller classes is unlikely to make much difference to attainment. The reason is that only at these very small numbers, beyond the reach of most schools, can teachers actually teach differently. Reducing a class from say 30 to 25 will still mean the teacher thinks and plans in terms of groups within the class. Only when numbers are really low is it possible to plan for and respond accurately to the learning needs of individuals.

Verdict: myth

Setting and streaming

Schools often seek to combine reducing class size with streaming, creating small sets where (in theory) lower-attaining pupils will get more personal attention. An extensive body of research over many years (Francis *et al.*, 2020), however, shows that placing pupils in streams or sets has no overall impact on attainment, and actively disadvantages those placed in lower sets or streams. In turn, socio-economically disadvantaged children (and boys in particular, perhaps because of behavioural issues) are more likely to be placed in lower sets and streams (Kutnick *et al.*, 2005).

The effects start early, even in KS1. Susan Hallam and Samantha Parsons (2013) used data from nearly 9000 children in the Millennium Cohort and found that 26% of children in Y2 were set for literacy and mathematics and a further 11% of children were set for mathematics or literacy. Boys were over-represented in the bottom sets for literacy (though not in maths). Children in bottom sets were significantly more likely to be part of a long-term single parent household, have experienced poverty, and less likely to have a mother with higher-level educational qualifications.

Becky Francis (2018) has argued cogently that setting leads to double disadvantage, since pupils from low socio-economic backgrounds are already disadvantaged on arrival into the education system, and then they are the recipients of school practices found to hinder their progress. Less academically, but equally cogently, the case against setting has been made in a 1996 episode of the Simpsons, in which one character (Bart) is moved to a remedial class: 'Let me get this straight,' he says, 'We're behind the rest of our class and we're going to catch up with them by going slower than they are?'

Grouping children flexibly by prior attainment *within* their class for specific activities or topics, such as literacy, has a better pedigree than setting or streaming. The EEF Toolkit concludes that such grouping practices, which enable tasks, activities and support to be matched to children's current capabilities, and may involve effective practices such as collaborative learning, on average benefit all pupils. The evidence suggests, however, that there are fewer benefits for lower attaining pupils than for others, and that within-class attainment grouping may have long-term negative effects on these pupils' confidence and engagement.

Laura Teague (quoted in Parr, 2019), highlights another potential negative impact: 'If you struggle in a particular subject and you're working only with students who also struggle, then you lose the opportunity for learn from one another. Similarly, if you are quite able in a subject, it is not always beneficial to work with others who have similar strengths to your own in terms of opportunities to consolidate your knowledge via explaining and teaching your peers.'

What can schools conclude from all this? I like this guiding principle from a report by Debbie Salmin, Jonathan Bell and Marc Rowland (2019):

Teachers and pupils should be clear that the purpose of grouping is to ensure mastery of key knowledge, not because they are 'less able', not clever enough or poorly behaved. Pupil perceptions of grouping may be different from those of the teacher. Further, where grouping takes place, it is important that groups who are low current attainers are not always working with less experienced or less qualified staff.

Verdict: myth

Allocating teaching assistants to work with lower attaining children in class

Also based on the assumed benefits of giving under-achieving disadvantaged pupils more individual attention, many schools choose to spend Pupil Premium funding on extra TA support. This practice has been called into question by the controversial but influential research findings from the Deployment and Impact of Support Staff (DISS) study (Blatchford *et al.*, 2009) that demonstrated a negative relationship between pupil progress and the amount of TA support that they received, after controlling for other factors that might explain this relationship (prior attainment, SEN, disadvantage, gender).

One reason for the surprising finding is that in many classrooms TAs had come to replace, rather than supplement, teaching from qualified teachers. In the study, researchers sat in classrooms observing pupils every ten seconds and coding their interactions. The results for pupils identified as having special educational needs are shown in Table 3.1.

You will see from the table that pupils with SEN had fewer interactions with their class and subject teachers than did pupils without SEN. A wise HMI

Table 3.1 Interaction patterns

Interaction by type of SEN	With teacher	With TA
Non-SEN	55%	27%
School Action	24%	32%
School Action+ or Statement	21%	41%

Source: Data from *Re-assessing the impact of teaching assistants.* Blatchford *et al.*, 2009

once said 'The DISS study does not show that the more time TAs spend with pupils, the less progress they make – it shows that the less time they spend with their *teachers*, the less progress they make.'

Practice has moved on since the original DISS study, but nevertheless I still meet many teachers and school leaders who view extra TA support as the solution for children in 'low ability' groups, particularly in primary schools. And as we have seen, these within-class groupings contain a disproportionate number of disadvantaged boys.

Some schools have even gone so far as to interpret the requirement to account for Pupil Premium spend as a discrete budget line as an indication that they should appoint a dedicated 'Pupil Premium' TA to support eligible children in class, irrespective of their actual learning needs and the effect this might have on their self-perceptions – and their progress. This particular wrong turning runs against all the evidence, but is an example of how well-meaning policies can have unintended consequences.

Schools are on much surer ground when they deploy well-trained TAs to work on time-limited intervention programmes with individuals or groups (on the basis of assessment of learning needs rather than labels or categories). We will review the evidence for programmes like these in later chapters.

Verdict: myth

Mentoring

Many secondary schools have developed mentoring programmes for their disadvantaged students, pairing young people with an older peer or volunteer, who meets with them regularly and acts as a positive role model. The business sector is often keen to partner with schools on mentoring initiatives which involve their staff, in order to fulfil their corporate social responsibility targets.

The aim of mentoring is usually to build confidence and raise aspirations, rather than to develop specific academic skills. In this sense, it seems possible that it will fall into the same class as other aspiration interventions, helping learners set goals without giving them the means to reach them.

This does indeed seem to be the case. The EEF find that on average, mentoring appears to have little or no effect on academic outcomes. Results do vary from study to study, however, with some researchers finding positive impacts for disadvantaged pupils, and for non-academic outcomes such as attitudes to school, attendance and behaviour.

Meta-analyses and research reviews have identified features that are common to effective mentoring programmes (Whybra *et al.*, 2018):

- Matching the young person with the right mentor, for example on the basis of shared interests
- Including structured activities, particularly ones that are driven by the needs and interests of the young person
- Specifically targeting young people with social, emotional and behavioural difficulties
- Building in fairly frequent contact between the mentor and mentee; one review found that programmes encouraging mentors and young people to meet at least once a week were more successful
- Sustaining the mentoring over time; relationships lasting for 12 months or longer have a more positive impact

A variant of mentoring by volunteers or peers is the role of Learning Mentors, first introduced in the UK in 1999 as part of the Excellence in Cities initiative and still widespread in schools. Learning mentors are trained adults that are employed by the school to tackle barriers to learning for individual pupils, including attendance and behaviour. Their role involves building a traditional mentoring relationship, but may also involve work with families and brokering services from other agencies.

The survival of the role suggests that schools find it effective, but I could find no research evidence to back this up. An overall evaluation of Excellence in Cities (Kendall *et al.*, 2005) did find some positive impacts on pupils taking part, but this was not an experimental study and did not look separately at the different strands of the programme, which also included learning support units, work with gifted and talented students, and increased access to technology. The evaluation notes only that 'pupils referred to a Learning Mentor had lower levels of attainment than otherwise similar pupils, but there was evidence to suggest that early mentoring (in Year 7) had enabled some pupils to overcome barriers to learning.'

Verdict: mixed evidence

What about just plain good teaching?

There is good evidence that being exposed to higher quality teaching makes more difference to disadvantaged pupils than others. One analysis (Sutton Trust, 2011) categorised teachers as high-quality or poorly performing, on the basis of the value-added results of the children they taught. They found that the effects of high-quality teaching are especially significant for pupils from disadvantaged backgrounds: over a school year, these pupils gain 1.5 years' worth of learning with very effective teachers, compared with 0.5 years with poorly performing teachers (Figure 3.1).

To me this has always meant that the first port of call for raising the achievement of disadvantaged pupils should be making sure they are taught by the very best teachers. This is not always the case, when those teachers are not allocated to the lowest-performing children, but to those on the cusp of exam success, and where, as we have seen, the lowest-performing children sometimes spend more time with less qualified adults (TAs) than they do with teachers.

We also need to unpick the *specific* elements that make up high quality teaching for disadvantaged children, and disadvantaged white pupils in particular. Research to be discussed later in this book suggests that these will involve a focus on building strong and supportive teacher–pupil relationships, on oracy in the classroom, on collaborative learning, on teacher language that builds self-efficacy and self-regulation, and on approaches which link to the child's own experiences and make learning relevant for them, plus best practice in supporting memory and metacognition.

Verdict: Good evidence

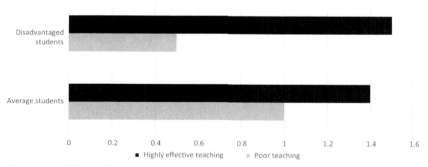

Figure 3.1 Effect of teaching on student in years of progress
Source: Data from *Improving the impact of teachers on pupil achievement in the UK*, Sutton Trust (2011)

But ensuring access to the best teachers alone will not be enough; to close the gap we need to ensure that disadvantaged white children get *more* great teaching than others, which can probably only be achieved by additional intervention programmes delivered over and above the regular curriculum.

An overview of what works

Table 3.2 summarises the EEF's analysis of what works – and what doesn't – in raising attainment, with a particular (but not exclusive) emphasis on disadvantaged pupils. Professor Steve Higgins, lead author of the EEF Toolkit, suggests that a feature of many of the less successful interventions is that they

Table 3.2 Summary of the international evidence on teaching 5–16-year-olds

Extra months' academic progress	Type of intervention	Caveats
-4	Repeating a year	
-1	Setting or streaming	
0	Raising aspirations	
0	Changes to the built environment	
0	Mentoring	
+1	Performance-related pay for teachers	
+1	Teaching assistant support	Can work when well-trained and supported TAs deliver small group and 1-1 intervention programmes
+2	Summer schools	Highest impact (+4 months) if includes small-group tuition with a trained teacher. Can be difficult to engage disadvantaged students.
+2	Breakfast clubs	Impact on attainment only for KS1 not KS2, and evidence applies to one particular breakfast club programme – Magic Breakfast
+2	Extended school time	
+2	Arts participation	
+2	Sports participation	
+2	Learning styles	
+2	Homework (primary)	

Extra months' academic progress	Type of intervention	Caveats
+3	Reducing class size	But only if class size is reduced below 20 or even 15
+3	Within class attainment grouping	But less benefit for lower attaining pupils than others. Some studies also show longer term negative effects on the attitudes and engagement of low attaining pupils, for example by discouraging the belief that their attainment can be improved through effort.
+3	Individualised (personally tailored) instruction	
+3	Behaviour interventions	
+3	Parental engagement	
+4	Social and emotional learning	
+4	Phonics	
+4	Outdoor adventure learning	
+4	Digital technology	When used to supplement rather than replace the teacher
+4	Small group tuition	
+5	Early years interventions	
+5	Peer tutoring	
+5	Homework (secondary)	
+5	Collaborative learning	
+5	Oral language interventions	
+5	One-to-one tuition	
+5	Mastery learning	But mainly as an occasional or additional teaching strategy, and when pupils work in groups or teams and take responsibility for supporting each other's progress. The approach appears to be much less effective when pupils work at their own pace.
+6	Reading Comprehension strategies	
+7	Metacognition and self-regulation	
+8	Effective feedback on learning	

are structural, whereas the more successful are relational – they affect the way adults and children interact and relate to one another in the classroom (Tall, 2019). Repeating a year, changes to the physical environment, placing pupils in sets do not necessarily change the way teachers interact with children. Reducing class size only works if the numbers become small enough for teachers to change the way they teach. Allocating teaching assistants to support children in class can actually limit the amount of time children spend with their teacher.

Now let us have a closer look at some of the interventions that the EEF highlight as likely to have a high impact – saving for later chapters a more detailed exploration of those relating to reading, oral language, social and emotional learning and parental engagement.

Starting early: high quality nursery provision in the early years

There is extensive international evidence that high quality pre-school education and childcare can reduce income-related gaps in later attainment. In the UK the Effective Pre-school, Primary and Secondary Education (EPPSE) longitudinal study, for example, has followed over time a cohort of approximately 3,000 children born in England in the 1990s, finding a strong association between the use of high-quality group-based pre-school provision and children's early cognitive development and long-term school attainment (Sylva *et al.*, 2010).

More recently, the interim findings of the Study of Early Education and Development (SEED) (Melhuish and Gardiner, 2020) suggest less impact overall, when looking at the amount of time children spend in early education rather than whether they attend or not. The SEED study did find some significant impacts on the 40% most disadvantaged children, however. If they started to use a minimum of ten hours per week of early care and education no later than age two, and continued with over 20 hours per week of such provision between age two and the start of school, they had a higher chance of achieving expected standards of development in their Reception year and showed improved verbal ability in Y1.

The evaluation of the pilot of government-funded provision for disadvantaged two-year-olds (Smith *et al.*, 2009) also found a positive impact, in this case on the children's early language development – which as we will see in later chapters is fundamental to narrowing later attainment gaps, particularly for disadvantaged boys.

So starting pre-school provision early is really important. Many schools understand this and as a result have used government funding to develop their own provision for two-year-olds. Since take-up of the entitlement of 15 hours of free early education is very variable across the country, and fell back in 2019 to 68% of eligible children (National Audit Office, 2020), with lower take-up and poorer-quality provision in disadvantaged areas, there is considerable scope for schools to get involved.

Another important factor is working with families. There is strong and consistent evidence (Asmussen *et al.*, 2018) for providing two-generation programmes (that is, programmes targeting the home learning environment through support for parents alongside centre-based care for children) to low-income families where children are at particular risk.

Quality is also vital – but what actually constitutes 'high-quality early years provision'? The EPPSE study looked at the characteristics of pre-school centres with 'good to excellent' child outcomes (Siraj-Blatchford *et al.*, 2002) and suggests that these settings had staff who engaged in more adult–child verbal interaction, and in particular, used 'sustained shared thinking' – working alongside children to solve a problem, clarify a concept, evaluate an activity or extend a narrative. There was an equal balance between adult-led and child-initiated activity, and staff were skilled in helping parents to support children's learning at home.

Finally, it is worth noting that high-quality nursery provision will not in itself narrow the disadvantage gap in the long term. It has to be followed by high-quality provision in the school years. This was the finding in a US randomised controlled study (Pearman *et al.*, 2020) that looked at the effects of early years provision in Tennessee on children's attainment in the short term and later on when the participants were nine. Only when children were exposed in the primary years to both high-quality schools and high-quality teachers did those who received the pre-kindergarten provision show significantly greater achievement in English and maths than the control group.

Additional time in schooling before the age of five

A fascinating study (Cornelissen and Dustman, 2019) made use of the historical variations in the rules for starting school across local authorities to investigate the effects of age at school entry. Up until 2005–2006 some schools could defer entry for children born later in the year until the second or third term of Reception. Information from the National Pupil Database on more than 400,000 children in England born in 2000–2001 was combined with information on more than 7,000 of these children from the Millennium Cohort Study. The researchers found that additional time in school was linked to higher test scores in language and numeracy at age seven for all children, with pupils' age at the time of testing controlled for, but that the effects were particularly marked for disadvantaged boys. An additional term of schooling before age five reduced the achievement gap between boys from low and high socio-economic backgrounds at age seven by 60–80%.

There could be a number of explanations for this finding, including the fact that pre-school provision children attended in this period was generally part time, whereas in school it was full time – so it needs to be treated with caution. Although the rules have now changed so that only parents can apply for deferred entry, the research does suggest that early exposure to the more formal aspects of schooling can be actively beneficial to disadvantaged boys – or at least not harmful. It also implies that those who argue that we should delay the age of formal schooling for all children need to consider carefully whether this might inadvertently widen the disadvantage gap.

Behaviour interventions and social and emotional learning

Particularly for older pupils, there is evidence that behaviour interventions can contribute to improved attainment. The interventions may be universal – aimed at developing a positive school ethos and better behaviour in classrooms – or targeted at students with specific behavioural issues. Examples would be anger management and social skills programmes.

These programmes overlap with another category of intervention with extensive international research, including a number of meta-analyses – social and emotional learning (SEL). SEL interventions seek to develop the fundamental skills which underpin positive behaviour: self-awareness, self-management, social skills, relationships and social problem-solving. They involve active teaching rather than just 'managing' behaviour via teacher responses, rewards and sanctions. SEL approaches have been found to be effective in primary and secondary schools, and early years settings, and will be discussed further in Chapter 9.

Increased access to technology

Schools sometimes choose to spend their Pupil Premium on increased access to technology for disadvantaged pupils. New kit can feel exciting for both adults and children, and there is a possibility that digital technology might be particularly motivating for boys, and for disadvantaged children who do not always have the same access to technology at home as their better-off peers.

The EEF find both technology for students (where learners use programmes or applications designed for problem solving or open-ended learning) and technology for teachers (such as interactive whiteboards or learning platforms) to be associated with learning gains.

A recent systematic review of the impact of education technology (Escueta *et al.*, 2020), paints a slightly different picture. It found that at ages six to 18, equipping students with a computer and internet access generally had no effects on academic outcomes. The review also found that computer-assisted learning programs were effective in maths but not in reading.

Some approaches – like drill and practice programmes, or programmes which aim to assess where each pupil is in their learning and take them through appropriate sequenced activities, seem to be less effective than others. Much 'remedial' software is based on this principle, and many teachers have hoped that pupils could be left to progress independently through computer-generated activities that would enable them to catch up. Unfortunately, the evidence shows that this is rarely effective; there is as yet no substitute for the interaction between teacher and child. Technology, it seems, should be used to supplement other teaching, rather than replace it. It works best when it enables teachers to actually teach differently, and where its potential as a tool for group work and collaborative learning is fully exploited.

Peer tutoring

Peer tutoring involves children taking a formal role in helping each other to learn. In cross-age tutoring, older pupils are paired with younger ones; in same-age tutoring peers in a class work together several times a week using structured approaches for mathematics and reading; in reciprocal peer tutoring, learners take turns to act as tutor.

The EEF Toolkit concludes that there is strong evidence for peer tutoring programmes at both primary and secondary level, and in a variety of subjects. Two recent EEF evaluations for reading and maths (Lloyd *et al.*, 2015a, 2015b) failed to show impact, but this may be because whole classes took part, rather than targeted pupils needing support.

Paired reading is commonly a focus; here pairs of pupils chose reading material together, with the tutor then supporting the tutee using a standard sequence:

- Tutor and tutee read aloud together
- The tutor then stops reading aloud while the tutee continues reading on their own
- When the tutee makes errors or struggles to pronounce a word, the tutor waits for five seconds before intervening with the correct word
- The pair then read aloud together again until the tutee signals they want to continue on their own
- The process repeats, alternating reading together and tutee reading alone
- The tutor and tutee question one another, before, during and after the reading
- The tutor praises the younger pupil (tutee) throughout.

Peer tutoring ought to be of great interest to schools, since apart from managing a project and training and supporting tutors, the costs are minimal. Interestingly, academic benefits have been found for both tutors as well as tutees.

Some studies suggest that a two-year age gap is ideal for cross-age tutoring, that short-term blocks (four to ten weeks) of tutoring are more effective than longer-term programmes, and that the best use of all kinds of peer tutoring is to help children consolidate rather than undertake new learning.

Homework for secondary pupils

The evidence for the impact of primary school homework on attainment is weak, but for secondary students there is no doubt that pupils who complete between one and two hours per school day do better academically (EEF, 2018). It is important that tasks are linked closely to main class teaching, and that students get high-quality feedback on their work. Disadvantaged pupils of course often have nowhere to do homework and may lack access to technology, and effective schools provide them with both. They also help parents understand the importance of regular homework routines, whilst making clear that what matters is their support for these routines, encouraging their child and showing interest rather than being directly involved in the actual tasks (Patall *et al.*, 2008).

Collaborative learning

Many systematic reviews and meta-analyses have provided consistent evidence about the benefits of collaborative learning. A review by Jonathan

Sharples and colleagues (2011) found positive impacts on low-achieving pupils in disadvantaged schools for programmes that coached teachers in how to develop cooperative learning, in which pupils work in small groups to help each other learn – for example, in reading. Cooperative Integrated Reading and Composition (CIRC), for example, had positive effects in several studies involving white working-class pupils. Other examples are the whole-school Success for All approach, and the PALS approach (Peer Assisted Learning Strategy) – a type of peer tutoring, in which teachers pair lower- and high-performing pupils, and the partners work on different activities that address the skills that they are struggling with. The pairs are changed regularly, giving all pupils the opportunity to act as coaches and players.

Both primary and secondary students can benefit from collaborative approaches, and there are good impacts for maths as well as reading. It is worth noting that Ruth Miskin's successful approaches to teaching early reading have a strong emphasis on cooperative learning.

A recent meta-analysis of 'peer learning' (Tenenbaum *et al.*, 2019) defined it as any occasion when two or more students come together to discuss a learning activity. The review found that children working with peers learned more effectively than children doing the same task individually. The researchers observe that following up direct teaching with work in a group supports children in their understanding, perhaps because pupils have to explain their thinking. Interestingly, the study found that there was little difference between the positive impact of pairs versus larger groups of children. Peer interaction was found to be more effective when children were specifically instructed to reach consensus than when they were not.

The EEF suggest that cooperative learning tasks need to be designed carefully so that children will perceive benefits of working together, or else some pupils will opt out and work on their own. Children will need to be taught how to work effectively in groups and have plenty of support and practice. We will look at how this can be achieved in Chapter 4.

Additional one-to-one and small group tuition

A huge weight of evidence summarised in the EEF Toolkit demonstrates the impact of one-to-one and group tuition delivered by teachers or TAs to low-attaining pupils. Programmes involving TAs or volunteers tend to be less effective than those using experienced and specifically trained teachers, which on average have nearly twice the effect. As a rule the smaller the group the better; one-to-one tuition has the largest impacts and effects start to diminish with group sizes of six or more. For reading, one-to-one teaching of early reading is more effective than group tuition, though for older pupils working on reading comprehension in groups can be effective. In early maths, some evidence suggests that small group tuition in twos or threes can be just as effective as one-to-one tuition. We will look in more detail at interventions for reading, maths and oral language in later chapters.

Slightly different from these intervention programmes delivered by TAs and teachers are approaches based on tutoring by graduates. There has been funding in England recently for a national tutoring programme (NTP), in which paid tutors not on the school staff provide extra tuition for disadvantaged pupils. If successful, the programme offers a real chance to narrow the disadvantage gap, given the fact that private tuition paid for by parents is very common for parents who can afford it, with one in four pupils outside London having accessed it (Nichols, 2020). The NTP best practice guidance (2020) suggests that:

- Tutoring programs conducted in school time tend to have larger impacts than those conducted after school.
- For one-to-one tuition, regular short sessions appear to result in optimum impact. Longer tutoring sessions can be effective for older pupils who are more able to concentrate for extended periods, however.
- Tuition needs to take place over a reasonably long period (perhaps six to 12 weeks) so that relationships can be built; the NTP recommended 15 hours of sustained sessions.

The evaluation of the national programme will be interesting, but so far the UK evidence on such external tutoring is limited, based on two EEF randomised controlled trial studies. In one (Torgerson *et al.*, 2018) the Tutor Trust charity deployed trained university students to tutor Y6 pupils. The children who received tutoring made an average of three months' additional progress in maths, and there were indications of particular benefits for FSM-eligible pupils and those with lower prior attainment. In the other (Lord, 2015), four secondary schools introduced their own Perry Beeches graduate coaching programme, involving regular academic tutoring for Y7 pupils struggling with reading and writing. Pupils involved in the intervention made five months' additional progress in literacy, compared to other pupils.

A recent meta-analysis of international evidence on all types of additional tuition (Nickow *et al.*, 2020) found that effects are stronger on average for teacher and paraprofessional (TA) tutoring programs as opposed to nonprofessional tutoring. Nevertheless, the study notes that paid volunteers and recent college graduates are all promising tutoring candidates.

Feedback, metacognition and self-regulation

The categories of interventions highest-rated by the EEF, on grounds of both effectiveness and cost, are giving pupils effective feedback on their learning, metacognition and self-regulation approaches.

Providing feedback on learning that is specific about what the pupil did that was effective and specific about what they can do to improve on previous performance works for all pupils, though not necessarily more so for disadvantaged children. We will explore feedback in more detail in Chapter 7, in the context of building self-efficacy.

Metacognition and self-regulation approaches aim to help pupils reflect on their own learning and understand the strategies that work best for them. Pupils are taught how to plan, monitor and evaluate their learning and to self-regulate in the sense of motivating themselves, coping with setbacks and persisting in the face of difficulties.

In the UK the EEF has tested out a number of self-regulation programmes, finding positive impacts, although smaller in size than the average seen in the international literature. Encouragingly, three of these UK programmes had particularly strong effects for pupils eligible for FSM.

Key take-aways

- Some of the approaches commonly taken by schools to narrow disadvantage gaps have little evidence of impact. These include aspiration interventions, small reductions in class size, and allocating TAs to support low-attaining pupils in class.
- The evidence for mentoring and enrichment is mixed.
- There is very strong evidence for teaching approaches which develop metacognition and self-regulation, and the explicit teaching of reading comprehension strategies.
- Also well supported by research evidence are one-to-one and group tuition, oral language interventions, social and emotional learning, collaborative learning and peer tutoring, outdoor adventure learning, phonics approaches and digital technology when used to support rather than replace the teacher.

4 The word gap

I am absolutely convinced that no school will get far in closing socio-economic attainment gaps unless they attend to children's spoken language. There is just too much evidence showing that weaker language skills predict low attainment for disadvantaged children (particularly boys) to ignore – and as we will see, there is also evidence that this is not just a correlation. Weaker oral language is a *cause* of low attainment, across the age range.

There seems to be particular language problems for poorer children in our country that are not linked to low general ability, and not found to the same extent elsewhere in the world. At the age of five we have in the UK a gap of 16 months between the vocabulary of children brought up in poverty and the vocabulary of better-off children (Waldfogel and Washbrook, 2010). The gap in non-verbal cognitive skills is only half that size, and the vocabulary gap in the UK much larger than in other developed countries.

An average gap of 16 months at an average age of 60 months is a very big gap indeed. And these early language skills in Reception go on to predict attainment right through school – and beyond. Here are the statistics:

- Much of the observed socio-economic gradient in attainment at age seven may be explained by children's language skills at age five (Finnegan *et al.*, 2015).
- At age 11, children who had poor language at age five are six times less likely to achieve the expected standard in English and 11 times less likely to achieve the expected standard in maths (Save the Children, 2015).
- In secondary school, vocabulary at age 13 strongly predicts both English and maths at GCSE – in English Literature and maths,

DOI: 10.4324/9781003176442-5

> vocabulary is a better predictor of success than pupils' socio-eco-
> nomic background (Spencer *et al.*, 2017).
> - Vocabulary at age five is the best predictor of whether children
>   who experienced social disadvantage in childhood were able to
>   buck the trend and escape poverty in adult life (Blanden, 2006).

Language also predicts other difficulties that lead some white disadvantaged children to struggle in the school system – notably behaviour. At the
end of children's first year at school, lower language proficiency is associated with an increased risk of social, emotional and behavioural difficulties,
more so for children with English as their first language than English as an
Additional Language (EAL) (Whiteside *et al.*, 2016). In a study of secondary
pupils at risk of exclusion from school, two-thirds were found to have speech,
language and communication needs (Clegg, 2004); other research shows that
81% of children with emotional and behavioural disorders have unidentified
language difficulties (Hollo *et al.*, 2014).

Equipping disadvantaged young people to be able to confidently and effectively articulate information and ideas has the potential to make a significant
difference to their social mobility. There is some evidence that a key factor
in the over-representation of children educated in the private sector in elite
universities and in white collar professions may be the more developed and
confident communication skills developed in many public schools as a result
of very small class sizes and teaching styles. In a survey of 900 teachers
across the UK (Millard and Menzies, 2016), teachers in independent schools
reported fewer barriers to initiating talk-based activities than those in state
schools. They were also more likely to:

- Feel that it was very important their schools help pupils develop skills in
  oracy
- Report that their school had debating clubs
- Communicate formally with parents about the quality of pupils' contributions in lessons

Boys and language

Boys seem to be particularly at risk of language-related low attainment.
A Save the Children study (Moss and Washbrook, 2016) found that two-thirds

of the gender gap in achieving at least the expected level in Reading at age 11 is attributable to the fact that boys have lower levels of language and attention at age five.

As we saw in Chapter 1, boys are more likely than girls to experience language difficulties and delays. They are also more vulnerable to the wider impacts of language delays when they do occur. For boys, below-expected language in the early years is strongly linked to weaker later self-regulation skills, to the detriment of their conduct (Vallotton and Ayoub, 2011). A recent analysis of the Millennium Cohort sample, moreover, observed that language delays were associated with behavioural problems in boys during preschool, but were not for girls (Gibson, 2018).

Studies additionally observe that social disadvantage may have a greater impact on boys' language development than it does on that of girls (Barbu *et al.*, 2015). An interesting Early Intervention Foundation analysis of Early Years Foundation Stage Profile results in Communication and Language (Gross, 2020) found a larger gender gap in language outcomes for children eligible for FSM than for non-eligible children – driven by the particularly low achievement of FSM-eligible boys. Another study (Moss and Washbrook, 2016) found that the gender gap in early language and communication was highest in disadvantaged areas.

Correlation or cause?

Remembering the pot plant analogy, it is important to show that interventions to improve language do actually also increase attainment. There is considerable evidence of this from experimental studies:

- Reception children involved in the 20-week NELI (Nuffield Early Language Intervention programme) made two additional months' progress in early word reading, on average, compared to children who did not receive NELI, in addition to four additional months' progress in language skills (Dimova *et al.*, 2020).
- A rigorous study for the EEF (Jay *et al.*, 2017) found a significant uplift to attainment in English, maths and science after teachers introduced dialogic techniques in their primary classrooms.
- For Y5 children with poor reading comprehension, an intervention to boost oral language skills made a more lasting difference to reading comprehension than an intervention directly teaching reading comprehension skills (Clarke *et al.*, 2013).

- In the secondary years, KS3 pupils taking part in a vocabulary and oral narrative intervention ('Talk for Literacy') made three months' extra progress in reading (Styles and Bradshaw, 2015).

As a general rule, interventions evaluated by the EEF prove less effective for disadvantaged children than for the whole sample. This does not seem to be the case, however, for language-based programmes, such as Philosophy for Children and Thinking, Doing, Talking Science, where children eligible for FSM make greater academic progress after the intervention than the overall average.

What are the language issues for school-aged disadvantaged children?

Some time ago I noticed the lack of connection between the ways different expert groups think about language. On the one hand there are EAL specialists, and on the other those who focus on 'speech, language and communication needs' in special educational needs and disadvantage contexts. At the same time, I realised that models developed by EAL theorists had much to offer our understanding of language delay in disadvantaged groups.

The well-known EAL model developed by Jim Cummins (2008) posits two types of language: BICS (Basic Interpersonal Communicative Skills) and CALP (Cognitive Academic Language Proficiency). Cummins notes that it takes only two years or less of immersion for a child new to English to develop the everyday conversation skills involved in BICS. Teachers may at this stage think that the child is fluent. But developing CALP, the type of language used in academic situations, is not at all complete after two years. It can in fact take up to seven years before the child is working on a level with native speakers as far as the language needed for schooling is concerned.

A key feature of BICS is that the language is 'context embedded'. A good part of the meaning can be inferred from the situation, the shared knowledge of the speaker and listener, from gestures and intonation. The speaker can use conversational short cuts; they do not need to spell everything out. CALP, however, tends to be 'context reduced': there are very few clues to meaning outside the language.

To illustrate the difference I use the example of a boy whose mobile phone has been taken by another student in the playground. When speaking to the lunchtime assistant who saw the event and shares the context, all the boy might need to say is 'He dunnit - he's run over there now' (BICS).

But then if a teacher is summoned and comes out to investigate, not sharing the context, the boy might need to say something like 'A boy with ginger hair took my phone . . . he's standing with his back to us, by the water fountain' (CALP).

So what has this to do with disadvantaged learners? What I realised was that many of these pupils who are native speakers of English nevertheless may not have progressed much beyond BICS. The task for teachers of these children is not so different from the task for teachers seeking to help bilingual learners in the later stages of acquiring fluency in English. They need to explicitly develop vocabulary and scaffold the use of more complex, decontextualised and formal language – language where, for example, vocabulary is less conversational ('conceal' and 'obtain' rather than 'hide' and 'get'), where the passive voice might be used instead of the active voice. . . ('The questionnaire was administered . . .' rather than 'We administered the questionnaire . . .'), and where verbs or adjectives are often translated into nouns ('The army's overwhelming desire to expand further' rather than 'The army wanted to make Japan bigger no matter what').

In this chapter we will consider classroom strategies to move children in the primary and secondary years from context-dependent conversational language to the more formal, de-contextualised language they need for learning. But first let us look at what schools can do in the early years, so as to reduce the scale of the challenge teachers face when children are older.

Early years

Top tips

- Consider developing provision for disadvantaged two-year-olds
- Work with parents on initiatives to improve the home learning environment
- Develop more 'communication hotspots' in the learning environment
- Make time for conversations and train staff in the types of interaction that promote language development
- Share more books with target children
- Deliberately choose useful vocabulary to teach systematically
- Use the Early Years Pupil Premium to provide small-group language 'catch-up' interventions for targeted children

Consider developing provision for disadvantaged two-year-olds

We know that early education and childcare supports improved language development for disadvantaged children. For example, findings involving the Millennium Cohort observed a small, but significant benefit for disadvantaged children attending centre-based provision when they were later given language and attainment tests at ages three, five and seven (Côté et al., 2013). The evaluation of the government-funded 15 hours of early education for the most disadvantaged two-year-olds found a positive effect on language, where the provision was of high quality (Smith et al., 2009).

Starting early – before the age of two, or soon after – has the greatest effect. One study (Sylva et al., 2011) found that out-of-home group care (for more than 12 hours per week) before the age of two predicted gains in children's vocabulary at age five in comparison with children not receiving childcare.

Schools are rarely able to offer provision for under-twos, but more and more have become interested in developing provision for two-year-olds as well as the traditional nursery class. So if at all possible, that would be one strong recommendation for narrowing the language gap for disadvantaged children, and boys in particular.

Work with parents on initiatives to improve the home learning environment

Even more significant as a predictor of early language is the home learning environment: the extent to which parents engage in two-way conversations with their children, respond sensitively to their attempts to communicate, share books and sing songs and rhymes. Government and other agencies are attempting to help parents improve home learning environments, through campaigns like 'Hungry Little Minds' (DfE) and 'Tiny Happy People' (BBC). In Chapter 10 we will look at programmes and practices that schools can use to develop their own home learning environment initiatives.

Develop more 'communication hotspots' in the learning environment

A simple but very useful activity for early years practitioners is to identify aspects of the environment and daily routine which encourage lots of conversation (hotspots) and those that don't (coldspots). You can observe children at play and put coloured crosses on a map of the setting layout (inside and outside) to mark the hotspots for talking: one cross for places where talking takes place sometimes, more crosses if more often. With another coloured pen you then mark places where there is little talk.

Once coldspots have been identified, you can make plans for change. One setting, for example, noticed that in the outside area the children were spending most of their time riding round and round on bikes and cars, but not talking, so they turned a coldspot into a hotspot by setting up a pit-stop area with tools one day, and an improvised petrol pump made with bendy washing machine tubes attached to boxes on another. One early years setting in Stoke-on-Trent turned a fence between the setting and the primary school playground into a talking hotspot by the simple device of attaching ribbons to the fence for children on each side to thread.

Small changes can make all the difference, like not having all the equipment out for an activity, so children have to ask for what they want. Just defining an outdoor space with a circle of tree stumps, putting out a circular table with four chairs round it, or putting out old mobile phones (which immediately prompt de-contextualised talk) are all good conversation creators. Other settings have created hotspots by revamping book areas to include story props and puppets.

Make time for conversations, train staff in the types of interaction that promote language development, and share more books with target children

Two-way conversations are very important in the early years setting as well as at home. Research with disadvantaged two- and three-year-olds (Perry *et al.*, 2018) has found a positive association between a teacher talking and children's language development – but only when that teacher talked to the child in a back-and-forth conversation. Yet such conversations are often a low priority in classrooms because by their nature they are 'in the moment' and cannot form part of teachers' planning.

Early Years expert Penny Tassoni (2016) makes a simple suggestion for increasing the number of conversations with targeted children. She recommends that staff list the children who need help with their language on a flip chart or whiteboard. Next to the names are a series of columns. Every time a member of staff has a conversation of five minutes or more with a child, they put a tick in the first column next to the child's name. Another conversation means another tick, in the next column – and so on. Using this visual record means staff can monitor and target those 'wandering' children who flit from activity to activity and may not be engaging with adults for sustained periods.

11/03/21				
Andrew	☑			
Jason	☑	☑		
Conor				
Brooklyn	☑			
......				

Figure 4.1 Counting conversations

Some types of conversations are more successful in promoting language development than others. What doesn't work well is using closed questions ('What colour is it? Where does it live? How many are there?) Speech and language therapists suggest that instead we should use the 'hand rule' (Figure 4.2), in which adults use a ratio of no more than one question to four alternatives:

- Repeating back what the child has said ('Yes, you drew a picture of a peacock')
- Expanding on what the child has said, adding additional words they may not know ('Yes you've drawn a really detailed and colourful peacock picture')
- Commenting on what the child is doing ('it looks like you might have seen a peacock maybe . . . perhaps in a book, or when you went to the park?')
- Explaining an idea or concept ('Peacocks fan out their tail feathers to make the female [lady] peacocks notice them')

Figure 4.2 Hand rule
Source: Photo by Sincerely Media on Unsplash Adapted from *Communication Development*, a blog by Sophie Alder, developed after ELKLAN training

The hand rule also applies to sharing books, another highly effective way of building vocabulary and exposing children to de-contextualised, sophisticated language that is beyond the here and now. Book-sharing has been called 'the rocket fuel of language development,' because research consistently shows that children who read regularly with adults in early years learn language faster, enter school with larger vocabulary and become more successful readers (Mol *et al.*, 2008).

The greatest effect on language development is found when adults use a conversational style, talking around and about the book and encouraging the child to join in, rather than simply reading the story aloud (Rowland and Noble, 2016). It is important to link a story to the child's own experience, follow their interest, and ask open-ended ('Why do you think . . .') rather than closed ('What's he doing?') questions – or simply make comments that invite conversation ('He's asking his Dad for an ice cream. My favourite ice cream is that one with chunks of cookie dough in it . . .').

An interesting study of three-to-five-year-olds (Read *et al.*, 2019) found that using dramatic pauses that invite prediction led to greater word learning from a shared book than reading without the strategic pauses. It has also been found that children remember more words if they hear them through repeated reads of the same book rather than hearing them the same number of times but in several different books (Horst *et al.*, 2011; Damhuis *et al.*, 2014). So it seems that children really do know what's best for them when they ask for the same book again and again, however tedious that is for the adult. This finding was the basis of an innovative project in North Tyneside:

Over and Over: a project in North Tyneside

Ten North Tyneside primary schools with nursery provision each selected a group of disadvantaged children who were showing little interest in books and stories, including children with speech and language difficulties. The project involved school staff reading two books to the same group of children for 15 minutes daily, moving through a set of ten books over a six week period. Each book, from a box specially provided by the Schools Library Service, was shared five times as a minimum. Practitioners found that children previously unlikely to visit the book corner began to do so if they could see familiar books from the project on the shelves, and some also began to participate voluntarily in related activities which develop oral language, such as role-play.

Other ways of targeting children for extra shared reading include posting films of staff reading bedtime stories aloud on Facebook, allocating volunteers to read to them in school, and using Penny Tassoni's 'counting conversations' method described earlier, only this time with children receiving a tick against their name each time an adult shares a book with them.

Deliberately choose useful vocabulary then teach it systematically

Book-sharing is a great way to move children's language from the conversational to the more formal and de-contextualised forms. It can be one of the best ways of building vocabulary if it is followed up by planned opportunities to use the new words, such as small world play and props in role-play areas.

In book-sharing, as in all vocabulary teaching, we need to explicitly choose the words we want children to learn to master – the 'Goldilocks' words described by Stephen Parsons and Anna Branagan in their excellent 'Word Aware' books and training (Parsons and Branagan, 2013, 2016) as words that are 'not too easy, not too hard but just right.' The Goldilocks words are those which are just beyond children's everyday conversational vocabulary, but not specific to a particular topic. The words you might choose for a book or topic about pirates, for example, could be treasure, hook, adventure and explore, rather than the 'too easy' words (sword, ship, fight) or the 'too hard' words (compass, booty, ransack). The choice of words is a professional decision, based on your knowledge of the children; there can be no 'approved list'. To understand why, think of the words 'village' and 'chimney'. For children who live in blocks of flats in the city, these will be Goldilocks words. For those who actually live in a village, and in a house with a chimney, they will not need to be taught.

When it comes to the 'too hard' words, you will of course briefly explain what some of them mean if they are encountered in books or other contexts. Children with advanced vocabularies may well then remember them as a result. But children with fewer words in their store need explicit teaching, practice and review if they are to add the words to their vocabulary store. It will be a great deal more useful to focus that sustained process on the 'just right' words that will be useful to the child across multiple contexts.

The football nets

The football net metaphor helps explain why many disadvantaged children, and boys in particular, need to have new vocabulary explicitly taught.

Imagine all the words a child knows when they start school. For some children, there will be lots of words, with lots of links between them – like a strong football net. When an adult explains a new word to them, it is like throwing it into the net. The tight net of links will catch it. But some children come to school with just a few words in their net, and the words are not well connected to each other. Their football net has lots of holes in it, so when you introduce a new word it goes straight through the holes and is not remembered. These children do not easily pick up the vocabulary from one-off adult explanations or from a language-rich environment. It has to be explicitly taught in a sustained way, with regular recap and review.

EAL learners may not need the same approach. Many (though not all) come into school with a strong football net made up of words in their first language. Their task is to link the new English words with those they already know – but there is already a network of connections in which to embed them, so they may retain the vocabulary more easily.

Teaching the 'just right' words in the early years will involve building a web of links between the new word and other known words and schema. So, for example, you might teach the word 'hook' using the 'Word Magic' framework (Figure 4.3) from ICAN's Communication Cookbook (Lee, 2008).

Children will then need opportunities to hear and use the word repeatedly: for example, you might suggest they paint pictures of Captain Hook, put out a fishing game with a hook, bring in different types of hook to look at, talk about how you are hanging a picture and so on. One of the simplest ways of building vocabulary is often to use more complex words yourself – why always say 'Get your coat,' for example, when you could just as easily say 'Get your jacket/Get your parka/Get your mac?'

Some schools hang up their chosen Goldilocks words above relevant activities, so that everyone who interacts with children will be reminded to use

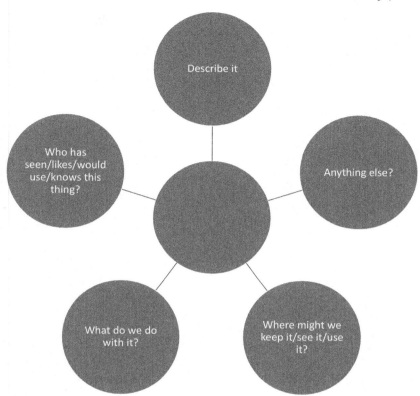

Figure 4.3 Word Magic
Source: Adapted from ICAN's Communication Cookbook (Lee, 2008)

the words repeatedly. In one setting, for example, I saw the words 'pouring', 'filling', 'scatter' and 'tiny' above pots of pasta and beans with jugs, funnels and bottles.

Use the early years pupil premium to provide small-group language 'catch-up' interventions for targeted children

A final suggestion is to target disadvantaged children in the early years for specific interventions. The 'Well Comm' tool published by GL Assessment allows practitioners to assess children's language then develop a tailored programme using its 'Big Book of Ideas.' Infant Language Link from SpeechLink provides online assessment and profiling, with suggested activities for individuals or groups identified as in need of a boost. Then there is the popular ICAN 'Early Talk Boost' small-group programme for nursery-aged children, and for Reception the Nuffield Early Language Intervention (NELI) which is marketed by Oxford University Press with training provided by ELKLAN. In the hands of skilled practitioners all of these represent really good value in terms of likely impact on language and later literacy skills.

Primary and secondary

Closing the word gap for disadvantaged children is just as important in the primary and secondary phases as it is in the early years. Again, there needs to be a balance of targeted intervention and whole-class strategies. Figure 4.4 shows a model I use to capture the core features of effective practice.

The model suggest that every school needs to have in place agreed, evidence-based methods for identifying and teaching key vocabulary, in the context of language-rich classrooms where children have many

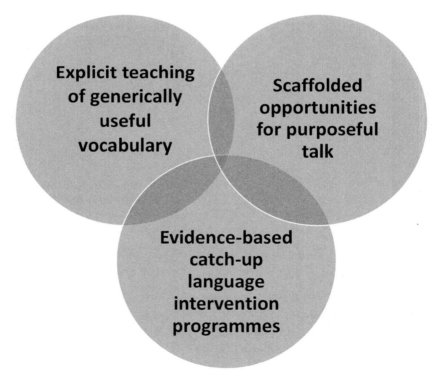

Figure 4.4 Core features of effective practice

opportunities to apply their learning, as well as targeted interventions. Let us look at each of these in turn.

Explicit teaching of generically useful vocabulary

Disadvantaged children continue to experience the 'football net' problem described earlier. In addition, it appears that we may inadvertently compound their vocabulary gap once they are in school. Research has found that teachers serving economically disadvantaged areas explain words less often and are less likely to explain sophisticated words than teachers in economically advantaged areas (Neuman and Wright, 2014). Grouping practices based on 'ability', too, may reduce opportunities for children with weaker language to learn from their peers. So we need to be mindful of this and make extra efforts to grow the vocabulary of disadvantaged pupils - including EAL learners and those disadvantaged white boys in particular.

Relatively easy ways of expanding vocabulary are modelling new words in everyday classroom talk ('Oh bother I left the door ajar' . . . instead of 'open') and using the expansion technique we looked at earlier in this chapter. This involves reflecting back what a child has said and adding vocabulary. For example, if a child complains to a head of year about one of his teachers ('She were going on at me'), the head of year can say 'OK, she was going on at you, *criticising* you . . . I wonder what that was about?' This example also illustrates the most effective technique for dealing with grammatical errors - simply repeating back what the child has said in the correct form.

Many teachers believe that wide independent reading is the best way for children to broaden their vocabulary. Unfortunately, in order to deduce the meaning of unfamiliar words from context a reader needs to be able to read and understand 95-98% of the *other* words in a passage. Many disadvantaged children will be nowhere near this figure. It works for good readers with wide vocabularies, but not for others, and so the vocabulary gap will widen year by year unless other strategies are in place.

Reading aloud *to* children, of course, helps overcome the problem, and increasing the number of read-alouds for disadvantaged children is as important in the primary as in the early years. Even in secondary school, form tutors can read aloud to the tutor group, using books carefully chosen to be of relevance to the students' lives.

One primary school scheduled daily whole-school story time; in Term 1 adults positioned themselves around the school with a favourite book to read aloud to groups, in Term 2 older children read to younger ones, and in Term

3 children within the same class were paired, with stronger readers reading aloud to partners.

When we come to explicit teaching of vocabulary, there are several models we can use:

- The Word Aware STAR approach (Parsons and Branagan, 2013) that we touched on earlier, which suggests four steps (**S**elect, **T**each, **A**ctivate and **R**eview) and provides a range of game-type activities.
- Alex Quigley's SEEC model (Quigley, 2018) in which the teacher **S**elects key vocabulary carefully, **E**xplains this in class (getting students to chant the word and its definition back to the teacher), **E**xplores the word through questioning and **C**onsolidates the key word later.
- A model based on the work of Isobel Beck (Sealey, 2019) in which the teacher first asks whether certain words are examples or non-examples of the target vocabulary. So for the word '*sleek*', for example, the teacher might offer hair, cat, porcupine, duck, tree, car and seal. S/he might then have children come up with concrete examples of the use of the target word – how might a cook, a musician, a teacher show they are, for example, *versatile*, or *industrious* or *expert*? Finally, teaching will involve true/false questions; for example, 'If you are *toppling*, you are the best at something. True or false?' or 'Toppling means something that might happen if you are unbalanced. True or false?'
- The closely linked 'Frayer model' (Table 4.1), a graphic organiser for the teacher and class to complete together.

What all the models have in common is an initial careful selection of words to teach – the just-right 'Goldilocks' words described as Tier 2 by Isobel Beck *et al.* (2002) – see Figure 4.5.

Tier 2 words for a primary topic on Victorian England might, for example, include petticoat and hoop but not gruel and workhouse. For a Y7 secondary science class studying the environment and feeding relationships, Tier 2

Table 4.1 The Frayer model

Definition	Characteristics
Examples	Non-examples

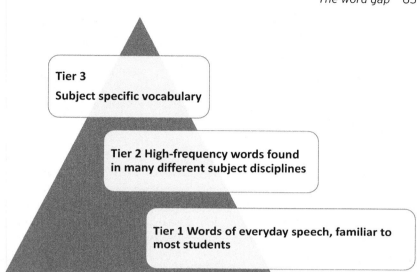

Tier 3
Subject specific vocabulary

Tier 2 High-frequency words found in many different subject disciplines

Tier 1 Words of everyday speech, familiar to most students

Figure 4.5 Isobel Beck's tiered vocabulary model

words might be produce, consumer and migration but not climatic stress or overwintering. This is not to say that these words should not be explained – they should, or else children will not understand the topic. But they do not all need to be taught to mastery level.

This is a really important distinction. Suppose children come upon the word 'incandescent' in their reading. It is a word they may enjoy, but are they going to need it regularly in their schooling? The word 'constructed', however, is going to come up in technology, in art, in literacy. So 'incandescent' will be briefly explained, and some children will catch it in their football net. But 'constructed' must be explicitly taught and practised until everybody can understand and use it.

We should never underestimate the gaps in children's knowledge of apparently 'easy' words. A headteacher told me recently how he asked a Y5 class who knew the meaning of the word 'fortnight' (as distinct from the computer game). Only two hands went up. Another told me about children who didn't understand the instruction 'circle the answer' in tests. For many disadvantaged children we need to check, check, check – and be prepared to teach when necessary.

The choice of which words to teach to this level is one for the teacher, for reasons explained earlier. Nevertheless, there are some useful lists of core academic vocabulary you can draw on - like the Berkeley Unified School district (BUSD) Grade Level Academic Vocabulary publication, freely available on the web.

We should always, across all subject disciplines, make sure to teach the key vocabulary used in tests and exams (Table 4.2).

Teaching of vocabulary should aim to build the football net by building multi-sensory links in the child's brain - phonological, semantic and grammatical. The sequence can go like this:

- First explore with the class what the word sounds like - what does it begin with, end with, rhyme with, how many syllables?
- Then look at its structure (prefixes, suffixes, root, morphemes). A morpheme is a unit of meaning, so the word unbreakable has three: un- (a morpheme that means 'not'), break (the root) and - able (a morpheme that means 'can be done').
- Then explore the word's meaning with questions like 'Where would you find it?, 'What category is it?' or 'What do you do with it?'
- Have the class make up an image, sign, gesture or movement to help them remember it.
- Put the word in a sentence and discuss whether it is a noun, adjective, adverb and so on.
- Finally, get children to think of words that go with it. You can ask them to tell a partner the first word that comes into their head when you say the target word. This helps link the new word to other words and concepts in the child's 'football net'.

All vocabulary teaching models emphasise the need to apply new vocabulary - with words on cards on the wall that children pull off to use in their writing, for example. In one school I met, teachers paired up; a Y5 teacher taught new words to a Y6 class, who then had to use the word appropriately in their conversations with their Y6 teacher. Her job was to guess the target word.

Table 4.2 Top test terms

Tick   Underline   Circle   Match   Re-write   Complete   Correct   Copy Calculate   Identify   Describe   Explain   List   Analyse   Compare   Contrast Outline   Comment on   Examine   Define   Discuss   Indicate   Persuade/argue Summarise   Demonstrate   Evaluate   Explore   Interpret   Infer   Illustrate Justify   Conclude

The next stage is to consolidate newly learned words by returning to them regularly. I always suggest we draw on the science of memory and use spaced practice, reviewing a word at progressively greater intervals: at the end of the lesson, at the end of the day, at the end of the week, at the end of the half term, at the end of term and end of year. Effective teachers will keep a word bank of all the words taught and regularly pull out one or two for a quick True/ False or matching game.

Opportunities for purposeful talk

Teaching word lists in isolation will not be effective unless children have many opportunities for using words in the classroom – and not simply words, but also the phrases and sentence structures in which they are embedded. Yet it appears that in the majority of classrooms such opportunities are rare. Studies (National Literacy Trust, 2011; Gregersen, 2014) have found that the typical pupil contribution to a class discussion is just four words, and that the average child aged 6–18 only asks one question per month for each subject they attend, while teachers ask an average of 291 questions a day.

Opportunities to contribute may not be equally distributed. When we look at the distribution of talk opportunities in classrooms, it is often the more advantaged who are getting more than their share of dialogue and discussion.

It is possible to address this imbalance, using simple classroom techniques such as:

- Scrapping quick-fire 'hands-up' questioning and asking every child to discuss an answer with a peer partner
- Asking more open-ended questions (Why? How?) rather than closed questions to which you already know the answer
- 'Bouncing' children's answers to others for comment: 'Thank you for making that point, Jo. Andrew, what are your thoughts on what Jo just said?,' or 'Can you build on what Jo just said/summarise what she said/compare her ideas with Andrew's/give reasons for agreeing or disagreeing?'
- Always asking the class 'What questions do you have?' rather than 'Has anyone any questions?'

Activities such as debating ('Would you rather drop a puppy or an I-pad?'), delivering TED talks, interviews, making podcasts or becoming museum or tour guides all develop language skills whilst also reinforcing subject knowledge.

Coastal Ilfracombe Junior School became aware that spoken language was a significant issue for their children, who tended to use simple structures and vocabulary ('They did this and I did that and then . . .'). The school wanted their disadvantaged children to be able to talk knowledgeably and confidently in a range of contexts. Staff taught the children that sometimes we need to elaborate and use what the children came to call 'David Attenborough' language.

Units of work were developed which begin by using Rosenstein's well-known principles of instruction to teach core subject knowledge. Once this was mastered the unit moved on to discussion and dialogue, where children learn that there are questions that don't have a 'right' answer, and are invited to express opinions backed up with facts.

In a Y5 geography unit on rivers and the water cycle, for example, a big question is posed at the beginning (Should dams be built on rivers?) Children then spend time acquiring solid knowledge before moving on to the dialogic stage. Knowledge builds from year to year; for example Y6 pupils discuss 'which civilisations have been most successful' drawing on their history learning in previous years.

Pupils also learn to prepare and make short speeches using key principles of hooking the listener in, providing background, giving their ideas and the evidence for them, then taking a different point of view and exploring that before reaching a conclusion.

The school has compiled a list of 4000 words to be systematically taught in daily vocabulary sessions, applied in shared and independent writing and consolidated at the end of each week with games and quizzes.

Voice 21 (https://voice21.org/) is the organisation to go to for brilliant training on how to develop approaches like these, and their website also provides many free resources like sentence starters to provide children with essential scaffolding. Another excellent site is Oracy Cambridge (https://oracycambridge.org/resources/).

One approach I particularly recommend for both primary and secondary schools in disadvantaged areas is Philosophy for Children (P4C). Here, children are presented with an initial stimulus, which might be a picture, a piece of film, or a text. They come up with relevant questions they would like to discuss. A class vote is used to decide which question to explore. In P4C sessions children lead the discussion; the teacher acts as a facilitator. Children learn to listen actively to one another, to think before they speak, and give reasons for what they say.

In one primary class, for example, Michael Rosen's book *Sad* formed the stimulus. The children formulated questions like 'Do people like to be on their own when they are sad?,' 'What is sadness?' and 'Why do people cry?' They decided to focus on the question 'Is it alright to be sad?' and pursued this line of enquiry. They agreed that it was alright to feel sad and that sometimes as humans we cannot control this.

P4C has been evaluated by the Education Endowment Foundation (Gorard *et al.*, 2015) and found to have a positive impact on KS2 attainment. Overall, pupils using the approach for just under a year made approximately two months' more progress in reading and maths than a control group. For the purposes of this book, an important finding was that the impact was even greater (four months for reading, three months for maths and two months for writing) for children eligible for FSM. A later evaluation did not replicate these effects, but half the schools involved did not actually implement the programme at the expected level.

Teaching children debating skills has also been shown to impact on attainment – and is, as we have seen, particularly important for disadvantaged pupils. Yet a recent study (Donnelly *et al.*, 2019) found that schools with the highest proportion of FSM-eligible pupils were half as likely to offer debating clubs as those with the lowest proportion.

Geoff Barton (Millard and Menzies, 2016) describes how he prioritised debating when he was headteacher at a Suffolk school serving a disadvantaged area; he used to take his students on the debating competition circuit, where they would come up against children from independent schools, fluent in what he calls 'the language of power'. His mission was to make sure that the children in his school had equal access to this kind of language.

I'm also a big fan of role-play areas and props in the primary classroom, linked to whatever topic the class are studying (and for secondary, the use of drama within other curriculum subjects). For a KS2 World War II unit of work, this approach might be as simple as providing two battered suitcases found in a second-hand shop, which children use to explore the evacuee experience, or with more effort a mocked-up 1940s sitting room for children studying the novel Rose Blanche, or a simple Anderson shelter area. I've seen the booking office on the Titanic with children taking calls from anxious relatives, a Viking museum, and an Astroturf-covered hut with slits cut for windows and inside a sleeping bag, binoculars and a bird-watching book – a hide, linked to work on habitats. What is vital is that children help to plan and design the role-play area, that adults model the language and vocabulary they expect children to use within it, and that they allocate proper curriculum time for children to use the resource. A role-play area is not somewhere you go to play when you've finished your work; for all children and for disadvantaged children in particular, practising new language *is* work, of a very important nature.

Scaffolding talk

Simply providing opportunities for meaningful talk is not enough. Children like Jason will also need structures and supports that move them from conversational to academic language.

I'm often struck by the way teachers put children into groups and expect them to have a reasoned group discussion. Group collaboration is a skill, and one that many adults struggle with – think back to an INSET day where people in your 'group' meandered, cut across each other, let the most confident speakers dominate, split off into pairs to chat, or simply gave up.

So we need to teach children to listen to each other, build on one another's views, make sure everyone contributes, and manage time. Voice 21 and Cambridge University's Thinking Together[1] programmes have many ideas for achieving this, for example through allocating roles (chairperson, ideas person, timekeeper, note-taker, reporter) and developing protocols for talk. I like the idea of asking children to come up with ideas about the behaviours that one would see in 'the worst group in the world' and then turn these into their opposites, so as to create ground rules for effective collaboration.

Another good form of scaffolding, which helps bring in less orally skilled children who might opt out (and prevents more verbal ones from dominating), is using talk counters. A pile is given to each child at the start of a class or group discussion, and each time the child makes a contribution, they put one of their counters in a pot. When they have used their counters they can say no more. The group learns to look out for those who are not spending their counters, and draw them in by asking for their ideas or opinions.

Teachers can scaffold academic language very easily in their responses to what a child has said – 'Can you use "moreover" to link to a second piece of evidence?,' for example.

Finally, every teacher of disadvantaged children needs to know about and use talk frames, which provide children with the scaffold of sentence starter or structure appropriate to the particular language purpose – recount, persuade, agree/disagree, justify and so on. If you search online for 'Tower Hamlets progression in language structures' you will find a set of very useful age-related talk frames covering all of these purposes and more.

At Parkside Primary in Bradford each teacher has a pack of these frames for their year group, in the form of laminated speech bubbles. Children have these out on their desks and on the walls to support discussion. If for example they were comparing a book with a film, the teacher would pull out the talk frames of comparison. For Y1 these might be simple: 'They are the same because . . .,' 'They are different because . . .,' while for Y6 they might be 'In some ways x and y are alike. For instance, they both . . .,' 'Another feature they have in common is. . . .' For every lesson, the type of talk is chosen and identified in the teacher's planning.

Schools can also develop subject sentence stems for each curriculum subject – in history, for example, 'This artefact shows that . . .,' 'This source illustrates that . . .,' 'This source is biased because . . . .' In English, a teacher might make a list of key vocabulary that is useful when analysing a text (words like juxtapose, evoke, underscore, elicit, symbolize, convey, allude to), then develop familiarity with the vocabulary by asking pupils to analyse forms they are more comfortable with, such as artwork or songs ('What do the blues in this painting evoke?,' 'How does Adele convey a particular tone in this song?') using talk frames:

This artist's use of _____ evokes _____
The singer conveys _____ by _____
The repetition of _____ underscores _____
In juxtaposing _____ and _____, the song ____

Older students like the idea of learning 'talk moves': examples might be a structure for building on others' contributions ('I would like to add to what XX said'), or to press for reasoning ('Why do you think that? What is your evidence?').

Evidence-based catch-up language intervention programmes

Even the most language-rich classrooms are unlikely on their own to close the language gap for many disadvantaged children. As with literacy, maths and social and emotional learning, what is needed is a three-Wave approach (Figure 4.6) in which there are opportunities for small-group, time-limited intervention programmes delivered by TAs or teachers, as well as access to speech and language therapy where the children need more specialist support.

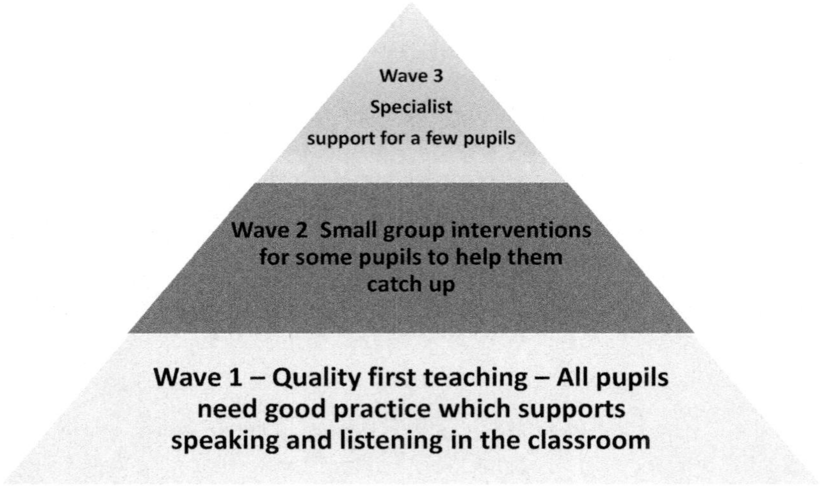

Figure 4.6 The three-Wave approach to language

Assessment tools such as WellComm and ICAN's Universally Speaking booklets can help identify those who need intervention. There is no short-age of evidence-based small group intervention programmes available for primary pupils at Wave 2:

- Key Stage 1 Narrative, Key Stage 2 Narrative (Black Sheep Press)
- Language for Thinking (Speechmark)
- Talking Partners (www.educationworks.org.uk)
- Talk Boost KS1 and Talk Boost KS2 (www.ican.org.uk)
- Infant Language Link and Junior Language Link (https://speechandlan-guage.info/)

Secondary programmes are thinner on the ground, but include

- TalkingPartners@Secondary (www.educationworks.org.uk)
- ELCISS (Speechmark) - evaluated by EEF as Talk for Literacy
- Talk Boost Y7 (www.ican.org.uk)
- Talk about Talk (www.ican.org.uk)
- Talk Fitness (https://speechandlanguage.info/secondary)

When well-trained staff deliver Wave 2 programmes to the right children (those whose limited language is linked to environmental factors rather than biologically based developmental language disorder), progress can be remarkable. Evaluation of Talk Boost KS1, for example, found that after the ten-week programme 83% of children reached age-expected levels in under-standing and using vocabulary, and over three-quarters of children reached age-expected levels in their ability to talk in sentences. After Talk Boost KS2, nearly three-quarters of children were working at age-expected levels in tell-ing stories and explaining what has happened.

Finding help for children who need specialist support (at Wave 3) may seem daunting, given the pressures on local NHS speech and language therapy (SLT) services. But more and more schools serving disadvantaged populations are deciding to buy in SLT time themselves. A recent guide from the NAHT and the Royal College of Speech and Language Therapists (NAHT, 2020) provides welcome advice on the nuts and bolts of investing in this way, as does the second edition of my book *Time to Talk* (Gross, 2018).

Finding out more

Readers might want to go to 'Time to Talk,' and to excellent books by Alex Quigley, Amy Gaunt and Alice Stott, for more detail on how to develop chil-dren's spoken language.

I would also recommend undertaking in-depth, whole-school professional development. You might, like the schools described in the following sec-tions, work on a sustained programme with your local speech and language therapy service, or contact organisations like ELKLAN, ICAN, Voice21, Educa-tion Works and Thinking Talking for training. I'd also recommend the online courses developed for Future Learn by expert advisory teachers at Babcock Education, and their Teaching Vocabulary CPD programme of six short ses-sions which one person in school can deliver to all staff.

Sustained professional development in a primary school

In one primary school in Worcestershire, staff noticed that increasing numbers of children were arriving at school not talking in sentences and with very limited vocabulary. The school made many referrals for speech and language therapy (SLT), but waiting lists were long, so they decided on a different approach. The governing body agreed to fund a day of SLT time a week for a year. Over this period the SLT trained staff to introduce one new strategy per half term. One strategy was the Word Aware approach to teaching vocabulary. Another half term, staff learned how to develop children's listening skills. All training was backed up with in-class coaching.

In addition the school introduced the online Infant Language Link programme in Reception, and small group intervention programmes to develop children's narrative skills. At the start, 60% of Reception children had speech and language difficulties but by the end of the year 87% were at age expected levels. A few children still required specialist SLT support, but the numbers were now manageable.

Sustained professional development in a secondary school

A secondary provision for boys with social, emotional and behavioural difficulties worked on a sustained staff development programme with the children's communication charity ICAN. Staff learned how to increase opportunities for discussion in class, asking more open and fewer closed questions. Bit by bit, they introduced changes like explicitly teaching students how to work in small groups, and providing generic talk frames. Independent evaluation showed that the majority of staff made changes to their teaching practice: they talked less, gave students more thinking time, and were more skilled in facilitating whole-class discussion. Staff fears that moving from teacher-dominated talk would lead to behaviour getting out of control were not borne out. The teachers reported that as a result of the CPD programme their students were more confident and able to work independently.

Key take-aways

- Evidence suggests that under-developed oral language skills are a cause of low attainment across the age range, particularly for disadvantaged boys.
- In the early years, schools can try to develop provision for disadvantaged two-year-olds. Increase the number of conversation 'hotspots' in the environment, train staff in the types of interaction

that promote language development, and increase the number of books shared with target children.

- In all age groups it is important to systematically teach, apply and revisit carefully chosen, generically useful vocabulary.
- Learning word lists alone is unlikely to be effective; children need scaffolded opportunities for collaborative groupwork, role-play and drama, debate and open-ended class discussion.
- Short-term, small group language intervention programmes can have a big impact on closing the word gap, as long as the right children are targeted.

Note

1   http://thinkingtogether.educ.cam.ac.uk.

5 The literacy gap

In this chapter we will examine some of the difficulties disadvantaged children, and boys in particular, may experience with reading and writing. We will look at effective class-based strategies for developing the core skills, and at short-term 'catch-up' interventions. But first, let us look at examples of schools where our group of pupils are doing well in literacy.

Broken Cross Primary Academy and Nursery serves an area with high unemployment in Macclesfield, once a thriving industrial and silk-manufacturing town. Almost all pupils are of white British origin. Forty-two per cent of pupils receive the Pupil Premium, but in 2018–2019 the school's reading progress and test results were above the national average, with maths at the national average.

Five years ago the school set up its own resourced provision for children with language difficulties, as a response to the numbers coming through from the nursery with significant needs. The provision is led by a specialist teacher, whose expertise has (in the words of headteacher Donna Lewis) 'had a huge knock-on effect on all staff.'

The school's nursery offers places to two-year-olds as well as older children, and developing spoken language skills is a major focus of its work. Very generous staffing ratios at the start of the year make it possible for adults to have many back-and-forth conversations with children. This year the school will also offer the evidence-based NELI (Nuffield Early Intervention Language Programme) to children in Reception who need help with their language.

The school has an Oracy lead as well as leads for Reading, and Writing. The lead teacher has undertaken Voice 21's three-day course and

DOI: 10.4324/9781003176442-6

developed an oracy action plan for the school. All staff receive training on good classroom oracy practice and have been trained in the 'Word Aware' approach to building vocabulary.

Headteacher Donna is a trained Reading Recovery teacher. The principles of Reading Recovery – such as the reciprocal relationship between reading and writing – are embedded in literacy teaching across the school, from the Reception Literacy package that is in place, through to helping parents understand their key role in building children's pace and fluency in home reading.

Phonics is taught through the Letters and Sounds programme and supplemented by Y5 and 6 children going into Y1 regularly for ten minutes of phonics flash card work with the children.

There is huge emphasis on reading for pleasure. A few years ago every child received a free gift of a pack of books to create a home library. Children are encouraged to borrow lots of books to read at home, and no-one will be worried if they don't return them. Parents have become enthusiastic about reading and enjoy challenges and competitions at parents' evenings.

Donna is an accredited trainer for the Inference programme developed in Leicester, a group intervention for pupils in KS2 and KS3 who decode adequately but fail to get full meaning and enjoyment from their reading. The intervention typically involves groups of four pupils, for 40-minute sessions twice a week over a period of ten weeks. Donna herself delivers sessions to Y6 pupils; other staff have also had the training.

To teach writing the school uses the IPEELL programme, which emphasises metacognition and self-regulation, and provides a clear structure that helps pupils to plan, monitor and evaluate their writing. The scheme has been evaluated by the EEF and shown to improve the writing skills of lower attaining children.

Interventions for children struggling with reading and/or writing are individualised and carefully tailored to identified gaps in learning. They are delivered by teachers as well as TAs.

Scalby secondary school in Scarborough serves a coastal community which once had a large fishing industry, now largely defunct. The catchment area is mixed and includes a relatively affluent village as well as poorer areas. Ninety-three per cent of the pupils are from white British backgrounds, and 25% are disadvantaged. Five years ago only 25–30% of pupils eligible for the Pupil Premium achieved five good GCSEs including English and maths; now more than half do. The Progress 8 measure for this group formerly stood at -0.4, but now hovers at around zero, with non-disadvantaged students at around 0.5.

The school's leaders attribute the change in part to a focus on improving the quality of everyday teaching. There has been a strong CPD programme based on incremental coaching; every member of staff takes part in a coaching cycle in which they work on a small aspect of their practice (such as 'How can I give lower-attaining disadvantaged students more time and more opportunities to answer questions?') for two or three weeks at a time.

Maths and English departments are over-staffed so that students who need extra tuition can receive this from skilled teachers. For students with literacy difficulties, the school uses a programme called 'Thinking Reading,' a whole-school strategy with one-to-one intervention at its heart. It targets children with the most serious reading difficulties and enables them to catch up completely. Staff are trained to use detailed diagnostic assessment and provide intensive teaching, usually one-to-one in Y7 and 8, several times a week. Six members of staff at Scalby have been trained including the literacy lead, the SEND manager, a subject teacher and three assistant teachers. Lessons begin with key vocabulary, which is then rehearsed in texts. Students can be expected on average to remain in the programme for about six months and typically gain five years or more in their reading.

In Y9 students may move on to Accelerated Reader, a well-evidenced online programme which assesses pupils' reading levels and suggests reading materials at the right level. Pupils take comprehension tests on the texts they have read and earn points and rewards as they progress through the scheme.

Reading

We should never, ever underestimate how difficult it is for some children to learn to read. Year on year, around one in ten boys leave primary school with the reading skills of an average seven-year-old, unable to read the simplest secondary school texts. These are the children who inevitably become profoundly disaffected, with an increased risk of truancy and exclusion from school.

The majority (though not all) of these children are disadvantaged, and are male. As we saw in Chapter 2, in 2018, 30% of children eligible for free school meals in England failed to meet the expected standard on the national phonics test at age six, compared to 16% of all other children. Thirty-eight per cent of white boys eligible for free school meals failed to reach the expected standard. At re-sits when they were seven, *one in five* such boys still had not met the expected standard.

Reading difficulties are often familial; several studies have found a high incidence in children whose parents themselves found it hard to learn to read (Snowling and Melby-Lervåg, 2016). I link this with the 'cycle of disadvantage', in which disadvantaged children who struggle with reading go on to have children who experience the same difficulties, so that educational failure is often transmitted through the generations for one clear reason – poor early reading.

H is for Harry

Harry, a white working class boy whose story is told in the 2019 documentary 'H is for Harry,' started Y7 at the celebrated Reach Academy in Feltham unable to read and write. His dad, Grant, and his grandfather couldn't read or write either.

'I didn't learn nothing at school,' says Grant in the film. 'I've got no education, no qualifications. My sister said I kept walking out of lessons. That was probably because I was having trouble reading and writing. My dad is much worse than me actually. I've never seen my dad read a paper because I know he can't do it. Life does repeat itself. It's just like repeat, repeat, repeat. I've had it and now my dad's had it. And now my son's going to have it.'

Harry spends his English lessons in a withdrawal group with three other boys. His teacher, Sophie, works hard to teach them basic skills: phonics, spelling, writing a sentence. Harry makes good progress, but finds it hard to believe he can succeed. In Y8, back in the main class, he struggles to keep up and becomes frustrated and dejected. His behaviour goes increasingly haywire. Grant comes in regularly for meetings with pastoral staff, Sophie and senior leaders.

Eventually, the school makes the difficult decision that it can no longer offer the support Harry needs. He moves to a social, emotional and mental health provision in West London, where the film leaves him.

'For Harry it is just that lack of belief; it's hard to always be behind and I don't think he could really cope with that,' says Sophie. 'It did work really well, we just couldn't maintain it long enough to make the difference I wanted it to make, I think. That's what's really sad.'

Why is reading so difficult for some children?

The well-known 'reading rope' model (Scarborough, 2001) in Figure 5.1 helps us understand how the development of skilled reading involves multiple, interwoven skills.

If I reflect on what I learned as an educational psychologist from assessing Jason at various points, I can clearly see the many frayed strands in his rope.

Jason and the reading rope

In the word recognition strands Jason struggled with phonics from day one, as a result of poor phonological awareness – from lots of colds and blocked up ears, perhaps, or his history of late development of clear speech, or the family history of reading difficulties that had never been called dyslexia in those days but might well be now.

He had difficulty in detecting small differences in spoken sounds on one test I gave him, and was unable to blend a series of sounds spoken to him into a whole word. Because sounds were shifting and unclear to him, he was not able to link them consistently with print. He didn't retain phoneme-grapheme correspondences or high-frequency exception words like 'was' and 'said'.

In the language comprehension strands, when I first met him he could not point to a 'word' or 'letter', never mind understand what a phoneme was. He simply did not have the vocabulary levels or language structures he needed to make sense of even the simplest texts; on a reading test even if I read to him a passage he could not read himself he was not able to understand it well enough to answer questions about it.

Background knowledge was a real issue: one test had a passage about a surprise parcel. Jason did not know what a parcel was. Inference was an impossibility – how can you read between the lines when the lines themselves are incomprehensible?

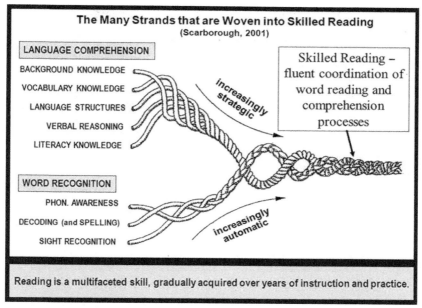

Figure 5.1 The Reading Rope

Source: Scarborough, H. S. (2001). Connecting early language and literacy to later reading (dis)abilities: Evidence, theory, and practice. In S. Neuman and D. Dickinson (eds.), *Handbook for research in early literacy* (pp. 97–110). New York, NY: Guilford Press. Reproduced by kind permission

For children like Jason it is the *multiple* barriers to learning that make their reading difficulties so hard to tackle.

What happens if you're finding early reading difficult

Early reading difficulties persist. Research has found that children who have poor reading skill at age six–seven years have an 88% likelihood of remaining below expected levels for their age for the following three years (Juel, 1988). Data from 2018 show that fewer than one in five pupils who fail to reach the expected standard in Reading at the end of KS2 go on to achieve the former Grade 4 or above in GCSE English (Quigley and Coleman, 2019).

Teachers tend to group children in KS1 according to their reading skills, which means that those who struggle (for a whole variety of reasons, from familial reading difficulties like Jason's to SEND, behaviour problems or being in the early stages of learning EAL) are exposed early to all the disbenefits of fixed 'ability groupings' that we examined in Chapter 3. Because of these groupings, these children also understand, very early, that judgements are being made about their reading. Boys, it seems, are more sensitive to this process than girls (Moss, 2002).

So if there is one plea in this book, it is that we tackle the issue early, with the basic skills in place before the end of KS1, on which further work on reading comprehension and reading for pleasure builds in KS2.

> The importance of getting children off to a good start in reading cannot be overstated. Success in primary school is virtually synonymous with success in reading – good readers are more likely to succeed in all subjects in secondary school and beyond, while poor readers are likely to continue to have reading problems, to struggle with other subjects, and to become unmotivated and develop problems with behaviour, self-esteem and attendance.
>
> Sharples *et al.*, 2011. *Effective classroom strategies for closing the gap in educational achievement for children living in poverty, including white working-class boys.*

One analysis of pupils permanently excluded in Year 9 (Gross and Members of the KPMG Education Advisory Team, 2009a) showed that those who entered secondary school with very low literacy skills (below the old National Curriculum Level 3 in English) had an exclusion rate five times that of pupils entering KS3 at the age-expected level or above. They were also over four times more likely to truant than those who entered with age-appropriate skills.

Another study (Parsons and Bynner, 2002) found that 73% of socially disadvantaged pupils who had been poor readers at age ten wanted to leave school at 16, compared to 48% of disadvantaged good readers and 31% of non-disadvantaged good readers. At age 16, over half of boys with poor reading skills thought that school was a waste of time.

What can we do to identify difficulties early?

We know from research that it is possible to predict which children are at risk of later reading difficulties on the basis of two key factors: whether they had language delay or difficulties in their early years, and whether there is a family history of reading and/or spelling difficulties. One study (Snowling *et al.*, 2019) found that 55% of children fitting these criteria at age three-and-a-half went on to have clinically significant reading or language difficulties at age eight.

On this basis, we can include these factors in information gathered from parents when their child starts school. It is possible to do this tactfully, by asking for example, 'Did anyone in your family struggle with reading or spelling when they were at school?' and explaining why you are asking: 'We're asking this because scientists have found that reading problems can be inherited, and we try to give extra help to any child who might need it, as early as we can.'

If children are at risk, you can plan specific work on phonological awareness and spoken language, using activities such as those in Phase One of the Letters and Sounds programme (DfES, 2007) or, the more intensive Nuffield Early Language Intervention (NELI), described later in this chapter.

Another thing to get checked is the child's hearing. Research on eight- to ten-year-olds (Carroll and Breadmore, 2017) has found that around a third of the children who had a history of repeated ear infections had problems with reading and writing.

When children are older, it will be important to use standardised diagnostic assessment tools, such as the YARC reading test, to establish exactly how far pupils have fallen behind and unpick which strands of the 'reading rope' need strengthening.

The importance of spoken language

Oral language is the foundation of learning to read (Lervåg *et al.*, 2018). It contributes not only to comprehension but also to decoding: studies (Cassano and Schickedanz, 2015) have found expressive vocabulary to be a good predictor of growth in phonological awareness in four- and five-year-olds. The more words a child has in their vocabulary, the more sensitive they become to small differences in words' internal sound structures.

Research at Bristol University (Moss and Washbrook, 2016) found that even after controlling for family background, children with lower language skills at five were at age seven likely to perform less well in KS1 reading assessment, as well as being less attentive, enjoying school less, liking answering in class less and trying less hard at school.

Boys' reading seems to be particularly affected by early language difficulties. The same study found that struggling with early language at age five discouraged boys from reading for pleasure at age seven much more than it discouraged girls.

So a focus on oral language in the EYFS is essential, as well as screening struggling readers of any age for language disorders, using assessments such as The Communication Trust's Progression Tools. One study (Snowling *et al.*,

2020) found that 58% of eight-year-olds with dyslexia also had a diagnosable developmental language disorder. Often, these subtle language problems will be unknown to their teachers, who see only the reading difficulty.

Language matters for older children too, when spoken language skills (language structures as well as vocabulary) overtake decoding skills as the most important element of literacy learning (Castles *et al.*, 2018).

Talk is a powerful means of improving literacy at all ages – and particularly for disadvantaged learners, according to evidence from the EEF.

> Talk is a powerful tool for learning and literacy. It can improve reading and writing outcomes, enhance communication skills and increase students' understanding across the curriculum.
>
> While all students benefit from classroom discussion activities, talk also appears to be particularly beneficial for low attaining students and those from disadvantaged backgrounds.
>
> Alex Quigley and Robbie Coleman, 2019. *Improving Literacy in Secondary Schools.*

Nor should we forget the evidence that oracy based whole-class teaching approaches such as Philosophy for Children and Dialogic Teaching, whilst not specifically directed at developing reading and writing skills, have nevertheless been shown to have significant impact on attainment in English in UK schools.

Developing vocabulary

Schools have become more and more aware that the reason many of their children do poorly in official reading assessments is that they simply do not understand the words in the tests. What is Jason to make of a KS1 reading assessment passage describing 'bushes laced with cobwebs,' or an infamous KS2 paper that started with 'Dawn broke over the savannah'? One teacher told me of her class, in a disadvantaged area, which had a child in it called Savannah, and a teaching assistant called Dawn. The children came out of the test distraught: 'Why was Dawn broked, Miss? And why was Savannah there?'

So schools with good reading (and writing) outcomes understand the importance of daily teaching of vocabulary, using some of the strategies we looked at in Chapter 4. In the early years this may be through repeatedly sharing core books. At Sheringham nursery school in London, for example, one core book or rhyme is introduced every three weeks and used as a basis for role-play and small world activities. Right through the age range, Pie Corbett's 'Talk for Writing' helps children internalise both vocabulary and language structures. Guided reading can be used effectively: one school I heard about plans for one of three guided reading sessions a week to focus solely on the vocabulary in the text. The other two sessions focus on making inferences.

Home reading and vocabulary

An ingenious strategy developed at Haytor Primary in Devon focused on using home reading to develop vocabulary. Parents' comments on children's reading had been brief and mechanistic ('We read three pages') so the school changed the format and gave parents and children a new guide:

- Was there a word here you enjoyed? Was there a word you liked the sound of?
- Find two or three words and write them in your book.

In class, when children change their reading books at the start of literacy lessons they share their new words and explore their meaning. Finding interesting new words is celebrated with certificates and in assemblies. The impact has been transformative; children remember the words because they have ownership of them.

They learn to question; one boy halted an assembly with the headteacher to put his hand up and ask 'What does that word mean?'

Some words really catch on; when one boy came in and said 'I got a new word – lavatory. It means toilet,' everyone in the class started to ask to go to the lavatory.

Parents engaged more with home reading, because the new system gave them license to talk about the book and enjoy words rather than just 'hearing their child read.'

In the secondary school, every teacher can improve children's reading and writing skills by teaching the core vocabulary for their subject. This is a key element of disciplinary literacy, as described in the EEF's 'Improving literacy in secondary schools' guidance (Quigley and Coleman, 2019).

For disadvantaged children, it is the way to move from conversational to academic language. As Geoff Barton (2011) writes, 'The child who tells us "In the book the writer says . . ." will do less well than the one who knows how to say "In the novel the author suggests. . . ." These are the key words of our subject – novel, play, dramatist, suggests, proposes, implies – so let's display them and teach them much more explicitly.'

So teachers in each faculty should identify the Tier 2 vocabulary for their subject – that is the words that will recur across different units of work, and teach them using strategies we looked at in Chapter 4. They might provide a template for students to fill in for each word, such as a concept map with branches (Figure 5.2), encourage application by having students highlight the

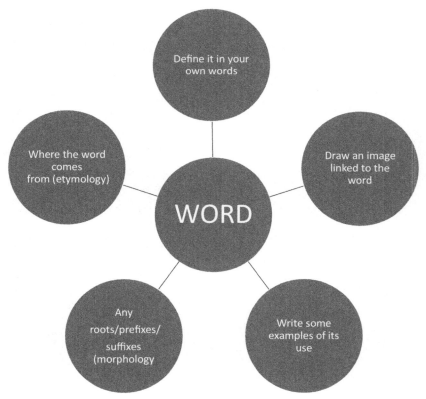

Figure 5.2 Template for learning vocabulary

words when they use them in a piece of work, and plan regular quizzes on all the words taught.

Every teacher in every subject can also develop generic word-learning skills – such as breaking words into their component parts: 'photosynthesis', for example, into the morphemes 'photo' (light), 'syn' (with or together) and 'thesis' (putting or placing).

In all work on vocabulary, what seems to work best is not the 'word of the week' or word list approach, but instead teaching children how to build their own word store. As at Haytor Primary in the case study, children need to learn to spot words they don't understand, discuss and make predictions about what they might mean and check their ideas using the internet.

Exposing all children to challenging texts

When children struggle with reading, they are at risk of experiencing the well-known 'Matthew effect' (the rich get richer . . . the poor get poorer); better readers read more, and read more challenging texts so gain a cumulative advantage in vocabulary and comprehension skills. It is important to mitigate this, for example by continuing to read complex texts aloud, as often as possible, and by providing all poor readers with laptops and teaching them to use screen-reading technology.

At Park Academy in Wolverhampton (Sargent, 2021), staff realised that guided reading sessions in ability groups, with texts tailored to the reading ability of each group, were restricting some children's access to more complex language and ideas. Disadvantaged children were often particularly affected, with the result that the gap between them and their peers was widening.

The school switched to whole-class guided reading in which everyone works on the same vocabulary-rich, challenging text – for four, half-hour lessons a week. Children all sit in mixed-attainment pairs. Adults read all or part of the text aloud, modelling tone and expression. This is followed by a planned activity based around one of the 'Vipers' (vocabulary, inference, prediction, explanation, retrieval and summarise/sequence). Two of the lessons each week are oracy based.

The new approach has had a significant effect on the progress of children eligible for the pupil premium and those not eligible, as well as for pupils with SEND, with the disadvantage gap showing clear signs of closing.

Phonics

There is, of course, extensive evidence that a systematic phonics programme is the most effective way of teaching early reading, and some evidence that good phonics teaching has particular benefits for disadvantaged children. I will not rehearse here the guidance on phonics teaching provided by government.

What is worth doing, however, is reflecting on Jason's story and the implications for phonics teaching. He and many other children like him can, as we have seen, struggle to 'hear' the separate sounds in words, or distinguish similar sounds (like 'e' and 'i' from each other). As a result it will take him a long time to learn phoneme-grapheme correspondences. His short-term or working memory capacity may be insufficient for him to hold a series of sounds in his head in order to blend them.

There are strategies that can help – like multisensory methods, Elkonin boxes, masking cards to draw the child's eye across the word from left to right or using chunks the child already knows in order to reduce the load on short-term memory when blending (for example, the 'and' in 'sand'). But what Jason will need is undoubtedly extra intervention, and sometimes this will only work if it is highly personalised – for example, teaching phoneme-grapheme links chosen to be of high salience for the child (perhaps occurring within the child's name, or on a book they are enjoying) and using the phoneme-grapheme links they *do* know as the basis for blending words, rather than a set sequence.

Reading comprehension and fluency

One of the more exciting findings from recent research involving disadvantaged children is that they seem to benefit particularly from teaching which unpacks and makes explicit the 'how to' of learning. Nowhere is this clearer than in reading, where the explicit teaching of reading comprehension strategies has been found to increase progress markedly, with children from disadvantaged backgrounds on average benefiting more than others.

Teachers need to model (and children practise) marshalling what they already know about the subject of a text (activating prior knowledge), making predictions, mentally framing questions about the text, clarifying strategies for making meaning by thinking aloud, and finally summarising what they have read.

Being able to summarise the key points of a text is an essential strategy, but one where many children need help.

One school regularly asks children to note three or four main points on separate post-it notes which they take home, using them to re-tell the story or information piece to a parent.

A good way of helping children internalise these reading comprehension strategies is by adopting the 'Reciprocal Reading' approach, applicable in both primary and secondary age groups (EEF, 2017; Quigley and Coleman, 2019). In Reciprocal Reading children work in groups; the teacher initially models prompts and questions but over time the children learn to use them, with each child in turn leading the group as the teacher did.

Another key message from recent research on reading comprehension is the need (particularly relevant for disadvantaged learners) to prepare children in advance for new vocabulary and make sure they have some background knowledge about the topic of any text they are studying. Class trips, classroom visitors, online searches, videos and the kind of structured subject teaching that builds knowledge cumulatively over time can all be used to bolster that domain knowledge.

One interesting recent study (Tyner and Kabourek, 2020) found that exposing pupils to rich content on topics such as history, geography and civics appears to improve reading skills more effectively than direct teaching of comprehension strategies. Surprisingly, the greatest effects on the reading comprehension of six- to 11-year-old children on this study came from the amount of time they spent on what are called 'social studies' in the US, rather than the time they spent in English or maths lessons.

Strategies which use repeated reads of the same text are important, too. There is evidence (Minero, 2019) that such fluency-oriented instruction significantly improves reading comprehension. In the 'five-step reading strategy', for example, children echo and choral read the same text every day over a week, each day focusing on a key skill – identifying the main point, annotating, identifying key details, analysing the author's craft, and summarising/drawing conclusions.

To build fluency, the books that children take home to read should include plenty of familiar texts as well as new ones – with a proper explanation for parents about the rationale for their child not getting 'a new book'. Paired or partner reading, which we looked at in Chapter 3, can also be used. If you use cross-age pairs and choose older partners who struggle with reading at their own class level, these older children will receive valuable fluency practice in reading simpler texts – all the while increasing their confidence by taking on a leadership role.

Reading for pleasure

Schools are not always good at getting children reading for pleasure. I'm reminded of a friend's story: her nine-year-old son had not always enjoyed reading, but during the coronavirus lockdown that changed, and one day she found him reading Robinson Crusoe in his bedroom. When he went back to school he stopped reading voluntarily. When she asked why, he told her it was because 'At school whenever you read anything you have to write about it.' She raised this with the class teacher, whose response was 'If they didn't write about it how would we know they'd really read the book?'

Other schools do things differently, often with advice and resources from the Reading Agency and the National Literacy Trust (NLT). The Reading Agency's reading challenges often appeal to boys, and its 'Reading Hack' is brilliant for secondary schools. Here, young people aged 13 to 24 'hack' reading by doing any activity with reading at its heart. The scheme involves engaging youth-led projects, such as volunteering, event planning and creative activities – anything from a poetry-themed DJ set or novel-inspired Minecraft, to book-related filmmaking or helping younger children read.

The NLT's offer includes the primary Premier League Reading Stars intervention and the secondary Skills Academy, which has online reading challenges featuring texts about football, breakdance and beatboxing. Completing the challenges enables students to watch how-to videos of football freestyle tricks and other skills.

Boys eligible for FSMs are more likely than those not eligible to say that they prefer to read on screen both at school and at home (Picton *et al.*, 2019). Because of this, digital resources are often their route into reading – such as the NLT's Virtual School Library, in which every week a popular children's author or illustrator provides free audio and e-books, videos and their top three recommended reads.

Some whole-school reading programmes like Accelerated Reader (described later in this chapter) and Pearson's Bug Club aim to increase reading enjoyment by carefully tailoring reading materials to children's interests. There is some preliminary evidence from a randomised controlled trial of Bug Club (Carroll *et al.*, 2020) that it may be effective in KS1; data from over a thousand Y1 and 2 pupils from 30 schools were analysed., with a new cohort of Y1 pupils recruited in the second year. Over five terms, experimental pupils in the first cohort were 11 months ahead on age equivalent reading scores, relative to their chronological age – though a replication study in the second year did not elicit the same significant gains.

Relevance is vital for secondary students. One good idea is to explore with students any problems in their lives they want to solve (how to cope when friends turn on you, for example, or how to be respected) and hand them two books in which people tackle the issue in different ways.

Another interesting idea for increasing children's interest in reading for pleasure is to make reading a *social* activity. Here, the teacher carefully puts children into same-age pairs or threes on the basis of their interests and friendships and suggests a book for them to read in instalments at home. Every day the pair or group have ten minutes in class to talk about their reading. The teacher can model these 'book talks' and provide guiding questions to steer their conversations, such as:

- How are you liking the book so far?
- What were the best bits you read?
- What feelings is this book evoking for you?
- Which character do you most closely relate to, and why?

An idea for group reading for pleasure for older pupils comes from Victoria Griffin, vice-principal at a school in south-west London (Griffin, 2020):

Logic Studio School in London takes students from the age of 14. Typically each new cohort is about 70% boys, the majority disadvantaged. Fifty minutes a week are dedicated to guided reading, in which small groups of seven to ten students with similar reading ages read together with a teacher.

Teachers from different disciplines run the sessions, and there is a sense of shared responsibility for promoting reading for pleasure.

Books are carefully chosen to engage the students emotionally and offer opportunities to relate the reading to their own experience. Staff also deliberately choose texts that require students to overcome the 'hump' of the first 50 pages – books like Kamila Shamsie's *Home Fire*, Alex Wheatle's *Crongton Knights*, Mark Haddon's *The Curious Incident of the Dog in the Night-Time* and Roald Dahl's *Skin and Other Stories*.

The purpose of the sessions is discussed with students; at induction staff share statistics showing the proportion entering the school with low reading ages (in one year, for example, half had a reading age of below 12 and nearly a quarter below 9) and the reading levels required to do well in exams. It is made clear that guided reading sessions are not English lessons and that there will be no testing.

The impact has been substantial. As a result of the weekly read and other literacy initiatives, reading age tests taken in June 2019 showed that, on average, students had made 20 months of progress. Student surveys revealed much more positive attitudes towards reading at the end of the year.

In the words of the school's vice-principal 'It turns out that teenagers might not choose to read on their own but they actually quite like it when they do it in a group, when they are not examined on it and when they can see the benefits clearly.'

In all these examples it is notable that pupils are reading whole books, not a series of extracts. A fascinating recent study (Westbrook *et al.*, 2019) found that reading aloud two challenging novels in their entirety, back to back in English lessons, enabled poorer Y8 readers to make rapid progress. Those with a reading age of 12 months or more behind their chronological age made 16 months' progress in their reading comprehension in a short period of 12 weeks. The authors noted that the intervention served to reposition 'poorer readers' as 'good' readers, giving them a different view of their own capabilities and greater engagement and enjoyment as a result of a reading experience not constantly interrupted to analyse a portion of the text.

Writing

With writing, as with reading, it is worth analysing what aspects of writing disadvantaged children may struggle with. Difficulties with the 'compositional' elements can include:

- Having little to write about because of lack of life experiences
- Limited vocabulary and language structures (for example, narrative): a child cannot write a story until they can tell one
- Lack of knowledge of 'academic' language forms

- Lack of working memory capacity, so that the child cannot hold all the words of a sentence in their head for long enough to write it
- Lack of motivation

Alongside these, Jason and others like him may struggle with the transactional or secretarial elements of writing. They may experience cognitive overload when writing, as the effort they have to make with spelling, punctuation, grammar and handwriting makes it difficult for them to think of what to say and how to say it.

Let us look first at spelling. It is not always well taught. In the primary school we have the ubiquitous weekly class spelling list, look-cover-write-check and Friday test. Research suggests, however, that list-and-test is much less effective than placing emphasis on analysing and using the words (Palmer and Invernizzi, 2015). Memory science tells us that it is also vital to revisit spellings previously learned, at progressively longer intervals (a week later, a month later, at the end of term, at the end of the year).

Jason will need his teachers to model different strategies for learning spellings, and help him find the ones that work best for him – tracing over a word, finding the tricky bit, looking at the word then looking up and to the left (for a right handed child) to visualise it, 'say it silly' (saying the sounds of an irregular word as in clim-b), learning a mnemonic (**b**ig **e**lephants **c**an't **a**lways **u**se **s**mall **e**xits for 'because') or making up and illustrating his own. He will need to be explicitly taught morphemes (for example, the -ed past tense to avoid the trapt/trapped error).

Marking should focus on just one or two errors and suggest a strategy for remembering those words, and every effort should be made to separate composition from transcription, so the child doesn't have to think about handwriting and spelling as well as compose. They should have opportunities to dictate a piece of writing to an adult, or work in a pair with a peer who is good at transcription but maybe not so good at coming up with ideas, as well as having as much access as possible to a laptop for their writing.

Above all, we should think about separating 'learning to write' (developing the skills of composition and transcription for their own sake) from 'writing to learn' (using writing as the medium for organising, consolidating and demonstrating what the child has learned in other curriculum subjects). There are many other ways (pictures, mindmaps, films, audio recordings) of fulfilling the latter function, and students can use choice boards to select how to demonstrate learning based on their strengths.

Let us look now at strategies for tackling compositional difficulties. As with reading, many disadvantaged children need explicit attention to developing background domain knowledge before they begin a piece of writing. The vocabulary they will need to draw on may have to be explicitly taught and displayed; teachers can ask children when editing their writing to highlight any taught words that they have used, and see if more need to be added. Children can also practise formulating and revising sentences *orally*; a fascinating recent study (Arfe *et al.*, 2021) found that this led to significant gains in the writing quality of 11- and 16-year-olds.

It seems easy to write a story, but many children lack the language structures to construct narrative. Many of the language intervention programmes described in Chapter 4 (such as NELI and ICAN's Talk Boosts) have a narrative element; Speechmark also publish specific narrative programmes for early years and primary.

For secondary schools the 'Talk for Literacy' programme is well worth looking at. This small-group, TA-led speaking and listening intervention combines two programmes: vocabulary enrichment, and narrative. The EEF's evaluation of the programme did not include a writing measure but did find that the intervention had a significant impact on overall reading ability, with a mean effect size of +0.20.

Lack of knowledge of 'academic' language (CALP) is probably the greatest obstacle disadvantaged children face in their writing. We can help by providing models and sentence frames such as 'On the one hand . . . but on the other . . .,' 'In conclusion . . .,' 'The evidence suggests . . .,' In summary. . . .' Turning the active ('This supports the theory that . . .') into the passive voice ('The theory is supported by the evidence that . . .') is a useful trick to practise. So is learning to combine sentences, as in the EEF example of changing 'Tudor clothing was uncomfortable. The Tudors dressed up for extravagant parties' into 'Despite the fact that Tudor clothing was uncomfortable, the Tudors dressed up for extravagant parties.'

Other forms of scaffolding include graphic organisers – visual tools that provide a structure for a type of writing. Try, for example, the Hamburger Paragraph, the Persuasion Map, the Pro-Con T-Table or Sequence Chart, all readily found through an internet search.

Adding visuals, like those in Figure 5.3, to planning structures, word banks and sentence stems is helpful for many children who struggle with spoken language. The Colourful Semantics approach and Widgit symbols are particularly useful in this context.

To tackle lack of working memory capacity, KS1 and 2 writers can use a recording device to record a sentence at a time, playing it back in order to transcribe it, so as to avoid the problem of not being able to remember a sentence for long enough to write it.

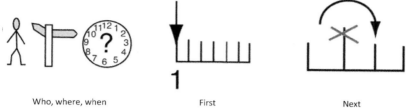

| Who, where, when | First | Next |

Figure 5.3 Visuals for planning structures
Source: Widgit Symbols © Widgit Software 2002-2021, www.widgit.com

As for lack of motivation, we can tackle this by making writing a social activity, as for reading, with pupils writing together in pairs and giving each other structured feedback. We can also create vivid experiences as a basis for writing – like the school I met who had a week-long simulation of World War I battlefields, with trenches dug in their field in which children sat (in the rain), a field hospital with bandages and fake blood, and a field kitchen where children baked bread and made soup.

Ofsted have a good description of the use of techniques, including drama, to promote engagement in writing, in their report on white boys from low income backgrounds (Ofsted, 2008).

In a Y8 lesson, boys discussed the novel *Stone Cold* to explore what they would want to take with them if they were leaving home for good. Among the items they identified were medication, money, family photographs, sleeping bags and mobile phones. Each group noted its ideas on a laptop before sharing them with the whole class. The boys showed high levels of motivation throughout the lesson.

The IPEELL writing programme (Introduction, Point, Explain, Ending, Links, and Language) exemplifies many of the principles we have explored here, and as a result is likely to be particularly helpful for disadvantaged writers. It uses memorable experiences, such as trips to local landmarks, as a focus for pupils' writing. Frameworks and mnemonics help with organisation, and pupils use self and peer assessment. They set goals for their writing and evaluate what they produce. The initial evaluation of the programme (Torgerson *et al.*, 2014) found that it had a strong positive impact on the writing outcomes of low attaining Y6 and 7 pupils at the transition from primary to secondary school, with a mean effect size of +0.74 for primary writing. A second evaluation with

Y5 and 6 pupils (Torgerson *et al.*, 2018) also showed a significant effect on writing – though sounding a warning note that the children involved made less progress in reading, spelling and maths than the pupils who did not use the intervention – perhaps because the increased focus on writing reduced the time spent on other skills.

Reading and writing interventions

In the previous sections we have looked at what might constitute high quality classroom teaching that is geared to the particular issues faced by disadvantaged pupils, and disadvantaged white boys in particular. This is unlikely to be enough for many, however, given the high prevalence of literacy difficulties in this group. We need to provide additional intervention programmes.

But which ones? There are a large number of programmes which claim to boost reading, and a rather smaller number for writing. In the next chapter we will look at the general principles of effective interventions, but here we focus on choosing programmes with the most robust research evidence.

A useful source of data was formerly the Evidence4impact website, which until 2020 reviewed evidence for different interventions, categorising it as strong, moderate or no impact, based on the number of high-quality experimental studies and the average effect size. The website has now closed, but I have summarised its evaluations in Table 5.1, and added in newer evidence from the EEF's more recent trials.

This list only includes interventions evaluated using control groups. There are many others that have a lesser level of evidence (pre- and post-test results). The 'Interventions for literacy' website provides a searchable database of these. Some, like the brilliant KS1 Project X Code, DigiSmart for nine-to 12-year-olds, and Inference Training for both primary and secondary, seem

Table 5.1 Literacy interventions

Intervention	Target group	Description	Evidence
Abracadabra	Struggling readers in KS1	Group, online or paper version with TA, 20 weeks. Covers phonics, fluency and comprehension activities based around a series of age-appropriate texts.	** Moderate for primary reading, with evidence of a greater impact on disadvantaged pupils than others. Effects still visible one year after intervention.

Intervention	Target group	Description	Evidence
Accelerated Reader	Primary and secondary pupils who need extra practice but already have some reading skills	Online programme which assesses pupils' reading levels and suggests reading materials at the right level. Pupils take comprehension tests on the texts they have read and earn points and rewards as they progress through the scheme.	*** Strong for Primary reading comprehension * Some evidence for Secondary reading (Y7), particularly for those eligible for FSM
Catch-Up Literacy	Struggling readers between the ages of 6 and 14	1-1 with a TA two X 15 minutes weekly	** Moderate for Secondary reading (Y7) No impact for Primary reading (Y3)
Lexia Core 5 Reading	Pupils from Reception to Year 6	Multicomponent blended learning	** Moderate for primary reading (KS1)
Peer tutoring	KS1,2 and 3	A range of approaches in which learners work in pairs or small groups to provide each other with explicit teaching support. Can be cross-age (an older learner takes the tutoring role and is paired with a younger tutee or tutees) or same-age peers. Four to ten week intensive blocks.	** Moderate evidence for primary and secondary, but recent UK trials have found lower effects
Reading Intervention	Struggling readers KS1	A variation of the Reading Recovery developed in Cumbria and widely used in North Yorkshire. Each pupil receives four 35-minute 1-1 sessions a week for 12 weeks with a TA.	* Some evidence for primary reading

(Continued)

Table 5.1 (*Continued*)

Intervention	Target group	Description	Evidence
REACH	Struggling readers in Y7 and 8	Adaptation of Reading Intervention with (in one version) supplementary material on language comprehension. In both versions, pupils received three one to one 35-minute sessions each week with a TA, for 20 weeks.	** Moderate for Secondary reading accuracy, though not comprehension
Reading Recovery	Lowest-achieving children in Y1 and 2	1–1 teacher, daily 30 mins for 12–20 weeks.	*** Strong for Primary reading
Read-Write Inc. Fresh Start	Struggling readers at the end of primary and the start of secondary	Teacher-led, group. The intervention starts with the systematic teaching of phonics and moves on to improving reading fluency and comprehension.	** Moderate for Secondary reading (Y7)
Reciprocal Reading	Whole-class or targeted groups struggling with reading comprehension, KS2	A structured approach to teaching reading comprehension strategies.	** Moderate for targeted primary reading (Yrs 5 and 6), with signs of promise for both the targeted and whole-class interventions on outcomes for FSM-eligible pupils, suggesting the programme could help schools close the disadvantage gap
Switch On	Struggling readers from KS1 to KS3	10 weeks of daily 20-minute 1–1 sessions with TA. Made up of alternate reading and writing sessions and based on detailed observation with strategy-based feedback.	** Moderate for Secondary reading (Y7) No impact for Primary reading (Y3)

to me to have particular promise for disadvantaged pupils. Project X Code appeals specifically to boys and has pre and post data from a standardised test showing an average reading age gain of 12 months after 4.5 months of support, with comprehension scores rising by 70%.

I'm also enthusiastic about the 1stClass@Writing intervention for pupils mainly in Years 3 to 5 who have fallen behind at writing and need a helping hand to get back on track. There are two versions: the Pirate Writing Crew is for pupils who need support to access Y3 expectations, and Dragon Hunters is for pupils who need support to access Y4 expectations. A trained TA delivers 60 motivating 40-minute lessons to a group of up to four pupils, four times a week, in addition to their daily class lessons. The pupils develop key skills of spelling, handwriting, grammar, and punctuation and complete daily writing tasks linked to thematic adventure stories.

Many schools, of course, do not use 'off-the-shelf' literacy interventions but develop their own. Pupil premium reviewer Richard Sutton (Sutton, 2018) describes a successful writing strategy he came across: the 20 day challenge. Here, each class or subject teacher 'identifies precisely why the three disadvantaged pupils in that class are not achieving well enough. Precise doesn't mean "spelling, punctuation and grammar." Precise means "using capital letters for proper nouns" and "using commas correctly."' The teacher then reflects on what they're going to do differently so that the pupils can improve, and makes a commitment that can be monitored: 'this is what will look different in their books in 20 days' time.'

For some children, the need for formal intervention programmes can be minimised by a combination of pre-teaching and consolidation, managed by the class teacher. Inclusion expert Daniel Sobel (Sobel, 2020) tells the story of two schools: School A introduced a new bought-in reading intervention, while staff in School B simply spent five minutes on pre-learning with target children (a preview of what would be coming up in the lesson, the key vocabulary and some background context) and five minutes on over-learning (going over key points after the lesson). Interestingly, it was in School B rather than School A that reading outcomes improved.

Many schools prefer group interventions, rather than one-to-one, on the grounds of cost. The EEF, however, have concluded that group support can be less effective. A meta-analysis of over one hundred studies (Gersten *et al.*, 2020) found that for early reading intervention (US grades 1-3) one-to-one instruction was more effective than small-group instruction (two to five students), with an effect size of 0.46 compared to 0.31.

Some one-to-one interventions appear to have long-lasting impact. Reading Recovery, for example, is targeted at Y1 children in the lowest 5-10% of the attainment range, who have made almost no progress in reading. It delivers an average 15 months reading age progress in four months of one-to-one daily teaching – five times the 'normal' rate of progress. Eighty-two per cent of children reach age expected levels within 12–20 weeks. Follow up to KS4 (Hurry and Fridkin, 2018) showed 49% getting five good GCSEs including English and maths, compared to 24% for a matched comparison group and 54% nationally for all pupils.

The following case studies illustrate the impact at both individual and whole school level.

St Mary's C of E Primary serves a disadvantaged and predominantly white community in Swanley, Kent, that includes a significant number of Traveller families. Fifty-one per cent of all pupils receive the Pupil Premium.

Over the last four years the school's KS2 results in English and maths have been in the top 10% of schools in England. In 2016 they were in the top 1% for reading. Children eligible for the Pupil Premium do as well as other children in SATs (as long as they consistently attend), in the proportion achieving greater depth as well as the proportion reaching the expected standard. They also equal non-eligible children in passing Kent's test for grammar school entry.

School leaders and staff believe that reading and writing are the key to the curriculum, and place great emphasis on the early acquisition of literacy skills. The Phonics International synthetic phonics programme is used from nursery onwards. Recently the headteacher introduced 'Destination Reader' in KS2, a structured whole-class programme which builds comprehension and love of reading. It focuses on developing learning behaviours that up-level children's discussions, through proven techniques such as language stems.

St Mary's has kept its school library going and well-stocked. It is a 'Power of Reading' school, with all staff having had training from the Centre for Literacy in Primary Education on the programme, which enables schools to deliver a whole curriculum based on high-quality texts. Children come to love reading as a result.

Many children at St Mary's struggle with spoken language skills, so the school employs a speech and language therapy assistant for half a day a week, to work with children in the Foundation Stage and beyond. The school has had a Reading Recovery teacher for many years. It offers one-to-one Reading Recovery teaching to its lowest achieving Y1 and 2 children, extra phonics lessons, and the TA-delivered one-to-one Better Reading Partnership programme to children with less severe literacy difficulties.

Reading Recovery has proved very successful with children of Traveller heritage, not only in quickly bringing them up to expected levels but also engendering a love of books and changing parents' attitudes to reading.

The Reading Recovery teacher's role goes beyond individual tutoring; she supports the intervention work of TAs, helps provide training on reading to all parents (particularly around phonics), and monitors all children's literacy progress across KS1 and 2, providing advice to their class teachers where needed.

The school employs two 'writing teachers', one in KS1 for one day a week, and one in KS2 for two days a week. They take children eligible for the Pupil Premium out of class for intensive support with the strategies that help them edit and improve their writing – the sort of work at an individual level that is difficult to manage in a busy class setting. This has been very successful in raising attainment.

Natalie (not her real name) went into foster care when she was in Y1, soon after she had started Reading Recovery tuition. She could not read at all at the time. In a few months she was moved to a new placement with a prospective adoptive family. In the area where she lives the local authority use some of the Pupil Premium Plus to fund a Reading Recovery teacher working with children in care or recently adopted from care. Natalie's teacher was appointed to the role, joining the Raising Health and Education for Looked After Children team.

This meant that she could follow Natalie to her new school and continue her programme there. Unfortunately, the placement with potential adopters broke down. Natalie was placed in emergency foster care outside the local authority boundaries, but again her Reading Recovery teacher followed her in her next and third school.

By the end of Y1 Natalie had gained 18 months in reading age, still just below her chronological age but now reading for enjoyment. Six months later she had made up the gap and was reading at age-related expected levels and passed the national phonics screening test. She was now 'very resilient and settled,' with a lasting love of books. Her Reading Recovery teacher remains in touch with her, having been a point of stability through many changes.

Every Child a Reader

I now need to return to Jason, and to my own story. Some years ago, troubled by what I had seen of children still struggling with reading year on year, despite their schools' best efforts to help them, I looked at all the evidence I could find on reading interventions that worked. Time and again I came back to Reading Recovery. Then I became head of children's services in Bristol, around the time that the council sold off its airport to a private company. We were asked to identify projects that might help close the disadvantage gap and bid for funding from the 'airport' pot. I asked for, and got, money for a number of initiatives targeted at early intervention in children's lives. One was Reading Recovery.

This money enabled the local authority to train its first Reading Recovery Teacher leader, who went on to train teachers in schools. The programme is still going strong in Bristol and has had a significant impact on the KS2 disadvantage gap.

Many years later, when I was working for the English government's National Strategies I had a visit from the head of the charitable foundation set up by the accountancy firm KPMG. She was researching literacy programmes in which the foundation could invest and had come to ask my advice. I talked about research we had commissioned from Professor Greg Brookes, showing that different approaches worked with different children. What was clear was that interventions delivered by trained TAs could work well as long as the children had started reading, but not if they were non-readers with the most acute difficulties. For these children with further to go if they were to catch up, Reading Recovery had been the only well-evidenced programme we had found.

It was a conversation that changed my future for a while. The KPMG Foundation employed me as Director of the Every Child a Reader programme, which aimed to expand Reading Recovery teaching for the lowest-achieving

5–10% of children, whilst encouraging schools to use their Reading Recovery teacher to support literacy learning across the school, whether by disseminating best practice in developing reading comprehension, or by training and supporting TAs to deliver less intensive reading interventions for those children with less severe difficulties.

Over the course of the initial 2005–2008 pilot, Every Child a Reader delivered Reading Recovery to nearly 8,000 children, the very lowest achieving six-year-olds in areas of high social deprivation. The results were impressive. Evaluators (Burroughs-Lange and Douëtil, 2007) found that the reading age of students exposed to Reading Recovery improved by an average of 21 months after just 40 hours of teaching. Eighty-six per cent of the children involved went on to achieve the level expected of children their age in National Curriculum reading assessments at age seven - two percentage points ahead of the national average for all children.

On this basis, the English government agreed to roll the programme out nationally at a cost of £35m per year, providing schools with half the costs they incur when providing Reading Recovery. A further 45,566 children received Reading Recovery over the next three years, and many thousands more received lighter-touch interventions. A DfE evaluation at the time (Tanner *et al.*, 2011) found strong evidence of impact. The programme as a whole improved school level reading attainment at KS1 by between two and six percentage points, and school level writing attainment at KS1 by between four and six percentage points at the end of Year 1. Reading Recovery itself had an impact of 26 percentage points on pupils attaining at or above the expected reading level for their age.

And then . . . there was a change of government, and the funding stopped in England - though strong implementation continued across the Republic of Ireland, and is growing in Scotland and proving very successful there (Goulay and Harmey, 2020). Since then the numbers of children receiving Reading Recovery in England have slowly declined, as school budgets contracted and schools faced the conundrum that while early reading intervention like this will pay for itself many times over in reduced costs of unemployment, crime and mental health difficulties, that return on investment goes to government and not to the schools who pick up the initial bill.

I remain convinced, however, that if any government really wants to close the disadvantage gap for children like Jason they should consider re-investing in a programme that demonstrably did the job for over 50,000 children, with a lasting impact on their life chances.

Key take-aways

- Reading difficulties are very common in disadvantaged white pupils, particularly boys, and contribute to the intergenerational transmission of disadvantage.
- It is possible to predict early on which children are at risk of literacy difficulties, and take action to develop their phonological awareness and spoken language.
- Effective class-based approaches for disadvantaged pupils will include those with an oracy focus, modifications to standard phonics teaching, explicit teaching of comprehension strategies and a focus on fluency.
- 'Boy-friendly' approaches and making both reading and writing social rather than solitary can increase engagement and motivation.
- Effective class-based writing approaches will include separating composition from transcription, strategy-based spelling instruction, interventions to develop narrative skills, and scaffolding the use of academic language.
- Schools have a wide choice of evidence-based literacy interventions, and these are an essential component in closing the disadvantage gap.

6 The maths gap

In this chapter we turn to the difficulties that under-achieving disadvantaged children may experience with maths. We will consider what good basic teaching might look like for this group, and at additional 'catch up' interventions. But first, let us look at how standards have been raised for disadvantaged white pupils in one school that has been successful in closing the gap.

St Ives School, an 11–16 secondary school in Cornwall, has a substantial proportion of disadvantaged students (27.3% eligible for the Pupil Premium). Very few pupils come from minority ethnic groups and only 1.8% are EAL learners. Tourism is the main local industry, with many parents in low-wage and part-time jobs.

Disadvantaged pupils do well at the school; in 2019 43.8% of students eligible for the Pupil Premium obtained a grade 4 or above in English and maths. In 2020 in-school tracking before the COVID-19 epidemic had been predicting that 60.9% of this group would achieve grade 4 or above, and that was borne out in final centre-based assessment results.

The school's priority in using the Pupil Premium has been improving the quality of teaching and learning across the board. In maths this has involved sustained CPD for staff on metacognition, for example, on changing pupils' attitude to mistakes, and how to help them persist with challenging tasks.

Students who come into Y7 below expected levels in maths, or in literacy, receive intensive support in the next two years. This happens in what the school call 'study time', a daily 40 minutes for all students

DOI: 10.4324/9781003176442-7

that is an extension of normal tutor group provision. Instead of having her own tutor group, a primary-trained member of the maths department works with individuals and small groups during this study time, using approaches that include Numeracy Ninjas, a free KS3 numeracy intervention designed to fill gaps in students' basic mental calculation strategies, and build the numeracy skills and fluency required to fully access GCSE maths concepts when they move to KS4.

Y10 and 11 students who need it receive additional maths, English and science tuition from their own subject teachers, on a rotation. There is also some bespoke after-school intervention, which is strictly time-limited and requires staff to demonstrate how they have accurately identified a student's learning gaps, what they will work on and what the endpoint will look like. The pupils buy in to the extra help because they are clear about timescale and outcomes; 'I need you in after school for four weeks . . . this is what you're going to work on . . . this is what you'll see at the end.'

Where are the gaps in mathematical attainment?

As with reading, there is a huge disadvantage gap in mathematical attainment. Forty-two per cent of boys (of all ethnicities) eligible for FSM fail to achieve the expected standard in maths at the end of KS2, compared to only 12% of boys who do not live in poverty.

The disadvantage gap in maths starts early and is particularly evident amongst white pupils. At the age of seven, the percentage of white British boys eligible for free school meals already failing to achieve the expected standard in maths (43% in 2019) is over twice that of non-FSM-eligible white boys (21%) and higher than any other ethnic group apart from children of Gypsy/Roma or Traveller heritage. Whilst white disadvantaged girls also struggle when compared with their peers at KS1, the issues are greater for boys.

When it comes to maths *progress* over the primary years, however, the picture is different, with girls doing less well. The group making least progress over KS2 (amongst White, Asian, Black, Mixed ethnicity and Chinese) is disadvantaged white girls who do not have English as an Additional Language (Nye, 2020).

At GCSE there are no DfE national data reports on maths alone - only English and maths, where we see that disadvantaged boys are again doing worse than disadvantaged girls, with particular issues for white disadvantaged boys - but also, on some measures, for Black Caribbean boys. There is some maths-specific information in data analyses undertaken by Teach First and FFT Education Datalab. One such report (Teach First, 2019) found that overall, two in five pupils from the poorest one-third of postcodes fail to achieve grade 9-4 in GCSE maths, nearly twice as many as those from the richest third. Unpicking ethnicity and controlling for disadvantage, an analysis for FFT Education Datalab (Thomson, 2020) highlights concerns about declining maths attainment for Black Caribbean pupils over the last four years.

As with reading, there is a core group of children leaving primary school with extremely limited mathematical skills. One report (Williams, 2008) noted that between the years 1998 and 2008, whilst standards in maths improved for most primary pupils, the proportion of children failing to achieve level 3 in maths (that is, with a maths level equivalent to that of the average seven- or eight-year-old) remained at about 6%. Another analysis (Gross and Members of the KPMG Education Advisory Team, 2009b) found that 55% of this group of very low-attaining pupils were boys and 45% girls. This over-representation of boys was much smaller in maths than it was in literacy, however (in literacy 68% of the very low achievers were boys). Children eligible for FSM were over-represented in the very low maths attainers, by a factor of over two.

More recent data confirms that we do indeed seem to have a particular long and hard-to-shift tail of mathematical underachievement in this country. Analysis of international comparator data on the maths skills of ten-year-olds (Jerrim *et al.*, 2017) shows that England had the third-largest gap between those doing well and performing poorly in maths among Organisation for Economic Cooperation and Development (OECD) member nations. Amongst 15-year-olds, the large gap between the highest and lowest performing students in England is equivalent to about eight years of schooling, and again one of the biggest across OECD countries (Jerrim and Shure, 2016).

Key take-away

In primary schools, we should be concerned about the performance of white FSM-eligible boys in maths in KS1, but also about the poor progress that girls in this group make in maths over their primary years. At GCSE level, disadvantaged white pupils are not the only group doing poorly; there are also signs that Black Caribbean pupils are not doing as well in maths as they should. The size of the overall maths gap between our highest achievers and lowest achievers is also of concern, as it is greater than the gap in most other countries.

What happens if you struggle with maths?

Numeracy failure becomes entrenched if not tackled early. Data from longitudinal studies (Duckworth, 2007) show that those who are very low attainers at seven tend to remain so at 11, more so in mathematics than in literacy.

There are two potential reasons for this. One is that later maths relies on the child understanding the basics of number, and the other is that early difficulties substantially increase the risk of children developing negative attitudes and anxiety about mathematics (Dowker, 2019).

Difficulties with maths have wide-reaching long-term consequences. Pupils with poor numeracy skills are much more likely to be excluded from school than their peers: one analysis by the Department for Children, Schools and Families (Gross and Members of the KPMG Education Advisory Team, 2009b), of all pupils permanently excluded in Year 9 in the 2004-2005 academic year, showed that pupils who entered secondary school with very low numeracy skills but good literacy skills (below the former Level 3 in maths but not English) had an exclusion rate twice that of pupils entering Key Stage 3 at Level 4 or above in maths, and were over twice as likely to be classified as persistent truants.

Beyond school, difficulties in basic numeracy are associated with higher risks of unemployment, mental health difficulties and involvement with crime (Gross and Members of the KPMG Education Advisory Team, 2009b). The proportion of the prison population with very poor numeracy skills, for example, is even greater than the proportion with poor literacy skills.

Why is maths so difficult for some children?

Jason's journey through maths learning will have been affected by many of the same factors that contributed to his reading difficulties – spoken language in particular. The vocabulary he met in maths will have caused him problems, particularly since so many maths terms mean something different in everyday life. Take 'remote', 'volume' and 'prime', for example, which he is more likely to associate with his family's TV. And what about take-away, operation and mean? And later on, factor, product and improper?

Maths language can be confusing. I will never forget the Y1 child (not Jason, but not unlike him) who piped up 'My Dad's been in one of those' when her teacher was describing the features of a prism.

Jason is also likely to struggle with comprehension of complex sentences, such as 'A number that is not a multiple of ten,' or 'How many more children in your survey chose football as their favourite sport than chose rugby?'

His history of intermittent hearing loss means he is likely to confuse '- teen' and '- ty', leading to problems in basic counting and in understanding the number system.

Jason's lack of regular exposure to conversations about events outside the shared context of the immediate here and now may mean he finds the level of abstraction involved in maths learning a challenge, particularly when it moves beyond manipulatives into a world of disembodied symbols.

He may have a more restricted working memory capacity than his peers, in which case it is less likely that new learning will be transferred to his long-term memory. It also means that he will struggle to hold numbers in his head while doing multi-step calculation problems (Gilmore *et al.*, 2018). He may also have difficulty with the working memory demands of multi-step word problems like 'In William's desk drawer there are 6 yellow highlighters. There are 12 more pink highlighters than yellow highlighters, and there are 3 more blue highlighters than pink highlighters. How many highlighters are in William's desk drawer in all?'

A great deal of maths work involves reading. As we saw in Chapter 5, reading difficulties are common in disadvantaged white children, and boys in particular. We also know that there is a strong association between reading comprehension levels and performance on maths word problems. Researchers (Vilenius-Tuohimaa *et al.*, 2008) attribute this either to simple difficulty in understanding the problem the child is meant to solve, or to difficulties in abstract reasoning that affect both reading comprehension and the ability to solve word problems. Either way, the words on the page will often be largely unintelligible to Jason. What is he to make of an instruction like 'Write an expression using a variable that shows how much 3 pairs of jeans will cost if you do not know the price of the jeans. Assume each pair costs the same amount'?

Finally, as a result of these multiple linguistic and cognitive challenges, Jason is very likely to lose all confidence in himself as a mathematician, and develop an 'I hate maths' attitude that his teachers will find hard to crack.

Let us now look at each of these factors in turn, to see what can be done to mitigate their effects, exploring the features of classroom teaching likely to work best for disadvantaged learners.

Maths and language

A focus on spoken language in the classroom can go a long way to improve the maths skills and understanding of all pupils, and is an essential for those who are lower-attaining.

Dialogic teaching is one such approach. Here, teachers elicit children's own ideas about the work they are engaged in and encourage them to discuss errors and misconceptions through extended conversations. A child's answer is seen as a starting point rather than the end point of dialogue. In an EEF evaluation (Jay *et al.*, 2017) of a whole-class dialogic teaching approach in KS2, the children involved made on average one additional month of progress in maths, compared to children in control schools. Children eligible for FSM made two additional months' progress in maths, which suggests that introducing more purposeful talk in classrooms may have a real gap-closing effect for disadvantaged learners.

Another way of achieving a language focus in maths is to draw on Cambridge University's 'Thinking Together' approach, in which primary and secondary pupils are taught how to have reasoned discussion in groups. The approach has been shown to have a significant effect on mathematics attainment.

Thinking together in maths

In an experiment carried out by the 'Thinking Together' team, over 300 children in Y5 took part in a study comparing the effect of talk-based maths activities with 'business as usual' in matched control classes in other local schools with similar catchments. Teachers in the experimental schools received training and then used 12 detailed lesson plans. The first five lessons actively trained children to work together effectively in groups using agreed ground rules like 'Ask people what they think and what their reasons are,' and 'Include everyone's ideas.' The next seven lessons applied a specific talk skill to work from the Y5 maths and science curriculum.

In one activity, children worked in groups of three using Function Machine software to consider what operation could be carried out on one number in order to end up with another. An initial dilemma – whether the function is for example 'halving' or 'subtract 2' is resolved by testing other numbers.

All children were assessed before and after the intervention using optional maths SAT tests. The results showed that the children in the experimental group made significantly greater progress on the tests.

The examples of children's conversation when using the Function Machine illustrate the difference in the children's learning.

Control group	Experimental group
Alan: I've got an idea. That's 14, then you're adding 2. **Sylvia:** I know – I've got it half the input. . . **Alan:** It's my turn. **Sylvia:** No – you don't know what to do – I know. **Alan:** Yeah but it's my turn. **Sylvia:** Wait . . . **Alan:** No. Me and Sabena should have two turns then. **Sylvia:** No, but wait a minute. I didn't have a turn before. I didn't have a turn. 33 and then add 5. *(Presses key to reveal answer.)* **Alan:** My turn. **Sylvia:** I've got an idea, I've got an idea. **Alan:** You're always having a turn. **Sylvia:** Yeah, but I'm faster than you and you can't do anything. **Alan:** No. **Sylvia:** Shut up.	**Kylie:** *(To Tony)* So what do you think? **Tony:** I think you have to add on two more. **Kylie:** No 'cos, I think like Rebecca, I think it's halving because we had 6, and it ended up 3. Now we've got 4 and it ended up in 2. Do you think half the number or subtract? Do you want to check? Do you want the reveal thing? **Tony:** No, I think it's what Maya said. **Rebecca:** What did you say? **Maya:** I said try 4 and it would come out half. **Kylie:** Tony, do you want to try a different number, try once more? **Rebecca:** Let's see if we put in an odd number and see what happens. **Kylie:** Yeah an odd number. Do you want to all try 5? **Rebecca:** Try 5 yeah? **Kylie:** Do we all agree? **Tony:** Yeah **Maya:** Nought . . . 2.5 **Kylie:** We thought it was half the number. *(To teacher, who has joined the group).*

Source: Neil Mercer and Claire Sams (2006)
Teaching children how to use language to solve maths problems
Language and Education, 20:6, pp. 22–23

It is interesting to note how schools using tutoring programmes have found that a key factor in their success is the increased opportunities they provide for children to *talk* about maths. One school, for example (Hallahan, 2021), noted that 'Teaching staff report that those who have had the tuition are much more articulate in their responses because of the constant discussion within sessions.'

To develop maths through language (and vice versa) teachers can also draw on the strategies discussed in Chapter 4, such as:

- Providing a running commentary on a child's activities: 'Looks like he has *fewer* than you,' 'Looks like you're putting the numbers *in order* . . .'
- Reflecting back what children have said in correct, expanded language (Child: 'My shape's got three pointy bits.' Adult: 'Yes, it has three corners.').

- Choosing 'Goldilocks' words for each maths topic and teaching them explicitly, with regular recap. The NCETM's list of Tier 2 and 3 words for the primary and KS3 maths curriculum is a useful starting point.
- Using questions that elicit different language functions and providing talk frames/sentence stems to scaffold children's responses, like those in Table 6.1.

It is also helpful to replace quick-fire 'hands-up' question and answer exchanges with opportunities for partner talk ('Of these three numbers, which is the odd one out and why? Think of an answer then explain to your partner how you worked it out'). The teacher can then call on a particular pair, and 'bounce' answers around the class for other children to comment on – 'Thank you for your idea. . . . Harper, what are your thoughts on it?'

A useful framework for this kind of bouncing is Voice 21's ABC model – Agree, Build on, Challenge:

Agree: That answer makes sense because, or I have the same result as. . .
Build on: The method I used was. . .
Challenge: A question I would like to pose is . . . or Have you thought about. . .

Table 6.1 Questions and talk frames

Language function	Adult Questioning	Talk frame
Deduce, justify	What conclusions have you reached? How do you know? What made you think . . . ?	My reason is . . . I decided . . . because I concluded/deduced . . . on the basis of . . .
Explain, report	Tell us how you got to that . . . talk us through it	When . . . then To find the answer you would . . . So far I have discovered/worked out that . . . I already knew that x . . . therefore I tried out . . .
Hypothesise, speculate	What do you think might . . . ?	It's likely that . . . What if we . . .
Compare	How are they similar/ different?	This . . . is . . . but the . . . is They are similar/alike in that . . . They are different in that . . .
Classify	How would you sort these?	This fits here because . . . This is the odd one out because . . .
Sequence	What might come next? Why?	The next item in the sequence would be . . . because . . .
Give instructions	What do I/they need to do?	First you should . . . then you . . .

The type of language that adults use with children is fundamental to developing their mathematical thinking. There is some evidence that teachers and TAs may differ here. The well-known Deployment and Impact of Support Staff research (Blatchford *et al.*, 2009) and the resulting 'Maximising the Impact of Teaching Assistants' project concluded that TA language was more likely than that of teachers to be based on task completion (Figure 6.1). TAs were also more likely to prompt pupils and supply answers, rather than engage them in discussion. Training for teaching assistants is therefore an essential arm of any strategy to improve maths attainment for children who struggle.

Finally, there are a number of specific oracy structures suitable for maths lessons: barrier games, hot seating, and various forms of structured collaborative group work.

In *barrier games*, a pair of children sit opposite each other, with a barrier such as a large piece of card between them. Each child is given equipment, but neither can see the other. One of the pair is given a task and must then give instructions to their partner so that they can reproduce a product of the task or locate an item. For example:

- One child makes a 3-D shape using linking cubes, Duplo or Lego and then describes to the partner how to make an identical shape
- One child is given a picture and has to use coordinates to enable the other child to reproduce the picture
- One child threads a pattern of beads of different shapes and colours and describes to the partner how to make the same pattern

There is then a 'reveal' where the partners can compare their models, pictures or patterns.

In *hot seating*, one child sits in the centre surrounded by the rest of the class. The child in the centre is privately given an item (a number, for example, or an equation) and the other children have to ask questions to find out what it is.

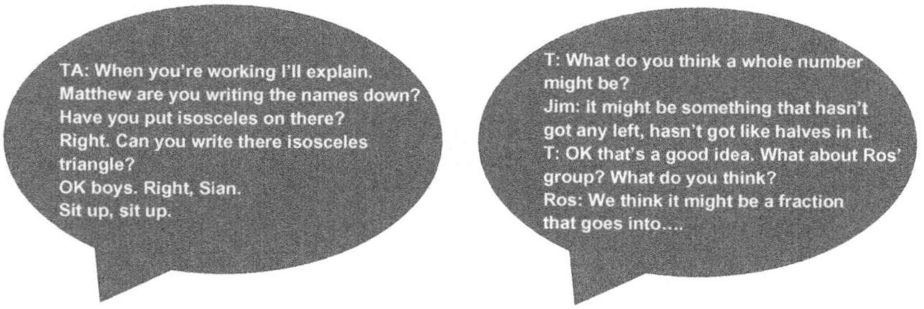

TA: When you're working I'll explain. Matthew are you writing the names down? Have you put isosceles on there? Right. Can you write there isosceles triangle? OK boys. Right, Sian. Sit up, sit up.

T: What do you think a whole number might be? Jim: it might be something that hasn't got any left, hasn't got like halves in it. T: OK that's a good idea. What about Ros' group? What do you think? Ros: We think it might be a fraction that goes into....

Figure 6.1 An example of the language used by TAs and teachers
Source: Paula Bosanquet, Julie Radford and Rob Webster, 2015, *The Teaching Assistant's Guide to Effective Interaction*

Think-pair-share involves pairs of children discussing a question (for example, how many people would be able to sit in the school hall) then feeding their ideas back to the whole group.

A variant, *snowballing*, has the pair of children join up with another pair to make a four to share their ideas, then join another group to make a group of eight. The pairs might for example be asked to come up with three facts about a given number, then five facts about the number in their group of four, then eight facts in their final group.

Well-structured group work is both motivating for many disadvantaged pupils (making maths social) and helpful in developing their mathematical language. The following box describes how one teacher used a '*Try it/talk it/colour it/check it*' structure in a remote lesson.

Try it, talk it, colour it, check it

Try it, talk it, colour it, check it is a strategy that increases student engagement, persistence, and collaboration.

Step 1 Try it: here students work on the problem independently for a few minutes and ask any questions they have come up with.

Step 2 Talk it: the students work together in breakout rooms, using conversation prompts and assigned roles (chair, timekeeper, checker, and scribe who records the group's conversation and the process they used to solve the problem).

Step 3 Colour it: students use the sticky notes on Google's Jamboard to indicate how confident they are in their answer. If they are super confident, they chose a green sticky note; if they are a little unsure, they chose yellow; if they are completely unsure, they choose pink. This step helps the teacher assess student learning.

Step 4 Check it: students return to the main room to feed back their process and answers – how they solved the problem and why they solved it in a certain way.

Other structures for group work include envoys, and the Jigsaw technique. *Envoys* means pupils working in groups then sending one of their group to share their product and look at how other groups have tackled a task. For example, each group might be given some data to represent using a method of their choice. In *Jigsaw*, children start off in 'home groups' of about five.

The teacher gives each child in a group a letter (A, B, C, D, E), then does the same for the remaining groups. S/he asks 'all the As' to move to another table and form an expert group to find out about the aspect of the topic that is the focus of the lesson. All the 'Bs' form another expert group, and so on. As an example, expert groups could each research a different way of presenting data (bar chart, pie chart, line graph, pictogram, frequency diagram or scatter diagram). Children then return to their home groups to share what they have learned. The home groups could be given some data and asked to choose which is the best way to represent it.

An adaptation of the Jigsaw technique

In a GCSE lesson on transformations, pupils worked in groups with each group member watching a video explaining a different transformation. They then had to teach what they learned to the other members of the group. To summarise the learning, the group matched transformations to pictures.

Dealing with abstraction

I once saw a teacher working with a child on subtraction. 'Looking at number two, if I took two away, what would I be left with?' she asked. 'Two,' he replied. She tried demonstrating with pictures, but to no avail. Next she got out some bricks but again the answer was 'two.' Then she remembered that his father ran a market stall and that the boy was knowledgeable about money. She tried 'If you have £2 and I take £2 away, how much will you have left?' 'Oh I know what you mean,' the boy replied. 'You mean b*&%er all, don't you?'

He might have needed to learn the more technical term of zero, but he understood the concept – when the teaching moved from the abstract to the concrete, with an example from his real-life experience.

Another example of anchoring learning in children's experience is asking them to create a poster showing what they know about a given number. Twenty-four, for example, might have a picture of a house number, a number 24 bus, the age of an aunty, a 20 pence coin and two-pence coins, and the time in minutes it takes the child to walk to school.

The traditional answer to making maths concrete has been the use of manipulatives, and more recently the maths mastery concrete . . . pictorial . . . abstract teaching sequence. But for some children this is not enough; we need to add a further, preliminary step (Figure 6.2) which presents a real-world object

$$\frac{1}{2} \; + \; \frac{1}{4} \; =$$

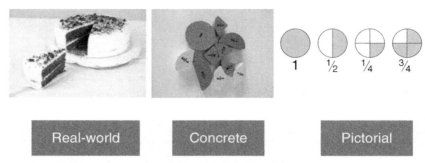

Figure 6.2 Concrete . . . pictorial . . . abstract teaching sequence

familiar to the child. When adding fractions, for example, the first step might be cutting up an actual cake. So 1/2 plus 1/4 would be explored by cutting a cake into halves then quarters and adding two of the quarters to one other. After this the children might cut up a photograph of the same cake, before moving on to manipulatives (fraction shapes) and pictorial representation of the fractions.

With extra steps like these, the use of concrete representations and pictorial images is likely to be very helpful for those disadvantaged children who have little experience of talking and thinking in the abstract. It is important to use several different representations. As an example, for place value asking the child to use base-10 apparatus to model 56 (concrete); put arrow cards together to make the number 56 (image); write the number (symbols) and explain what they have done and why. They might then use the base-10 apparatus to model 56 + 23 (concrete); draw a bar model or empty number line to show the calculation (picture); write the calculation (symbols) and use vocabulary the teacher has modelled to talk a partner through what they have done.

Visuals of many types are a source of support for children with weak language skills. There might, for example, be a colour-coded display of a circle in four segments, each a different colour and representing a different operation ($\times$, $+$, $-$. $\div$). Within the segment with the $\times$ symbol are written all the words that describe this operation, from 'groups of' through 'repeated addition' through 'times by' to 'a multiple of'. Or to help children remember the different forms of presenting data there might be a poster with an actual visual example of a bar chart, pie chart, line graph, pictogram, frequency diagram or scatter diagram.

Another element of dealing with abstractions is translating new learning into a practical 'real-world' task. One teacher in the Every Child Counts programme, for example, followed up class work on the tens and units structure of two-digit numbers by giving a child a typed letter from the headteacher.

> Dear Andrew
> Please will you count out the fruit for morning break time for me.
> Class 1 needs 20 apples and 10 bananas.
> Class 3 needs 32 apples.
> Class 2 needs 24 apples and 8 bananas.

Then the teacher showed Andrew bags of fruit – apples in bags of ten, oranges in bags of ten, bananas in bunches of 5. This prompted him to think hard about how to make 32 . . . 'You have to split open the bag of ten,' he said. His teacher went on to show him what this would look like using a superimposed 2 on top of the units in a 30 numeral card.

Memory difficulties

Teachers often comment on a particular difficulty shared by many children who struggle with maths: difficulty in remembering new information. If we unpack this, it might be because of capacity issues in working/short-term memory, or alternatively in long-term memory, or in both.

Working memory (sometimes called short-term memory) is the ability to hold information in your mind while you manipulate it. It is highly important in solving arithmetic and word problems in maths. Children can more easily circumvent working memory difficulties if we help them develop a secure and automatic knowledge of multiplication tables and number facts. This reduces the memory load, because it removes mental calculation steps from the problem-solving process. It also helps if we encourage children to use post-it notes to jot down each step as they work through a problem. Children may also benefit from intervention programmes which teach them to increase their ability to hold chunks of information in mind. Some of these are showing promise, and are described later in this chapter.

Long-term memory works differently. Children with long-term memory issues are those who seem to know something one day and forget it the next. We can help them by:

- Using the self-reference effect. Our brains are wired to remember information related to ourselves, so we can for example have pupils reframe word problems into 'I . . .' format.
- Using mnemonics.

- Which is the numerator, which is the denominator? Nice Dog (N before D).
- The mode is the **M**ost **O**ccurring **D**ata **E**ntity.
- All graphs need 'SALT' - **S**cale, **A**xes, **L**abels, **T**itle.

- Using work-arounds for times tables - like the finger method for the nine times table (you can find examples on YouTube), or this fun tables trick for multiplying large numbers by 11 (with thanks to Isaac and Mr Dixon): to calculate, say, 11x 43 you write down 4 and 3, leaving a space between them. You then add the outer numbers (4 and 3) and write the resulting number in the space - 473. Children enjoy working through a few examples to find out what to do when the outer numbers total ten or more.
- Creating knowledge organisers which outline key elements of the unit of maths work, to which children can refer.
- Using active revision methods, because we remember when our brains have to work. Children can teach another child the information or process they have learned, create their own flashcards of key facts or items and test each other in pairs, create quizzes for each other, or make a film of themselves explaining and demonstrating a concept or process, perhaps using the 'Explain Everything' app to show their parents how they have learned to go about a particular mathematical operation.
- Using regular retrieval practice, for example, using challenge grids and regular low stakes tests/quizzes.

Most secondary teachers are thoroughly familiar with the concept of retrieval practice and the need to interleave rather than block topics; they have become aware of the science of memory, which shows how memory traces soon fade unless they are topped up by going over the new learning at steadily increasing intervals (Figure 6.3). In practice this means that ideally we should revisit new learning after five minutes, an hour, a day, a week, a month, a term. Primary teachers are sometimes less aware of the memory curve. It

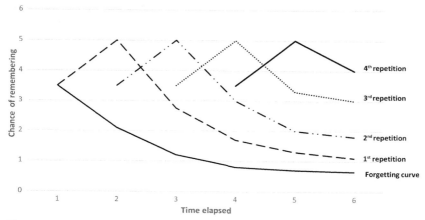

Figure 6.3 The memory curve

is important that they take a few minutes a day (perhaps using odd moments like lining up) to keep familiar information simmering – like number facts, right through KS2 as well as KS1.

Reading comprehension: word problems

One useful way to help overcome the barriers to solving maths problems arising from poor reading comprehension skills is for a skilled adult to apply the teaching sequence used for guided reading, using word problems as the text and developing some of the same comprehension-based strategies we would use in a guided reading session. This is different from guided maths where teachers might work with a small group of students to solve the maths problem. The children are not immediately being asked for an answer to the problem, but to learn and practise strategies for reading for meaning:

Before reading – being supported by the adult in identifying and activating prior experience of similar word problems or the subject matter, adult-led clarification of any challenging or technical vocabulary, setting one or two key questions to assist comprehension whilst reading.

During reading – looking for clues as to the mathematical operation involved, underlining key words and phrases, annotating the text, raising questions. A key role for the adult is to model reading the text aloud, pausing at appropriate points to 'think out loud' about the clues they have spotted, and model appropriate comprehension strategies. The children see and hear the way in which an expert reader automatically monitors their understanding 'in the moment of reading' (Clarke *et al.*, 2013).

Undertaken regularly, these steps in the process will help children ask themselves questions, such as

- What do I think this problem is going to be about?
- Does it remind me of anything else I've already read or seen?
- What type of operation might be involved?
- What clues in the text can I find to help me?
- What part of the text is confusing?
- Do I need to go back and re-read?

After reading - the adult leads a discussion, returning to the key questions identified *before reading*, helping the children revisit the clues and questions that have arisen *during reading* and supporting them in summarising the problem itself and the mathematical strategies they need to use to solve it.

The teacher can help students to model and represent their thinking in any way they choose. Studies show that when learners can represent their thinking visually, they develop higher levels of comprehension.

Confidence

Children's struggle with maths can be highly visible. If they are taught in ways that emphasise 'right answers', given publicly, it is easy to lose confidence, and at the extreme to develop maths anxiety. We know that maths anxiety can appear as early as KS1, and appears to increase with age (Petronzi, 2016). It is very real; Jo Boaler (2019) quotes research showing that when students with maths anxiety encounter numbers a fear centre in the brain is activated - the same fear centre that lights up when people see snakes or spiders. As this centre becomes activated, activity in the problem-solving centres of the brain is diminished and working memory capacity decreases.

Strategies to build confidence and reduce anxiety include:

- Putting a question to a struggling child after some other pupils have given examples of what is required.
- Giving thinking time or time to talk to a partner before answering a question, or saying 'I'm going to come back to you in a minute to ask you . . .'
- Scaffolding new learning using the 'I do - We do - You do' sequence.

One of the most effective ways of building confidence I have seen was a pre-teaching project devised by the Devon local authority maths team (Trundley *et al.*, 2017). The project targeted children in Y2 to 6 perceived by peers as 'low status' in maths. Their teachers gave them between five and 15 minutes a week of pre-teaching to prepare them for an upcoming maths topic. When the whole class began the topic, the target children were asked to teach what they had learned to a peer or explain it to the whole class, making them influential in the lesson and changing their classmates' preconceptions about their abilities. The impact was extraordinary, with the majority of children (initially not on track to achieve the expected standard in maths at the end of the year) achieving at least the expected standard in Y2 and 6 tests. Teachers reported that children who had no belief in themselves as learners were now confident in maths; the children themselves said things like 'I feel sort of clever because I already know what we're going to do in the lesson and it makes me feel happier about talking about things with everyone else' and 'I always put my hand up now even if I am not one hundred percent sure as I want to know if I'm right or not.'

To build confidence and reduce anxiety, we have to constantly make explicit what children have learned: 'You not only know numbers between 11 and 20, you now know what number comes next' and 'Yesterday you had to think for a long time about how to work out half of six, but today you knew straight away.' We also have to help children replace the thought 'I'm no good at maths' with 'I'm learning.'

Adults' attitude to mistakes are crucial in this endeavour. Mistakes are how we learn; indeed, research (Wilson *et al.*, 2019) shows that the best learning comes from an 85% success rate – that is, one 'mistake' to every five or six correct responses. I often tell the story of Edison, who is said to have taken many years to invent the light bulb and had many setbacks on the way. When asked what that felt like, he replied 'I have not failed 10,000 times. I have not failed once. I have succeeded in proving that those 10,000 ways will not work. When I have eliminated the ways that will not work, I will find the way that will work.'

That is an attitude we can cultivate in children in their learning, by conveying that mistakes are interesting. I have seen many teachers choose 'my favourite mistake' in a lesson, for example, and talk through what the class can learn from it. I loved the teacher who said to a child when marking her work: 'No mistakes. I can see I've wasted your time.' And another who said: 'So that's a useful mistake. What have you learned? What would you do differently next time?'

Confidence in maths at St Mary's

Standards in maths are high at St Mary's, the primary school we met in the last chapter. with skilled and confident staff delivering the small steps, mastery-based White Rose curriculum. In previous years, maths TAs delivered extra support, but this lost its impact as teachers were able to use intervention methods in class. Instead, a before-school Maths Club was set up. It runs daily for up to 80 children. Five TAs work with them on maths problem-solving, using assertive mentoring techniques. Attending is a choice, but if children are struggling with maths then staff will ring their parents to talk about the club and the benefits of sending their child.

Children at St Mary's do not fall into beliefs that they are 'no good at' maths – or indeed any other subject. The school has a strong growth mindset programme, with a weekly growth mindset assembly followed up by linked work in classrooms. The programme is based on key principles:

- We celebrate making mistakes – we can learn from them
- We never give up – perseverance is the key if we are to succeed
- We learn from each other
- We don't compare ourselves with others
- We challenge ourselves and take risks
- We remember that our brains are making new connections and growing all the time

Increasing girls' confidence

A study in primary schools (Lee *et al.*, 2021) showed significant gains in maths attainment when children read stories about mathematics journeys involving overcoming setbacks through hard work and persistence, and took part in sessions that challenged fixed ideas about gender – for example, guessing a person's job by their appearance and realising that gender stereotypes were not necessarily true.

Motivation

Motivation in maths lessons tends to be a result of feeling confident, but even pupils who do not suffer from maths anxiety can still switch off from a subject that can seem dry and irrelevant to their concerns.

Using teaching resources based on popular culture can help. The Mathematics Shed website is a useful source for resources based on pupils' interests, from Minecraft to The Walking Dead.

Technology too is an obvious way of engaging pupils, and the range of online and app-based maths programmes is ever increasing, On the face of it many – like Times Tables Rockstars – look promising as a tool to increase engagement and motivation for those who find maths a struggle. The evidence is somewhat mixed, however. In one EEF evaluation, a promising app-based programme, onebillion, led to an average three months more progress for the Y1 children using it (children who had been identified by their teachers as being in the bottom half of the class in maths) than a control group, but those pupils eligible for FSM made two months *less* progress than FSM-eligible pupils in the control group (Nunes *et al.*, 2019). On the other hand, an interesting whole-class computer-assisted programme called 'Stop and Think: Learning Counterintuitive Concepts' was effective in accelerating maths progress for Y3 and Y5 pupils (Roy *et al.*, 2019). The scheme aims to train children to inhibit quick intuitive responses and give slower, more reflective answers. The intervention consists of 30 sessions delivered for a maximum of 15 minutes, three times a week, for ten weeks at the start of maths or science lessons.

Perhaps a more guaranteed route to engagement is to make maths learning *social* through carefully structured group work. Children might, for example, undertake data surveys and decide how to present their findings. They might (in another example from the Thinking Together programme) be given the task of talking together in a group to agree a strategy for solving a magic square, in which each row, column and diagonal must add to the same number. Agreed ground rules for talk would be displayed and each group would use sentence starters on cards as prompts (What do you think? Why do you think that? I agree because . . . I disagree because . . . Any more ideas to share? Do we all agree . . . or shall we talk some more?) At the end each group explains their strategy, and (crucially) review how they organised their groups and arrived at solutions, and how they used the ground rules for talk.

Role-play areas can also be motivating and a good way of helping children to 'talk maths' together. I have seen the usual shops but also travel agents and a brilliant Y6 football manager's office, in which pupils planned fixtures, worked out budgets and transfer fees and made calls to bid for new players.

Additional interventions

So far, we have looked at ways of overcoming key barriers that lower-attaining disadvantaged children may experience when learning maths: lack of motivation or confidence, restricted language, a need for the abstract to link with the real world, a need to have visual support and use models and images that support their thinking, and to have repeated practice so that knowledge becomes automatic and fluent.

But however good the class teaching, it is likely that some disadvantaged children will need additional interventions. How and when these are delivered is a matter for debate.

As we have seen from the Devon project described earlier, there are many advantages to intervention in the form of pre-teaching. Ten minutes spent on a pre-teach yields much more than ten minutes of learning, since it can enable the child or group to engage fully with the subsequent whole-class lesson. To achieve this, the pre-teaching needs to focus on unlocking barriers to later participation rather than replicating the lesson that is to come. This might involve rehearsing prior learning, teaching vocabulary, allowing confusion to happen so that misconceptions can be addressed, introducing sentence starters that will go on the working wall so the child will use them in the lesson, or introducing images and resources that they can later draw on.

Adherents of the mastery approach to maths, which aims to keep all the children in a class moving forward at the same pace, argue that this method minimises the need for interventions, limiting them to 'keep up' interventions for individuals or groups delivered soon after the lesson to children who are not quite there with their learning. Certainly, mastery approaches have the potential to work for underachieving children, because they address the key barriers we have discussed for this group: they use objects and pictures, introduce mathematical vocabulary in a structured way, emphasise practice and consolidation and engage learners in exploration and investigation.

Children who have large gaps in their knowledge and understanding, however, will need more than short, ad hoc intervention sessions. Their need is sustained help to catch up, not keep up, in order that the level of attainment in their class can be brought up to within a sufficiently narrow bandwidth that teachers can realistically then teach a whole mixed-ability class together.

As with literacy, such sustained interventions should ideally happen early, because gaps in understanding of basic number will prevent the child accessing almost all of the maths curriculum later on, and to reduce the risk of the child developing negative attitudes and anxiety about maths. The research literature (EEF, 2018; Clark and Henderson, 2020) suggests that for maths, group interventions can be as effective as one-to-one, with children benefitting from collaboration and dialogue with peers.

There are fewer interventions for maths than for literacy, but still a good range to choose from. Table 6.2 provides a summary. As with the literacy interventions reviewed in Chapter 5, ratings of the strength of research

Table 6.2 Maths interventions

Intervention	Target Group	Description	Evidence
Accelerated Maths	Primary and secondary pupils of all abilities	Computer-based assessment with personalised assignments and practice	* Limited for primary maths * Limited for secondary maths Average effect size +0.08 primary, +0.05 secondary
Catch Up Numeracy	For pupils struggling with maths who have a maths 'age' of 6–11	15 minute one-to-one sessions twice a week delivered by teachers, TAs or mentors.	* Limited for primary maths One small RCT had average effect size +0.21. A second study gave some indication that the programme was effective but not necessarily more effective than 'home-grown' one-to-one TA interventions of similar duration and intensity
Numbers Count	One version for Yrs 1–3, and one for Yrs 4–6 (can also be used in KS3)	A specially trained teacher delivers at least three lessons a week for a term, individually and in groups of two to three	*** Strong for primary maths. One large randomised trial, average effect size +0.33.
1stclass@number	Mainly Y1 and 2 pupils struggling with basic numeracy	TA delivers half-hour sessions to a group of up to four pupils, three times a week over ten weeks	*** Strong for primary maths. Effect size +0.22.
Improving Working Memory Plus Arithmetic	Y3 pupils working below class average	TAs work with pairs of children to teach them memory strategies which children practise through adaptive games played online. Ten one-hour sessions over one term. Five sessions focused on working memory, five on arithmetic content.	*** Strong for primary maths. Effect size +0.24.

(Continued)

Table 6.2 (Continued)

Intervention	Target Group	Description	Evidence
Maths Counts	Y3 to 6 children struggling with basic maths	1-1 TA 30-minute sessions three times a week for ten weeks. Digital software suggests activities and resources for each lesson.	* Limited for primary maths Small positive effect on maths skills (effect size 0.13) but possible negative effect for FSM-eligible pupils
Maths Tuition (Third Space Learning)	Primary pupils in need of extra support	Online one-to-one tuition from maths graduates	No impact (Y6 evaluation)
The Tutor Trust	Upper KS2, KS3, KS4 working below expected standard	Tutors (university students) work one-to-one or in small groups for about 12 hours	** Moderate for primary maths (Y6). Effect size 0.19.

evidence for each programme are taken from the (now closed) Evidence4Impact independent organisation, plus newer evidence from recent studies.

Schools will want to watch out too for Connecting Maths Concepts, a secondary direct instruction programme of scripted lessons for students in Y7–9. The intervention is being evaluated by EEF, with some initially promising results reported by the schools in the multi-academy trust involved. We will also before too long have information about outcomes from the National Tutoring Programme (NTP), including further evaluation of the impact in KS2 and 3 of online tutoring such as Third Space Learning. Data from Third Space suggest that on average children make double their expected progress with their one-to-one maths interventions, calculated using the Rising Stars PUMA standardised assessments.

Other intervention programmes which have good 'pre and post' test data but have not been the subject of controlled trials include Success@Arithmetic and Talk4Number. Success@Arithmetic Number Sense targets children in Y3 to 5 who need support to understand the number system and become fluent with number facts. Success@Arithmetic Calculation is for pupils in Y5 to 8 who need support to understand calculations and develop fluency with written methods. Both are usually delivered by TAs working closely with a teacher. Children typically make 15 months progress over four months of intervention.

Talk 4 Number is delivered by a TA and targets pupils in Years 3 and 4 who need support to use and understand mathematical language, and talk fluently about their mathematics. Groups of four children work with the TA for half an hour a day, three times a week for eight weeks. Pre- and post-testing finds an average number age gain of 12 months over a three-month period. A similar programme is Talking Maths, from Education Works, which targets speaking and listening skills in the context of mathematical language for pupils in Y1 to Y7. It is delivered over ten weeks by a TA working with a small group.

Whatever intervention programmes you choose, it is useful to 'stress-test' them by asking the questions in the following box.

Stress-test your intervention programme

Be confident if. . . .	*Be wary if. . . .*
There are clear entry criteria, which identify the target group	The programme is unclear about its target group
There are clear exit criteria	The programme is indefinite rather than time-limited
There is guidance on diagnostic assessment and matching the intervention to learning needs	There is little scope for tailoring the programme to what the child knows and needs to know
The programme includes support with tracking progress and evaluating impact	
Regular review of pupils' progress is incorporated as an intrinsic part of the programme	There are no suggested ways of monitoring children's progress over the course of the intervention
The teaching plans are structured so that pupils will know what is to be learned, how it fits with what they know and can do already, and what they are learning/have learned	There are no suggested before and after measures to evaluate the impact of the programme
The teaching concentrates on misconceptions, gaps or weaknesses that pupils have experienced in their learning to date, and builds in additional consolidation	The suggested activities look unlikely to interest and motivate the learner
The suggested teaching approaches are likely to motivate the pupils – they have pace, dialogue, feedback and stimulating activities	The programme comes without training, or with training only for the staff delivering it directly
Training for the staff delivering the intervention is provided	There are no visible linkages with children's wider class and subject learning
Training and information for class or subject teachers is provided, so that they can help the pupil apply learning from the intervention	No research evidence of the programme's impact is provided
The intervention includes links for class teachers and suggests ways in which children can take their learning into the class situation	
The intervention includes ways of involving parents/carers and addresses different levels at which parents are able to support (including compensating for those who cannot)	
The programme is structured so as to build pupils' independence and self-efficacy	
The programme developers can provide research evidence demonstrating the rationale for the approach and impact of the programme	

Many schools, of course, devise their own 'home-grown' catch-up interventions for their pupils. If devised by subject departments or class teachers these can have the advantage of maintaining strong links between the intervention and the curriculum on offer in the classroom, and ensuring that class or subject teachers retain responsibility for children's progress. I saw this working well in one primary school serving a predominantly white disadvantaged community: here the Inclusion Coordinator retained a 'pot' of TA hours for which class teachers could bid. They could go to her to ask for a six-week block of time from a TA to work on a specific misconception/gap for a small group of pupils. The teacher identified the pupils, constructed the programme, monitored progress and reported on the results.

The stress-test questions for home-grown intervention, all based on research (Webster, 2020) might be:

- Is the intervention supplementary to high-quality classroom teaching, rather than attempting to make up for less than good quality?
- Is it based on detailed assessment of what the pupil knows and needs to know?
- Are there explicit and practical connections between the work the child does in the intervention and in class?
- Is the intervention time-limited, with clear success criteria for when the pupil's skills, knowledge and understanding are at a level where intervention can end?
- Are there plans on how to continue to revisit and sustain the new learning back in the classroom?
- Is intervention delivered by the most qualified and experienced adult possible?
- If the intervention is delivered by a TA, have they had extensive training plus ongoing support from experienced teachers?
- Does the child always miss the same lessons when taking part in the intervention, or always miss the subjects they are good at or enjoy most?
- Does the class or subject teacher retain ownership, responsibility and involvement from beginning to end of the intervention?
- Does a member of the senior leadership team have oversight of interventions and responsibility for careful monitoring of impact?

The following case studies illustrate the importance of these key elements. One is about how interventions in maths are managed at Broken Cross primary, a school we met in Chapter 5. The second describes the work of one secondary school visited by Ofsted because the attainment and/or progress made by disadvantaged pupils, especially those from white British backgrounds, was higher than the national average for these groups or improving strongly (Ofsted, 2013).

> At Broken Cross Primary maths teaching emphasises the use of manipulatives and visuals. The school uses the White Rose maths programme. Half-termly pupil performance meetings identify children who may need additional intervention; the Sandwell numeracy tests are used to provide a detailed profile of what the child knows and needs to learn. Intervention is delivered by teachers as well as TAs. Afternoon foundation subject lessons are often introduced by the class teacher, with the TA then supporting the learning while the teacher works with individuals or groups to plug specific gaps in learning, in maths or writing or reading. The regular pupil performance meetings, involving school leaders and class teachers, enable the impact of intervention to be carefully monitored and evaluated.

> In one secondary school visited as part of the Ofsted survey, a specific leader was appointed to reshape the school's intervention programme. Self-evaluation had shown that previous interventions had not always been successful because they had been delivered by nonspecialists. They had been delivered at the end of the school day. The school decided on radical changes. Students making slow progress in maths and/or English receive one-to-one tuition and mentoring from subject specialists during the school day – scheduled at different times to minimise disruption to other subjects. The head of English or maths designed an individual learning plan for each pupil, clearly identifying the skills or knowledge the pupil needs to improve. The tutor then planned a series of intensive lessons that addressed these weaknesses. After each session, the tutor completed a detailed review of the pupil's progress. Parents received regular information about the purpose of the tuition and their child's progress. School leaders carefully monitored the impact on pupils' academic performance.

Key take-aways

- Early maths difficulties generally persist unless tackled promptly.
- Under-achieving disadvantaged children are likely to benefit from approaches to maths that intentionally reduce anxiety, get children talking, link abstract ideas to real-life examples, provide visual support and build in strategies to overcome short- and long-term memory difficulties.
- Brief 'keep-up' interventions may not be sufficient; if children do not have the basic building blocks of numeracy they will need high-quality additional intervention programmes that are time-limited but intensive.

7 The seven secrets of self-efficacy

This is the most important chapter in this book. It is important because it introduces a concept which is relatively unfamiliar to educators, but profoundly important in improving outcomes for disadvantaged children.

Self-efficacy is the belief that you can make a difference to your own life and that of others – the belief that 'things can get better, and I can do something about it' (Gilbert, 2018). It is the inner sense of self, of being a director rather than a spectator of your own life. It is also sometimes described as having a sense of agency, or having an internal rather than an external locus of control (Figure 7.1). People with an external locus of control tend to believe that events in their lives are out of their sphere of influence, and even that their own actions are a result of external factors, such as fate, luck, the influence of powerful others (such as doctors, the police, or government officials).

You can take your own self-efficacy test with a simple activity. First, think of a job you got, a promotion you received, or any other success in your life – small or large. Then complete the sentence 'I succeeded in . . . because . . .'

If, for example, you answered 'I succeeded in getting the job because I did my homework . . . looked at the school's website . . . paid a visit . . . got a friend to do a practice interview with me' then it is likely that you have high

High self-efficacy =	High agency =	Internal locus of control
Low self-efficacy =	Low agency =	External locus of control

Figure 7.1 Self-efficacy, agency and locus of control

DOI: 10.4324/9781003176442-8

self-efficacy, attributing your success to internal factors. If, on the other hand, you said 'I don't think they had many applications,' 'They must have just liked my face' or 'I just had a lucky day' you were either being modest or you have low self-efficacy, attributing your success to factors outside your control.

Self-efficacy applies to failure as well as success. Those with high self-efficacy tend to believe that if they had worked harder or tried different strategies they would have done better. Those with lower self-efficacy see the failure as unavoidable.

It is easy to spot children with low self-efficacy by their responses in the classroom. Take a boy who is sent out of class, for example, because he got into an argument with the pupil sitting next to him. If he says 'It weren't me, Miss . . . he wound me up' that would be a sign of an external locus of control, low self-efficacy. If he thinks to himself that the other boy did wind him up but recognises that he could have chosen to ignore him, that would be a sign of high self-efficacy.

Self-efficacy is not the same as self-esteem. We do not actually have a single self-esteem, but multiple ones. I have good self-esteem in relation to being able to use words and get on with other people, but low self-esteem in relation to any task that involves coordination (like parallel parking) or making music (like singing). What I do have, however, is a generalised sense that there are strategies I could use to get better at things I struggle with, if I chose to. I know that I have had to practice parallel parking lately so as to park in the narrow street where my grandsons live, and that practising is working. I remember joining a school choir long ago and finding that with coaching my singing voice did improve.

Disadvantaged children are more at risk of low self-efficacy than their more advantaged peers. There are several possible reasons for this. First, if you grow up in a family where adults did not do well at school, that will affect your own view of education and your belief in your ability to make progress through your own efforts. You may, moreover, see your family frequently powerless in the face of events. Your dad is in a low-skilled job that gives him little autonomy, your mum loses her job, then the gas gets cut off, then you get evicted. You are always on the edge of disaster if you are part of what Michael Savage (2015) describes as 'the precariat' class: 'people living and working precariously, usually in a series of short-term jobs, without recourse to stable occupational identities or careers, social protection or relevant protective legislation.' Your life, in the wise words of Matt Pinkett (Pinkett and Roberts, 2019) is 'driven by other people's decisions.'

To my mind, some of the populist movements we have seen driving politics across the world in the last few years are a result of the lack of agency felt by many people who live in left-behind communities – often white, formerly white working class and now part of the precariat. What we are seeing is simply people trying to exercise some control in lives otherwise lacking it.

Schools, too, play their part in cementing low self-efficacy. If disadvantaged children experience early language, literacy and maths difficulties (as we saw with Jason in Chapter 1) and do not get the right sort of teaching, they have multiple experiences of trying hard but with little success. We also often inadvertently strip lower-achieving disadvantaged children of their sense of independence and capability through grouping practices and offering too much 'help'. I have never forgotten the boy who told one of my friends 'I'm in the bottom table group and we can't do anything by ourselves so we always have to have an adult working with us.'

Low self-efficacy both contributes to low attainment and results from it. The two factors exist in a mutually reinforcing cycle. This is why strategies to narrow the attainment gap need to tackle both, and as early as possible, before the cycle has established.

What the research says about self-efficacy

A large body of research (Feinstein, 2000; Gutman and Schoon, 2013) has shown that some non-cognitive skills (the ability to focus attention, and internal locus of control) are almost as important as cognitive skills for achieving educational qualifications by the age of 26. Schunk (1981) found that self-efficacy explained nearly a quarter of the score on a later mathematics test, taking into account prior mathematics achievement. Self-esteem, in contrast, though predictive of mental and physical health in adult life, is not a good predictor of academic attainment (Baumeister *et al.*, 2003).

It is not only academic outcomes that are linked to self-efficacy. Longitudinal studies (Goodman *et al.*, 2015) find that it emerges as a strong, independent predictor of a wide range of adult outcomes such as mental distress, self-rated health, obesity, unemployment, and involvement in crime.

Studies (Betthaeuser *et al.*, 2020) also show a link between social class and self-efficacy. Using data from the British Cohort Study, researchers found that children of working-class parents had lower (i.e. more external) locus of control scores on a questionnaire they completed at age ten than children whose parents were in managerial and professional occupations. The study found substantial associations between locus of control scores, children's later educational attainment, and their own social class position as adults. The authors suggest that locus of control plays an important role in channelling the intergenerational transmission of disadvantage in Britain.

Further evidence of the link between self-efficacy and disadvantage comes from the Avon Longitudinal Study of Parents and Children (ALSPAC), which has followed up a large group of children from their birth in 1990–1992 up to the present (Goodman and Gregg, 2010). The cohort included children from all ethnic groups but was heavily weighted towards white British families. At intervals, the children and parents completed questionnaires focused on the child's attitudes and behaviours. One questionnaire administered when the child was nine assessed locus of control.

Figure 7.2 shows the relative impact of different factors on children's attainment at age 11. After controlling for prior attainment at age seven, locus of control emerged as the most important attitudinal/behavioural factor in the attainment gap between the most and least well-off, more important than pupils' perceptions of their behaviour and more important than their belief in their abilities.

In the secondary years, young people from poorer backgrounds were also found to be more likely to report an external locus of control than young people from better-off families. With other factors controlled for, learners were more likely to do well at their GCSEs if they had a belief that events result primarily from their own behaviour and actions.

There is a direct relationship between self-efficacy and response to learning tasks. Studies suggest that students with higher self-efficacy are more willing to take on challenges, more persistent at working on difficult tasks and

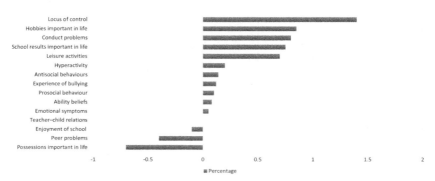

Figure 7.2 Decomposition of the attainment gap at age 11 between richest and poorest (accounting for prior ability): child and parent attitudes and behaviours
Source: Data from Goodman and Gregg (2010) *Poorer children's educational attainment: how important are attitudes and behaviour?* P. 32. London: Joseph Rowntree Foundation

better able to find solutions to problems (Multon *et al.*, 1991). Self-efficacy also affects pupils' willingness to use effective learning strategies; one study (Zimmerman and Kitsantas, 1997) found that it predicted the use of self-regulated learning strategies amongst a sample of adolescent girls. A two-year study of 15-year-olds (Berger and Karabenick, 2011) found that measured self-efficacy at one point in time predicted the use of learning strategies later in the school year (though not the other way round).

The finding of strong correlation between measured self-efficacy at one point in time and later academic attainment does not, of course conclusively demonstrate that low self-efficacy is necessarily leading directly to reduced success in school. Correlations, as ever, do not prove cause. There is, however, actual experimental evidence (Easterbrook and Hadden, 2020) that brief interventions targeting learners' thoughts, feelings and beliefs in ways that boost self-efficacy can have a large impact on attainment. Examples are experiments that develop children's growth mindset (their understanding that ability and personality is not fixed but can change), in which pupils are taught that the brain is like a muscle and grows with effort. Their subsequent attainment is typically significantly greater than that of control-group pupils who attended workshops teaching study skills (Sisk *et al.*, 2018).

Self-efficacy is not identical to growth mindset (Table 7.1), as it encompasses both the notion that success in learning is not inevitably predicated on prior ability/attainment *and* the notion that it is largely down to the individual to make changes happen – not the school, the teacher or the circumstances the pupil finds themselves in. But growth mindset interventions help make pupils feel powerful; they lay the groundwork for self-directed change.

Other examples of these brief intervention studies are experiments on what is called 'values affirmation', in which learners are asked to write about values that are important to them personally. Control groups are asked to write about values that are not important to them personally, but that might be important to other people. Two studies in England (Hadden *et al.*, 2019) found that this type of brief intervention (involving no more than 15 minutes writing, several times over the school year) increased the maths exam performance of disadvantaged students, reducing the gap with their more affluent

Table 7.1 The difference between growth mindset and self-efficacy

Growth mindset	Self-efficacy
The belief that personal characteristics can change – that you don't have fixed abilities or personality characteristics	The belief that change is *down to you* – that you can exert control over what happens to you and to others

peers by a remarkable 62%. It is tempting to interpret these effects as a result of a process by which that inner sense of 'I' – with choice and control – was cemented in the students who took part.

I am also struck, when reflecting on self-efficacy as an important but little-used concept in education, by the number of EEF evaluation studies demonstrating positive effects on attainment which involve putting pupils in charge of their own learning. Is part of the effectiveness of developing metacognitive skills (having pupils reflect on their own thinking and learning strategies) perhaps explained by their impact on self-efficacy? Might some of the spoken language interventions we have looked at in previous chapters, such as the Thinking Together programme, or Philosophy for Children, also have this element of giving pupils a sense of control over their own learning, a feeling they can have opinions that are listened to and valued? Did the Devon pre-teaching project we looked at in Chapter 6 work so well not simply because pupils mastered the maths content, but because they were invited to lead the whole class and teach others what they had learned?

The seven secrets of building self-efficacy

Secret number one: the words we use

Strategic praise for effort and strategies rather than success

When we praise children (openly for younger children, privately for secondary students), or tell them something wasn't as good as it should be, we want them to attribute both success and failure to things they can change – such as how much effort they put in or the strategies they used, rather than things that are out of their control (like luck, 'ability', or not having been taught particular content).

This means we should draw on the work of Carol Dweck to guide our language. In a typical example of her research (Mueller and Dweck, 1998), 11-year-old children were given moderately challenging logic problems to solve. The children were randomly assigned to receive intelligence praise ('That's a really high score. You must be very smart at these problems.'), effort praise ('That's a really high score. You must have worked hard at these problems.') or neutral praise ('That's a really high score.'). Then the children were all given a very difficult set of problems, on which they all performed poorly (a failure experience). Finally, they were given problems at the same level of challenge as the first set. The effect of the type of praise was significant. On the final set of problems, children who received neutral praise performed no better and no worse than they had on the first set. Children who received effort praise did better and asked to do more challenging problems in the future. But children who received intelligence praise solved 30% fewer problems and asked to do only easy problems from then on. Being praised for ability and then having that belief in their own ability challenged by tougher tasks led them to avoid future challenge – and thus future learning.

So we should stop praising children for ability. We should also stop praising them for success. If children receive praise for getting all their spellings right, or meeting the required standard on a test, those who struggle with learning will rarely get a look in. And those who get the praise will actually make greater progress if, as Dweck's work has proved, their parents and teachers ignore success and instead praise effort and strategies.

There are some words we often use, as teachers and parents, that we should try hard to avoid (Figure 7.3). Instead we can, for example, say 'Well done for getting stuck into learning your spellings this week – you must have practised every day at home' or 'You've put a lot of hard work into your maths lately – and it's paying off.' Praising successful strategies is even more effective: 'Well done for having a go at writing that word by yourself – you listened very carefully to the sounds.' Or if, for example, a boy's school football team won a home game and the boy attributes winning to external factors ('It's always easier to win at home') we can try to shift him to an internal locus of control ('Well yes sometimes it is easier to win at home, but what do you think you've been doing lately that helped you play well?'). We can also notice and praise successful behaviour strategies: 'So yesterday you didn't let yourself get distracted for the first half of the lesson – what was it you did to help you focus?' or 'You've done really well to get yourself to school every day lately – 100% attendance up from 80% before. How did you do that?'

Noticing and praising effort without strategies requires some care. Some teenagers, often boys, will deliberately not try hard so that they can then

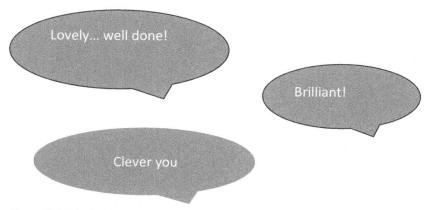

Figure 7.3 What not to say

attribute any failure to lack of effort rather than lack of ability. Praise there-fore should be given in relation to the specific social and emotional capabili-ties that underpin sustained effort ('You showed persistence there; I noticed you didn't give up'). The aim is not to make children feel good, but make them feel powerful in their own lives and learning.

Adults need not only to point out successful strategies, but get children themselves to reflect on what's working for them, so that they may develop this as a habit. As Ian Watson writes (Watson, 2018) 'Agency and control are developed through the reflexive process of relating our success or failure to the means and approach we take.'

Great teachers regularly draw children's attention to strategies they have used to help themselves. I'll never forget the skilled Reading Recovery teach-ers I watched, who would turn back to a specific page in a book a child had just finished and say 'Show me all the times on this page when you made a mistake and you sorted it out, all by yourself. Do you remember how you did that?' Or the secondary teacher who said to a boy who had just done a pres-entation to the class, 'It looked like everybody was really listening . . . what do you think you did to get everyone's attention?'

If we tell children enough about the strategies that are working for them, they will eventually internalise these messages – like the six-year-old girl who reflected on why her reading had improved (Figure 7.4), using the words that

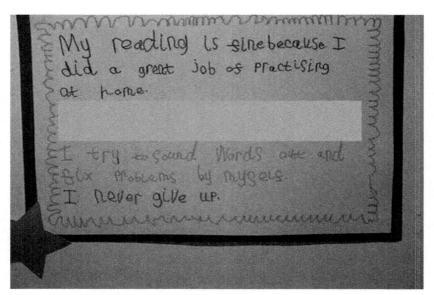

Figure 7.4 Internalising the self-efficacy messages

her teacher had used with her, over and over again. I know that not only had this child learned to read, but she had also learned some important lessons about her own capacity to make change happen, that will stay with her for the rest of her school career. Her experience had made her feel powerful in her own learning, perhaps for the first time.

Using growth mindset language

As we have seen, understanding that abilities and personality features are not fixed but can change can contribute to pupils' self-efficacy – as long as adults communicate that changes are ultimately made by the pupil him or herself, rather than by others.

So it is useful to engage learners in short growth mindset workshops (there are plenty available on the web) and consistently deploy adult language in ways that challenge fixed mindset beliefs (Table 7.2).

Walls festooned with motivational posters and stirring assembly speeches suggesting pupils can do and be anything they want to in life are less likely to be successful. The most effective way of developing a true growth mindset will be practical experience of specific change. We need to enable pupils to experience and reflect on trying a piece of learning, struggling, having setbacks and with scaffolding (not 'support') finding their way through. Doing and improving will work better than slogans.

Another problem with some schools' work on growth mindset is expecting pupils to believe they can change when teacher language suggests otherwise – as in any school where teachers talk about or plan for 'my low ability' (instead of low-attaining) pupils or groups. And haven't we all heard ourselves saying things like 'The thing with Jason is . . . he's bright but doesn't want to

Table 7.2 Adult language that challenges fixed mindset beliefs

They say . . .	You say . . .
I can't do it	OK so you haven't mastered it yet. Let's see which bits I didn't explain well enough.
That was easy	What was it you did that helped you do it so well/quickly?
I'll never be any good at . . .	You can definitely get better at it. How can I help?
This is too hard	It's making your brain work hard – that's good, you're learning.
I give up	Maybe try a different way?
I'm stuck	What helped you last time you got stuck?
	Let's talk about what you've tried, and what you can try next.

learn . . . he doesn't try . . . he's just like his brother.' Fixed teacher beliefs can apply to personality as well as intelligence.

Most damaging of all to pupils' growth mindset and self-efficacy is the practice of setting by 'ability'. Geoff Barton (2017) writes movingly about pupils placed in lower sets from the start of secondary school, 'with frequent implicit reminders that that is where they belong. Thus they become the disappointed, the disaffected, the disappeared.' In-class groupings can have a similar effect. One teacher told me about her Y6 class leavers' final performance, in which each child spoke about their best memory of school. She was saddened to hear one child say 'My best memory is when I was in Y4 and I got out of the yellow group.'

Valuing mistakes

Low-attaining disadvantaged students are likely to make lots of mistakes, but adults can build their self-efficacy by communicating that mistakes are essential, and even interesting, as described in Chapter 6. They can frame children's times of challenge as a need to find a better strategy – and help them do so.

In the early years, they get alongside a child whose construction has fallen down and say 'How can we work this out?' With older children, they say 'You've had a setback. What would you do differently next time?'

They provide feedback on elements that the pupil did get right: 'I can see you used that new formula we learned yesterday.' One teacher's response to a child who got only three out of ten on a test was 'You're a plus three.' Another's might be 'What was it you did that stopped you only getting one, or two?'

These teachers also avoid comfort words when children get things wrong. Academics (Rattan *et al.*, 2012) have found that teachers who themselves believe that ability is generally fixed are more likely to use feedback such as 'Don't worry, you'll do better next time' or 'This was a hard test!' They also found that this type of language lowered motivation, led to the pupils predicting that they would not improve in future and resulted in worse outcomes. Instead, when giving critical feedback we can emphasise our high standards and our belief that the student is capable of meeting those standards.

Equally, the most successful teachers try to avoid the very British type of praise that has a sting in the tail: 'That's good, you got all your spellings right but why don't you use the spellings correctly in your writing?' This can be replaced with 'You're getting all your spellings right most weeks. Tell me what strategies you are using to learn them. . . . Now what do you think might be the next step for you in spelling?'

Other useful approaches include:

- Explicitly labelling activities across the curriculum, from writing to maths to drawing and science, as 'rough-drafting thinking'. This gives students an opportunity to sketch initial solutions without worrying about correctness.
- Modelling struggles (and the associated feelings) yourself. In one fascinating piece of research (Schunk *et al.*, 1987), academics randomly assigned low-achieving students aged nine to 13 to receive maths instruction from an adult who used either coping modelling, mastery modelling, or no modelling of the learning task. In coping modelling, the adults demonstrated the anxieties and struggles that students might experience, but gradually improved their performance. In the mastery condition, the models demonstrated faultless performance from the start. Children who were assigned to the coping model had significantly greater growth in self-efficacy than either the no modelling or mastery modelling groups.

Feedback and assessment

To build self-efficacy, we should use assessment systems that demonstrate progress, often in small steps. Summative assessments that assign scores or grades often have a negative effect on lower achieving pupils, because they do not see change. If time after time they get only three out of ten on a spelling test, they soon begin to believe they are useless at spelling. Similarly, if they get low scaled scores year after year on maths tests, they soon say they are no good at maths.

Small-steps assessment (particularly self-assessment that is then moderated by adults) prevents these 'I can't' attributions. At The Harbour Pupil Referral Unit in Portsmouth, staff use grids of 'I am able to . . .' statements, providing a progression from a preschool developmental stage through to the skills needed to be successful in the upper secondary years. The progression includes social and emotional learning. The grids are printed on a blue background and progressively coloured in green when students demonstrate the skills. The system is very motivating for students, who can see the blue grids gradually changing to green as their skills develop. 'For example, all our students want to belong to a group but don't always know how,' say school staff. 'But after six months when they have a lot of green growing on their social skills grids, they see "I can learn how to do this."'

In an EEF-funded project across schools in Bexley, teachers developed new forms of assessment.

Adults used specific feedback rather than generalised praise and asked questions like 'What could your next step be?' when marking. Pupils learned how to set or reference their own goals, including success criteria, to self-assess their work against the success criteria or exploit peer feedback.

At the start of the project, without exception disadvantaged pupils evaluated themselves on a Survey Monkey questionnaire as less able to work independently, more in need of adult help or affirmation, and less willing to take risks than other pupils.

By the end of the year their self-efficacy and self-regulatory learning skills improved significantly. Fewer pupils felt they were totally reliant on external support (teacher/TA) and the proportion answering 'Yes' to the question 'When I'm asked to do something I'm not sure about I'm happy to have a go, even if it means I might get it wrong' rose from 39.1% to 52.4%. Teachers reported that the project had made a difference, and children were making faster progress.

Adapted from *Raising Standards Through Effective Feedback*, a presentation to Catch Up Conference by Beverley Gardner (2015)

Checking your teacher expectations

I remember well from my Every Child a Reader days the teacher who said of a child in her class 'If you can teach him to read, I'll eat my hat.' We did teach him to read; whether she ate her hat is less certain. What I hope happened is that the experience challenged her fixed expectations about what children can achieve.

Teacher expectations tend to be lower for disadvantaged learners (Rubie-Davies *et al.*, 2006) and disadvantaged learners are more susceptible to the detrimental effects of reduced expectations than their more affluent peers (Hinnant *et al.*, 2009). Expectations are also subtly lower for boys than girls. Girls who do well and boys who underachieve are both seen by teachers as typical of their gender (Myhill and Jones, 2004).

The effects start early: a study using data from the Millennium Cohort (Campbell, 2015) looked at seven-year-olds and found that children from low-income families, boys, pupils with any recognised diagnosis of special educational needs (SEN), and EAL learners were less likely to be judged 'above average' at reading by their teacher even when they had performed at equivalent levels on a standardised reading test. In maths there were fewer differences, although boys were more likely than girls to be judged relatively highly at maths, again even when they did no better on a standardised maths test. Black Caribbean pupils were significantly less likely than their equivalently performing white counterparts to be judged 'above average' in maths – along with children from low-income families, and those with any recognised SEN.

Such bias in teacher beliefs can directly affect pupils' future attainment. A recent systematic review (de Boer *at al.*, 2018) looked at the effects of 19 different teacher expectation interventions on student achievement in primary and secondary schools and found a significant overall effect on pupil achievement (an average weighted effect size of 0.30). Teachers in these interventions were trained to be aware of any pupils for whom they might hold low expectations and provide them with more opportunities to respond in class, more challenging instruction and more praise.

The impact on pupils' attainment was greatest when strategies were used to increase teachers' buy-in (many of them based on building teachers' own self-efficacy), such as teacher collaboration with researchers to select behaviours they wanted to work on. It also helped when teachers' assumptions were challenged using personalised information, such as observations of their own behaviours in class, and information about the achievement of their own pupils.

One study (Rubie-Davies *et al.*, 2015) tested a year-long intervention in which primary school teachers took part in four day-long workshops. They received a thorough introduction to teacher expectation research and the impact of high expectations on pupils' achievement.

They also looked at and practised the classroom behaviours typically shown by teachers who hold generally high expectations of all their students. These included using mixed ability grouping, providing challenging learning activities, promoting a positive class climate in which students could exercise autonomy, and helping students set goals.

To promote ownership of the intervention, the teachers were able to choose which of the behaviours they would practise. During the year, the researchers met several times with the teachers to discuss how things were going and to provide support. At the end of the school year, the experimental students had significantly higher maths gains than the control group.

So what can teachers and other adults learn from studies like these? Here are some ideas, with a focus on socially disadvantaged children:

- Challenge your own expectations by looking as a staff group at data from the EEF's family of schools to find examples of schools similar to yours, where disadvantaged pupils do well.
- Ask a colleague to observe you teach – do you give all students the same opportunities to respond in class? Do you give them the benefit of an equally long wait time when you ask questions? Do you show greater warmth to some pupils than others?
- Use the observation to choose a specific behaviour you want to change, and work on it.
- Reflect on the way you group pupils – could you use more mixed ability groupings?
- Emphasise high expectations in feedback: 'This particular piece of work is a little below what I think you are capable of,' 'That was not the behaviour I expect from a considerate person like you' or 'Some people may have decided you're not that good at maths. I'm not interested in that. I think you have it in you to surprise a few people – maybe surprise yourself.'

Teacher expectations, mistakes and growth mindset at St Ives school

At St Ives secondary, which we met in Chapter 6, staff have had extensive CPD on cognitive and affective bias – such as the unconscious expectations they may have about disadvantaged boys. Data are analysed to look for evidence of bias. It was found, for example, that house points were being given more often to girls than to boys, and this was fed back to staff.

Positive discrimination is used to ensure that opportunities are equal for all. Disadvantaged pupils are given priority in considerations about which pupils will move up a set; they are deliberately over-represented (along with other vulnerable groups) in the house councils – pupils from each year group who feed back on the quality of education and have a role in important decisions, such as how some new funding the school received should be spent to improve students' experience of school.

The school has developed its own 'SIGMA' (St Ives Growth Mindset Academy) programme based on six key values: effort, resilience, high standards, taking on challenges, learning from mistakes and the power of 'yet'. Learning about these forms part of the daily study time in tutor groups, and pupils are awarded house points when they exhibit one of the values. Students know where their efforts and persistence can take them; post-16 progression routes to local colleges are clear, there are visits to universities and inspiring speakers are invited into school.

Subject staff know how to praise effort and strategies rather than success, and regularly celebrate mistakes. Monitoring data has shown that the top two values for which house points were awarded were effort, and mistakes – rather than necessarily achieving high standards.

Pupil surveys of resilience, persistence and willingness to take on challenges have provided soft data showing the impact of work on growth mindset. Leaders also examined the proportion of pupils who attempted the harder questions at the end of maths GCSE papers, finding some quantitative evidence of greater persistence in the face of difficulty.

Secret number two: find the pivotal moment

Once, when my daughter Kate was in primary school, her teacher said to her 'You have a real talent for words.' Until that point, she had been a fairly plodding student with no particular enthusiasm for school. His words transformed her. She worked hard, enjoyed her learning – and went on to be an author.

Last year I heard a Durham headteacher speak about her own experience at school. She had been having a clear-out and came upon her primary school reports. Uniformly they said things like 'careless' and 'inattentive'. She had always come bottom-to-middle on tests. She recalled her first year at secondary school, when in a maths lesson pupils had to sit down in order of their performance on a test – those who came bottom sitting down first. She spoke of how she expected to be asked to sit down early on, and as pupils' names were called out one by one she kept expecting to hear hers, but didn't. She came nearly top. Reflecting on this, she identified the key difference in her experiences. In primary school she had not been able to meet her teachers' expectations, which were largely for neat work with no crossings out. This secondary school maths test, however, had called for reasoning rather than written calculation. This single experience, she said, changed her attitude to learning, and from that point on she began to do well, not just in maths but in other subjects too.

These stories represent what I call 'pivotal moments': moments when something a teacher said or did was able to alter the whole course of a child's learning, by altering their perceptions of themselves, by making them feel powerful as learners.

I had this in mind when suggesting to government, many years ago, that as well as having national targets for every child to reach the then Level 4 in English and maths at the end of primary school, we should have a target that every child would leave primary school with a Level 5 (above average) in *something*. This might not be in core subjects. It might be PE, cooking, art, gardening, kindness. The point was for every child to have that sense of being identified as having a talent, to provide that pivotal moment that would help them succeed more generally.

Sadly, I did not succeed in persuading civil servants or ministers. But primary schools can still individually identify an area where each child is working at greater depth as they move on to secondary. Every school can award a certificate of outstanding achievement in at least one curriculum or extracurricular area, each year, to every child. Every child can be outstanding in something. In Einstein's words, 'Everybody is a genius, but if you judge a fish by its ability to climb a tree it will spend its whole life believing it is stupid.'

We need not wait till the end of the year. At any time we can recognise children's strengths. We can ask them 'What are you good at? And what else?' We can have them reflect on successes and strengths and great learning moments, and then ask 'What did this tell you about what you might be capable of?'

Disadvantaged children often show strengths of which their teachers may be completely unaware. Writing in the brilliant book 'The Working Class,' Jaz Ampaw-Farr (2018) reminds us of this in her 'message to my teachers': 'The truth is I get myself and my three brothers up, dressed and to school every day so I already know a thing or two about perseverance. I have had to be incredibly resourceful just to overcome the disconnect between your class and my life.'

In the same book, inspirational teacher and trainer Martin Illingworth (2018) describes what life is like for a boy born in a former fishing and mining area, where there are few jobs. He recounts a catalogue of failure, of feeling written off by teachers, developing a sense that he is not clever and that a bright future is not for him. But then . . .

'There is a moment in your story when everything could change. Mr Wayment, your English teacher, sees your picture in the local paper. You have won a fishing competition and there you are in the paper holding a large trophy. And you have the biggest smile on your face, not one that we see too much of in school. What would happen if Mr Wayment remembered to congratulate you on your win, if he was to ask you about your interest, if he told your head of year to make a fuss of you? What if he contacted your mum to say how pleased he was to see that you won the fishing competition (and that it would be great to chat at parent's evening next week)? What if when Miss Ormsby, the art teacher, hears about your interest in fishing she gets you drawing fish? It turns out that you are rather good at drawing. Your stuff goes on the wall and you choose art at GCSE. What if that leads you to doing a talk about fishing, and then you are invited to set up a fishing club. After school on Wednesdays with Mr Oswald who loves fishing too? And with every little interest taken in you, you swell and grow.

As he puts the paper down and drinks his beer, Mr Wayment makes a mental note to speak to you. Let's hope he remembers. Let's hope he thinks on.'

Secret number three: give less help

There is nothing that strips children of self-efficacy more than leading them to believe they cannot function in classrooms without adult support. We must learn from the story told by HMI Charlie Henry, about a classroom where while the teacher was giving instructions he overheard one boy say to 'his' TA 'You'd better listen to this, Miss, because you're going to have to tell me in a minute.'

According to the latest figures, schools employ almost one TA to every two teachers. Yet the impact of TA support on attainment is clear only when they are delivering structured, time-limited interventions for which they have had good training (Sharples *et al.*, 2019), and research (Giangreco, 2010) shows that when a TA is nearby, children were more likely to seek help and less likely to work independently.

A first step in building self-efficacy, then, is to review the deployment of TAs to ensure that children do not become dependent on their support.

Children *can* learn to manage on their own if we help them. The teacher might, for example, set up a space in the classroom where pupils can go to find resources to scaffold their learning – a laptop with a PowerPoint of the lesson loaded up so they can review it, key vocabulary lists, sentence starters and writing frames. One primary teacher I met set up a table which she called the 'Enable Table.' As well as the lesson slides and key vocabulary she put there a quickread pen that scans words and reads them aloud, spelling resources, and maths manipulatives. Children are expected to use the Enable Table before asking for help from an adult. Other schools use the 'Brain, book, board, buddy, boss' system, or put up 'Ask 3 before me' posters.

At Mason Moor Primary in Southampton, children read the picture book *Stuck* by Oliver Jeffers. They then wrote down their strategies for keeping on learning when they were stuck. These were displayed on a working wall, and children were encouraged to use the ideas when they were struggling with a piece of work.

Where TAs are working with an individual or group, they can be trained to use a 'model and retreat' strategy, in which they first demonstrate the task, then tell the children that they are going to work with another group and will be back later to see how they are getting on.

TAs can also be deployed to produce resources that will enable children to work independently. I have seen, for example, laminated boards with series of photos stuck on to show the steps in a given task, and pre-prepared sheets of key words or pictures which the child circles when they hear the teacher using them in her explanations and instructions. As another example, instead of relaying what the teacher is saying (a form of 'stereo teaching' that actually makes it more difficult for a child to listen and understand) the TA can jot down key points on post-its for the child to order and discuss when the explanation is over.

It goes without saying that all teachers need to make clear to TAs that their role is to stimulate and scaffold children's independent thinking, rather than help them complete tasks. Professional development to develop questioning techniques and the types of adult feedback described in this chapter will be useful for TAs, particularly to help them avoid comfort words when children make mistakes or struggle, and instead learn to say 'So it didn't work that way. What might work, do you think?'

Secret number four: encourage children to set their own targets and challenge themselves

An alternative to setting and within-class groupings is to rank the tasks, not the learners. More and more schools are setting tasks at varying levels of challenge and asking students to opt for the one that is 'not too easy, not too hard but just right.' In this way children take ownership of their own learning rather than being passive consumers.

The system, influenced by the work of Guy Claxton and Alison Peacock, works best when combined with a process of teaching pupils about the three zones they can find themselves in when learning: their comfort zone, their stretch zone and their panic zone. I've seen laminated 'bulls-eyes' on pupils' desks, with a counter for them to place on the zone they feel they are in at any point in a task. They learn that though there may be times when we want to stay in our comfort zones (when we are feeling low or ill, for example), this is not the zone where we learn new things. Equally, we are not likely to learn when in the panic zone, because the brain centres that look after logical thinking (the 'upstairs' brain, or neo-cortex) stop working when the centres that mobilise us to handle stress (the 'downstairs brain' or limbic system) take over. The stretch zone is the one to aim for when learning.

Initially, pupils may find it difficult to choose stretch-level tasks. This is not a system that can be introduced overnight and expected to work straight away. Nevertheless, teachers consistently tell me that adopting it as a whole-school approach and coaching children in the system over time has worked well, with children increasingly able to gauge the right level of challenge.

Other ways of putting children in charge of their own learning include involving children in setting their own goals, which we will look at in Chapter 9, and using self-assessment in which they use clear success criteria (collectively arrived at by looking at a WAGOLL example – **W**hat **A G**ood **O**ne **L**ooks **L**ike) and decide on their own next steps in learning.

Pupils also need a way they can independently flag that they need help. This might be putting a counter onto the panic zone bulls-eye, putting out a yellow or red card on their desk, or posting a note in a wallet on the classroom wall if they are not clear about something.

Secret number five: giving pupils responsibility

Pupils taking the lead at parent-teacher meetings

At a secondary school in an area of industrial decline, parent–teacher meetings are always led by students. They are responsible for writing a letter inviting their parents or guardians to attend, coordinating with the office to schedule a time, and putting together a portfolio of their work and answers to self-reflection questions. This all happens about a month ahead, with pupils using a checklist to mark off each of the requirements.

The conferences typically last about 30 minutes, including time for parents to ask questions and for the pupil's tutor to give feedback on the pupil's presentation.

Pupils will lay out samples of their schoolwork, showing a mix of some of their best work and assignments where they struggled. They talk about which subjects are going well, ones where they need to make improvements, and what might help that to happen. They also share the results of questionnaires the school uses to help them assess attitudes to school and self, and discuss their social and emotional progress. Then they talk about their long-term goals and plans for the future.

The aim of the conferences is to end up with a plan of action that incorporates the student's goals and fosters parental support. Students appreciate not being talked about in the third person. Their motivation for learning has increased, as a result of their sense of self-efficacy. In the words of one student: 'I get to shape my own life.'

Before the new format for conferences was adopted, less than 20% of parents came to meetings about their child's progress. Now, more than 90% regularly attend.

This case study demonstrates one way of giving pupils responsibility. There are many others, often grouped under the banner of 'student voice'. Student councils, for example, can develop pupil self-efficacy as long as a wide range of students are involved, and they have a role in decisions on matters that affect teaching and learning as well as the menu for school meals and the state of the toilets.

Responsibility has to be real, and with this in mind it may be worth reflecting on where your school is on the ladder of pupil involvement (Figure 7.5).

At a primary school on the former Nottinghamshire coalfields, in place of a small student council there was a large, elected Children's Parliament, and child Cabinet Ministers for each subject area. The Ministers worked closely with the subject lead, taking important roles such as monitoring learning in classrooms and seeking pupil views.

Scalby secondary school, which we met in Chapter 5, has a Council for each Year Group, whose members are elected by their forms. The Councils feed into a 'Junior Leadership Team' (JLT) which works in parallel with the school's (adult) Senior Leadership Team, discussing topics on the SLT agenda and providing feedback. Staff invite applications to be on the JLT and can target pupils who might otherwise be under-represented to apply.

Panels of pupils who take part in interviews for new staff are similarly put together carefully to ensure balance.

Students have many other opportunities to exercise responsibility. They come to staff with causes they want to support and their own ideas for fundraising. Students from lower maths sets run a school shop with support from one of the maths staff; 'Digital leaders' go into primary schools to deliver workshops, such as on e-safety. There are student researchers and consultation groups, Community Ambassadors, and Primary Ambassadors. Y8 pupils support incoming Y7s in the first few weeks of transition, collecting them from lessons to take them to the next and helping them with routines and having the right equipment.

There is a real focus in the school on finding everyone's talent. The school offers a very wide range of activities so that all pupils can be good at something - from table tennis to a drama production in the Scarborough theatre, to working with a celebrity chef to cook and serve a banquet to the Mayor and other local dignitaries. Where students have a talent or interest, staff encourage this by funding opportunities and visits that are beyond a family's means.

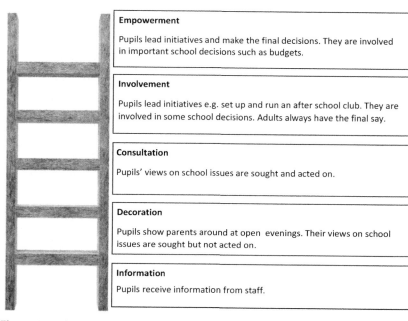

Empowerment

Pupils lead initiatives and make the final decisions. They are involved in important school decisions such as budgets.

Involvement

Pupils lead initiatives e.g. set up and run an after school club. They are involved in some school decisions. Adults always have the final say.

Consultation

Pupils' views on school issues are sought and acted on.

Decoration

Pupils show parents around at open evenings. Their views on school issues are sought but not acted on.

Information

Pupils receive information from staff.

Figure 7.5 The ladder of pupil involvement

At Surrey Square primary in London, Y5 and 6 children can become ambassadors for one of the school's core values (Responsibility, Respect, Enjoyment, Community, Perseverance, Compassion and Excellence). They write an application describing how they meet the Personal Excellence Learning Intentions (PELIs) for that value, and go through a formal selection process involving interviews. If successful, their role is to promote their value across the school community and help with the systems that are used to celebrate occasions when children demonstrate the value, in school or outside.

Another way of building self-efficacy is to set up peer mediation schemes in which pupils are formally trained to mediate conflicts and wear a badge or sash so that other pupils can turn to them for help. Anti-bullying programmes, too, are a type of work that should clearly be led by the pupils. I have seen great examples of pupils organising surveys, taking a camera out to photograph places in the school environment that are hot spots for bullying, and creating anti-bullying films. But any type of work is more likely to be successful if it puts pupils in the driving seat – like that at St Catherine's Catholic Primary School in Sheffield, where children in Y3 wrote their own book about the Romans. They then worked with staff at Waterstones to plan and organise a launch event. 'Surrounded by family and friends, the children proudly signed their books and posed for photographs. The books sold out within two days' (Lear, 2018).

Any project which involves pupils in exploring an issue affecting their lives or life in the local community and taking action to improve things will build pupil self-efficacy. One headteacher, for example, told me about her work with a group of Y5 girls who were not on track to achieve the expected standard. She wrote to them individually to invite them to join a lunchtime club called 'Leading Ladies.' Their task was to identify an issue that was important to them and take action to make change happen. What they chose to work on was marketing that targeted girls with all things pink. The girls wrote to the manager of the local Tesco store and were invited to a meeting with him, to put across their views.

At Netherfield Primary in Nottinghamshire, a Y4 class talked about how older people in the town perceived the younger generation. Children predicted what they might say, then constructed a questionnaire and went into the community to find out what people actually thought. The class came back to school to discuss ways of building stronger links between generations, and how their behaviour on the street when they were out playing impacted on residents' feelings.

Some everyday classroom teaching approaches (like mantle of the expert, and the reciprocal teaching we looked at in Chapter 5) are particularly helpful in building pupils' self-efficacy. Many of the oracy approaches described in Chapter 4, which engage pupils in questioning, debating and justifying their views, have a similar impact. 'Finding your voice,' the mantra of the oracy movement, has a dual meaning.

Then there are peer tutoring programmes in which older pupils are paired with younger tutees, or pairs of the same age work together in a structured way. One of the most successful projects I saw involved disaffected Y9 pupils with their own history of literacy difficulties going into the local primary to help Y3 children with their reading. In another, at Seabridge Primary in Newcastle under Lyme, staff invited children struggling with learning or behaviour to train as Forest School leaders for the Friday sessions offered to each year group in turn.

Less formally than in peer tutoring programmes, children can draw on their interests and talents to teach one another new skills. Netherfield primary, for example, set up a 'Try new things' project. The Y4 teacher put up a sheet asking 'Who would like to teach the class something?' Children signed up to teach others skills like tap dancing and boxing. They then planned and led the learning over three afternoons. In another school, children were asked to write a cartoon strip 'how to' guide for something they could do but others might not yet know how to. The guides were displayed in a class book.

A growth mindset experiment (Yeager *et al.*, 2019) is interesting in illustrating the potential effect of teaching something to others. In this large randomised controlled trial conducted with 15-year-olds, the intervention group completed two short online courses, which described successful strategies to develop ability but did not in any way instruct pupils to use them.

They then had to teach what they had learned to a pupil in the year group below who was struggling with learning. They were told 'This is where we really need your input. Think about new students coming to ninth grade next year. Imagine a student who is struggling in one of their classes and is feeling discouraged. Maybe the work feels too hard for them, or maybe they are having trouble staying motivated. What is the most important thing (or things) you learned today that could help them? Write a personal letter to encourage a 9th grader next year in the box below.'

Results showed a significant increase in grade point scores for lower-achieving students in the intervention group, compared to a control group. The proportion of lower-achieving students with very low grades dropped by 5%. This seems to me not only to show that growth mindset teaching can help increase attainment, but also that directly increasing self-efficacy by engaging pupils in learning for themselves and making their own choices (rather than being 'told'), and teaching another pupil information that could help them, are likely to have been important too.

A simple way of building this idea into everyday teaching is to ask pupils to reflect on their learning: 'What advice would you give to someone else who was learning this?' or 'How would you teach it to others?'

Exercising real responsibility

Inspirational headteacher Sharon Gray helped children at Netherfield Primary write their own account of their school experience, to put on the school's website. This is an extract from their document, which is called 'Our Sense of Pride.'

'This year I got to take my Peer Mediator Training. The training was pretty intense - a ten week course overall, the leaders have already been in role for a year - they are the experts, but I suppose it is a very skilled role and you can encounter some pretty tricky situations so you need to be well trained. There are now 12 of us who are Peer Mediators and we are all highly skilled in conflict resolution. If there is an argument or dispute, or if someone is upset or lonely, we're there to help.

Another of my major roles in school is as a Cabinet Minister for our School Parliament. I'm the Finance Minister for our school so I help to make sure we make the most of our budget and spend it on the things that are going to be the most beneficial to all the children at school. There are many other roles too, such as the Eco Warrior Team, the Learning and Teaching improvement team and Farm Association. We have lots of meetings where we can make real decisions. Last week we did some lesson observations of some of the teachers and gave them some really helpful feedback on how to improve their teaching so that we can learn better: Mrs Taylor says she is going to use more songs in her lessons after our feedback.'

Secret number six: give students choice and control

The last round of special needs and disability reforms brought in new ways of giving pupils and parents a greater involvement in decisions about them. The replacements for statements of SEN were expected to be called 'My Plan.' Families were meant to be given the option of personal budgets, which they could spend on forms of support of their choice.

Pupils were meant to be asked to help plan meetings where their needs and progress would be discussed – choosing people to be invited, deciding on how the room should be set out for the meeting, choosing music to play as people came in and snacks to be served. At the meeting, they would be asked about what was important to them, now and in the future. The child might be asked to describe what a good day in their lives looks like, and what a bad day looks like, so as to give clues about what actions and forms of support to retain, or do more of, and what needs to be changed.

Not all of this vision has been realised. 'My Plan' soon became a bureaucratic Education, Health and Care Plan, very few personal budgets are in place, and pupils are still not always even in the room when decisions are made about them. Nevertheless, many schools took imaginative steps to give pupils greater control.

At The Bromfords secondary school in Essex, for example, slots on staff meetings allowed pupils with SEND to talk to staff directly about the support they needed. A centrally held pot of unallocated TA hours was retained so that pupils could ask to book TA time for particular lessons of their choice, or to help them with specific pieces of homework.

Many schools also began to use the new kinds of pupil-led plans I recommended in my book 'Beating bureaucracy in special educational needs' (Figure 7.6) to replace individual education plans.

My Plan

What's important to me and my family	What's working, and needs to stay the same
My goals	What's not working, and needs to change
Who is going to do what to help me achieve my goals	
Who	By when

Figure 7.6 My Plan

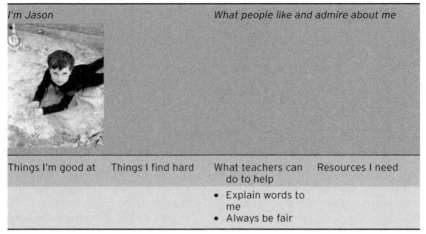

Figure 7.7 One-page profile

I think that there is much we can learn from the spirit of the reforms about how to build self-efficacy, not only for pupils with SEND but for all who are disadvantaged and lower achieving. Why not, for example, work with a wider group of pupils to develop one-page profiles like the one in Figure 7.7? Why not ask parents of all children to help their child, at the start of each school year, put together a one-page profile for their new class teacher or form tutor, with a photograph and headings like:

- My name is . . .
- What people like and admire about me . . .
- What I'm really good at . . .
- What I'm interested in . . .
- What my teachers need to know so they can help me learn . . .

I sometimes speak about the example of one boy with SEND whose family did have a personal budget. The boy was involved in discussions about how best to use it. He had been upset that the transport that collected him from school at a fixed time each day meant that he could never attend after school clubs with his friends, so everyone decided to spend some of the budget on a taxi pick-up on certain days.

Again, this kind of consultation should not just involve pupils with SEND. Inclusion expert Daniel Sobel (2015) tells how one boy eligible for the Pupil Premium was falling behind in maths. Maths was always the first lesson of the day and he was always late for the lesson. The school asked him why, but he wouldn't answer. They got no response from his parents. Eventually, they paid a home visit. They found that the boy was a carer for two younger siblings. Like all carers, this pupil found getting out of the house in the morning a struggle; he often missed the right bus to school and had to wait for the next. The boy and his teachers discussed what might help, and decided to use some of the Pupil Premium to buy him a bicycle so he could get to his maths lessons on time – and managed, through good communication, to make this feel fair to other pupils.

I sometimes ask groups of school leaders and teachers whether their school lets pupils and parents know that a pupil is receiving Pupil Premium funding. Very few say yes. Those who do have found ways of communicating this sensitively, in a context where the use of the Premium (including for spending on things like staff training or school-wide interventions designed to raise attainment for all) is transparent, and relationships with families have been carefully built over time. They also review spending choices by asking pupils whether the decisions taken on use of the Premium are working for them. Their perspective is that the funding actually belongs to the pupil and their family; it has not been provided so that the school can boost its Ofsted grading.

'No decision about me, without me' is a vision that the NHS is seeking to put in practice in interactions with patients. I think it should apply to the use of the Pupil Premium too.

Choice and control can apply to everyday learning as well as additional interventions. If pupils are not doing well, we can have an open-ended conversation with them, saying for example, 'I want to be able to teach you in a more effective way. So what's been going well, what hasn't worked well?'

In one interesting study (Hulleman and Harackiewicz, 2009), 15-year-old pupils were asked every three to four weeks to write down reasons why the material they had studied in their science lessons that week could be applied in their lives. A control group wrote a summary of the week's learning. This intervention led to a significant increase in the science grades of pupils with low expectations for success by the end of the school year. But when students were *told* why the schoolwork was important and relevant instead of coming up with their own reasons, the intervention had a negative effect. The pupils needed that sense of coming to conclusions themselves if they were to benefit from their learning.

Finally, choice and control can apply to the way we manage behaviour. Schools that emphasise behavioural choices in the language they use with pupils ('What happened when you did xxx? What other choices could you have made?') are building pupil self-efficacy. Schools that use restorative approaches are going even further, as they are handing responsibility for making reparation to the pupil after things have gone wrong, and hurt or damage has been the result.

Secret number seven: teach children about the concepts of agency and locus of control

Learning about self-efficacy

A Y1 class make a list of some of their achievements on the whiteboard. Their teacher asks the children questions about how and why they were successful.

- Did you learn to count in threes because the sun was shining?
- Did you learn to ride a bike because you kept practising?
- Did you . . . because you listened carefully to the instructions?

She comments that she's noticed that they seemed to have succeeded because of their own actions.

A Y3 class are given a set of cards: 'I did well in the spelling test because the spellings were easy,' 'Kylie doesn't want to be my friend because I wasn't very nice to her when she first started at this school.' They are asked to work in pairs to sort the cards into two piles, one of cards that showed the person was taking responsibility, the other of cards where they were blaming things outside themselves.

At a secondary school, Y7 learn the terms external and internal locus of control. They then sort situation cards like 'He made me laugh so I got thrown out of class' into piles of 'internal' or 'external' locus.

In Y9, pupils are given a 'What's my style' resource sheet describing three characters: Mr It'smeagainsttheworld, Mr Theworld'sagainstme, and Mr It'suptome. The teacher explains that they represent ways we explain to ourselves what happens to us (attributions).

The class talk briefly in pairs about which of the characters best matches their way of looking at events, then role-play how the three characters would respond to various scenarios.

Finally the class are divided into three groups representing the characters, and asked to think about a situation where they have a project to do, three weeks to do it but leave it to the last minute. The teacher returns the work saying it is not up to their usual standard and they will need to do it again. Each group has to say what they would think, say or do. In a whole class discussion they explore which type of response is most likely to get them where they want to be. The teacher puts an 'It's up to me' poster on the wall for pupils to add examples of this sort of thinking over the week.

All these are lesson ideas from the national SEAL (**S**ocial and **E**motional **A**spects of **L**earning) programme that I played a part in developing some years ago, in which many schools took part – and many still use. They show that we can teach pupils to understand self-efficacy, using age-appropriate language.

As with all social and emotional learning, direct teaching like this will only work if it is backed up by opportunities for pupils to apply the learning across the school day, in a climate that actually gives pupils opportunities to experience the exercise of responsibility and choice. So after lessons in self-efficacy, we need to apply the school's reward system (praise, points, certificates or whatever) to occasions when pupils demonstrate an internal locus of control – when they move, for example, from saying 'The glass fell' to 'I dropped it,' from 'The dog ate my homework' excuses to 'I put it off. I will get it done tonight.'

Key take-aways

- Self-efficacy, internal locus of control and agency all mean that we believe we can make a difference to our own lives and those of others.

- There is evidence that disadvantaged pupils on average may have lower self-efficacy than their more advantaged peers, and that this is an important factor in predicting attainment.

- When a disadvantaged child is underachieving, we need to ask ourselves what we can do to make the pupil feel more powerful in their own lives.

- To build self-efficacy we can praise strategies rather than success, use growth mindset language, monitor our expectations of pupils, find a talent in every learner, give less help, rank tasks not children, enable children to independently choose tasks at the right level of challenge, give pupils responsibility and choice, and explicitly teach them to understand concepts of agency and locus of control.

---

8 No excuse for no excuses?

Experienced headteacher Gill Kelly described her shock when she took over a Lincolnshire Pupil Referral Unit (PRU) to find that the large majority of pupils from Foundation Stage to KS4 were disadvantaged boys. 'My first headship was of a large academy with 75% free school meals that was particularly boy heavy. However to see 95% of the 252 places in our PRU taken up with boys from impoverished backgrounds threw their context into stark relief for me' (Kelly, 2018).

Many disadvantaged white pupils behave well, attend school regularly and engage fully with learning. Nevertheless, the statistics unfortunately demonstrate a much higher overall average risk of conduct and emotional problems for this group than their peers from wealthier families (Goodman *et al*., 2015).

The disadvantage gap in conduct problems is evident as early as age three, and appears to be wider now than it was among children born in 1970. One study (Gutman *et al*., 2015) used a composite measure of mental health problems (conduct problems, hyperactivity and inattention, emotional problems and peer problems) and found that the gap in prevalence between more and less disadvantaged children has widened since 1999, with children from the lowest income families now four times more likely to have mental health problems than those from the highest-earning backgrounds.

The effects of prolonged poverty

Researchers (National Scientific Council on the Developing Child, 2020) have documented the various routes through which prolonged poverty may affect the developing child through the stressors it brings with it: the metabolic consequences of inadequate nutrition, the developmental burdens of chronic disease or disability in the family, the physiological disruptions of air pollution, the interpersonal challenges of maternal depression and parental addictions,

DOI: 10.4324/9781003176442-9

the psychological threats of maltreatment and community violence. Any of these stressors may persistently and intensely activate a developing child's stress response systems. Whilst small amounts of stress can actually be helpful in terms of later mental health, chronic long-term stress can result in a brain that is 'stuck' in a state of high alert, overly primed to activate fight-or-flight responses even when threats are relatively low. It is this that at least in part appears to determine the link between disadvantage and behaviour problems.

Such links are not inevitable, however. There appear to be protective factors which can increase the child's resilience and reduce the impact of early risk factors.

Risk and resilience

It is not inevitable that children exposed to adverse experiences will develop long-term problems. Researchers (Latham *et al.*, 2019) followed up a large group of children who had experienced abuse, neglect, bullying, or domestic violence during their childhood. When participants were 18 years old, they were interviewed about the qualifications they had achieved, and their psychosocial wellbeing. A number of factors emerged which appeared to have protected the young person from negative outcomes – having a warm relationship with their mother, having an adult to turn to for support, having good quality friendships and living in a neighbourhood with a strong sense of community.

Ethnicity and behaviour

The relationship between ethnicity and behaviour issues varies by age. In school-age pupils, government statistics show that in 2019 Gypsy and Roma, and Traveller of Irish Heritage pupils had the highest school exclusion rates (both permanent and fixed-term). Mixed white and Black Caribbean, and Black Caribbean pupils also had high exclusion rates, and were both nearly three times more likely to be permanently excluded than white British pupils. The rate for Asian pupils was consistently below the national average. I was not able to find any data breaking exclusions down by both ethnicity and free school meals status, which seems a significant gap that ought to be addressed.

Although there are gaps in the data on school-aged pupils, there is some information on younger children; in a sample of 800 children in 40 schools in very disadvantaged areas across England, nursery-aged children speaking only English had more parent-rated social and emotional difficulties (on the Strengths and Difficulties Questionnaire) than bilingual children, particularly for conduct problems (Dockrell *et al.*, 2020).

Boys, girls and behaviour

The millennium cohort studies (Goodman *et al.*, 2015) all show a greater prevalence, persistence and combination of social and emotional problems for boys than girls, particularly conduct problems. So why are boys more vulnerable?

Researchers (Kraemer, 2000) suggest a blend of biological and cultural influences shaping the behaviour of boys and girls from infancy on. Perhaps because as a group they are more vulnerable to complications at birth, infant boys seem on average to have more difficult temperaments. Boys are more vulnerable to the effects of maternal post-natal depression than girls, the effect extending into the nursery years, long after the depression has lifted. In turn, mothers' depression is linked to inattentiveness and hyperactivity in their sons, especially in boys from disadvantaged families (Chowdry and McBride, 2017).

For children brought up in stressful environments, there can as we have seen be an over-production of the stress hormone cortisol that leads to the brain and body being 'stuck' in a state of high alert. Boys may be less able than girls to offset the effect of cortisol on emotions, because of lower levels of oxytocin, and this can make for lower levels of empathy and increased social withdrawal. 'This, in combination with the presence of testosterone, makes it more likely that boys under stress will react with aggression and show less empathy towards those they disagree with. A recipe for school punishments and exclusions' (Tomova *et al.*, 2014).

Equally, however, there are social and cultural explanations for gender differences in empathy and aggression. Parents behave differently towards boys. In a study of communication styles of mothers with their three-year-old children (Fivush, 1989), the mothers did not judge any of their daughters to be angry, only their sons. By the age of three, clear differences have emerged in how children perceive and respond to emotional states, with boys showing less sympathy for others' distress. But this may be because girls are praised more for showing tenderness and care for others. When pupils are of school age, there is clear evidence that we expect different things of boys and girls, and treat them differently. Boys are more likely to be seen by teachers as unable to sit still, noisy and disruptive, lazy or apathetic (Myhill and Jones, 2004). Both boys and girls feel that girls are more likely to get away with poor behaviour than boys, and that boys are more likely to be told off (Myhill and Jones, 2006).

Intervening early

Behavioural and emotional problems have long-term consequences. Research-ers (Chowdry and McBride, 2017) have found that such problems at age five contribute to emotional and behavioural problems at age ten, and to lower cognitive scores (on maths and reading tests) at age ten, which in turn contrib-ute to lower cognitive scores at age 16 (on arithmetic and vocabulary tests). As a result, the authors suggest, early social emotional and behavioural problems 'can cast long shadows.'

Such problems can be addressed at any age, but evidence suggests that outcomes are better and easier to achieve when interventions are provided earlier – through evidence-based parenting programmes, for example. Some of these work on the parent–child relationship with babies and pre-school chil-dren, but there is also good evidence for parenting programmes with school-aged children. We will look at some of these in Chapter 10.

In support of the need for early intervention, whilst pupils are still in pri-mary school, Chowdry and McBride found that the statistically significant link between behavioural and emotional problems at age five and cognitive scores at age 16 could be fully accounted for when they controlled for cognitive scores and behavioural and emotional problems at age ten. They say 'In other words, after this is taken into account, there is no independent link between behavioural and emotional problems at age five and cognitive skills at age 16. One potential way to interpret this is that early childhood behavioural and emotional problems need not present a risk for future educational attainment if they can be turned around by age ten.'

Solutions to behaviour problems: zero tolerance and 'no excuses' policies

There has been a trend in recent years for schools serving disadvantaged areas to see ever-tighter discipline as the solution to behaviour issues. First we had zero tolerance approaches, imported from the United States, in which every misdemeanour, however minor, is picked up on. More recently, 'no excuses' policies have come into vogue, where every aspect of pupils' behav-iour is governed by tight rules (such as not talking in corridors, and standing up when a teacher enters a room) and sanctions are applied uniformly to every student, no matter what the circumstances.

The US information organisation Child Trends (Boccanfuso and Kuhfeld, 2011) has summarised research on zero tolerance policies, and concluded that there has been a lack of rigorous research, but analyses of suspension and expulsion data suggest that they do not deter misbehaviour.

We can contrast the lack of evidence for zero tolerance with the rather better (though still not quite conclusive) evidence for a very different approach – restorative practices, in which pupils confront the effects of their behaviour on others and make reparation. A recent review (Darling-Hammond *et al.*, 2020) looked at the past 20 years of quantitative studies of restorative justice in US schools. Across these studies, the approach consistently improved discipline, discipline disparities and school climate, and reduced misbehaviour. As an example, a three-year study compared middle and high schools in California participating in the Whole School Restorative Justice programme to similar schools that did not. In the restorative justice schools, suspensions were cut in half (34% to 14% – very significantly more than the change seen in control schools). Chronic absences diminished in the restorative schools, while increasing in the controls, and more pupils graduated successfully from high school.

What works in reducing behaviour problems?

Learning Together is a secondary school-based intervention grounded in schoolwide policies and systems, restorative practices, and social and emotional education.

Forty secondary schools in southeast England participated in a trial of the programme, with 20 randomly assigned to deliver the intervention over three years, and 20 continuing with existing practices. In the intervention schools, staff and pupils collaborated in an 'action group' to change school rules and policies, with the goal of making it a healthier environment. This included focusing on improving relationships rather than merely punishment-based approaches to discipline.

Schools in the trial delivered classroom-based social and emotional skills education in stand-alone PSHE lessons, and/or integrated it into tutor time or subject lessons. Students received five to ten hours of teaching per year on restorative practices, relationships, and social and emotional skills. Lessons were based on the Australian Gatehouse Project curriculum. Schools selected modules on topics such as managing emotions, understanding and building trusting relationships, exploring others' needs and avoiding conflict.

All pupils completed a questionnaire at the start of the trial, and this was repeated three years later. Results showed that self-reported experiences of bullying and victimisation were lower in intervention schools than in control schools. Pupils in intervention schools also had higher scores on quality of life and psychological wellbeing measures, and lower scores on a psychological difficulties measure. They also reported lower rates of having smoked, drunk alcohol, being offered or trying illicit drugs, or being in contact with the police in the previous 12 months.

Adapted from Bonell *et al.*, 2019. *Modifying the secondary school environment to reduce bullying and aggression: the INCLUSIVE cluster RCT*

No excuse for no excuses?

When writing this chapter I came across a poem by an American writer (Dickerson, 2014). It speaks for itself:

'Cos I Ain't Got a Pencil

I woke myself up
Because we ain't got an alarm clock
Dug in the dirty clothes basket,
Cause ain't nobody washed my uniform
Brushed my hair and teeth in the dark,
Cause the lights ain't on
Even got my baby sister ready,
Cause my mama wasn't home.
Got us both to school on time,
To eat us a good breakfast.
Then when I got to class the teacher fussed
Cause I ain't got no pencil.

Reflecting on occasions like this when 'no excuses' policies might not be appropriate does not, however, mean that we should not have behaviour policies at all. As behaviour expert Adele Bates writes (2020) clear rules and routines provide boundaries that make children feel safe. They can prevent the kind of disruption to classroom learning that in the long run impacts most on disadvantaged pupils, because they often end up in setted classes where disruption is most common. Ninety-nine per cent of the time it is important to uphold the rules. But 'no excuse' policies should never let us off the hook of taking time to listen to pupils, to find out whether there might be a reason for not applying a sanction in a particular case, or longer term issues about a pupil's mental health or family circumstances that need to be addressed.

We also need to check how well any no excuses system is actually working. If the same set of students end up in detention time and time again, it probably isn't. If any group – disadvantaged, or of a particular ethnicity – is disproportionately represented in exclusions, something is going very wrong.

It may be that your school needs a more nuanced approach to discipline, based on understanding that there are different patterns in misbehaviour, different motivations and reasons, different causes – as at Broken Cross, the primary school we met in Chapter 5.

When the current headteacher joined Broken Cross Primary, there had been 43 fixed term exclusions in the past year. In the five years since, there has been only one. The school's behaviour policy is tight, but each child is treated as an individual. 'We work hard to understand our children,' says Donna. Staff are trained in relational practices, rooted in research and theory from the fields of attachment and trauma. Children who need help are assessed using the Boxall profile so as to design individual nurture programmes.

There is a social and emotional learning programme (Zippy's Friends) for all children in Y1 and 2, and in KS2 a programme called Mind Mechanics, an evidence-based wellbeing intervention, which teaches a set of sustainable skills and strategies to help children self-manage overwhelming feelings. It is delivered in small groups to targeted children but the aim is that by the end of KS2 every child will have taken part.

Why children don't behave

Grant is 12. He rarely does what teachers ask him to do in class, and constantly gets into fights at lunch and breaktimes. Nevertheless he is seen as a leader and has plenty of friends and admirers. When something interests him he can stick at it for hours.

Scott is also often in trouble for fighting. He flares up easily and flies off the handle if anything winds him up. In class, he finds it hard to work in groups and gives up easily if he doesn't see quick success with a task.

Conor is in many ways a model student. He generally works hard and gets on with teachers and other pupils. Sometimes, however, he seems to start the day off on the wrong foot and may end up swearing at a teacher or storming out of class.

Rhys is also unpredictable. He sometimes has intense bursts of anger, for no apparent reason. At other times he is withdrawn and listless. He is often involved in bullying, and has followers rather than friends. Staff find him hard to reach.

Grant, Scott, Conor and Rhys have all had many detentions and several fixed term exclusions since starting at secondary school. None of them have modified their behaviour as a result.

I think there are four main but overlapping reasons for behaviour problems, represented by these four pupils and shown in Figure 8.1.

Some children and young people – those in the top circle in the diagram – *can* behave appropriately, but don't choose to. Grant probably falls into this group. He has the underpinning social and emotional capabilities he needs in order to succeed in school. He can get on with others and can motivate himself when he wants to. He is choosing not to apply these skills, however, because the rewards for not doing so (like making peers laugh, or getting out of a tedious lesson) outweigh those for behaving well, and are of more interest to him than any sanctions.

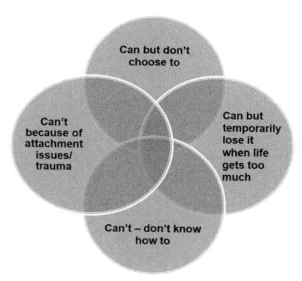

Figure 8.1 Four reasons why children don't behave

Grant values the attention and respect of his peers. He is gaining this right now by making classmates laugh, challenging teachers and picking fights. Detentions don't actually bother him much, and fixed term exclusions even less, as he can spend time at home gaming and watching YouTube.

Grant could relatively easily change his behaviour if the types of rewards and sanctions he experiences were adjusted, and more time was taken to find out what would actually encourage him to make better behaviour choices.

Scott, however, is different. He most likely falls into the second group of pupils – the bottom circle in Figure 8.1, those who 'can't' behave appropriately because they don't know how. These children actually lack some social and emotional capabilities and need help to develop them. Providing more rewards or adjusting the type of sanction won't work for Scott, because he doesn't know how to recognise and manage his feelings. He doesn't know how to handle frustration or control his anger. Nor does he have the social skills needed for working in groups.

Conor falls into yet another group – the right-hand circle in the diagram. He does not lack social and emotional skills, but is under stress. Perhaps he is caring for a sick or disabled parent; perhaps he is witnessing domestic violence; perhaps he has experienced a recent bereavement. When life gets too much, he simply 'loses it'.

Rhys 'loses it' more often and more intensely. He has a short fuse and swings between moods in ways that are hard to understand. He has great difficulties forming any sort of relationship, with adults and peers. It is very likely that he has experienced early attachment difficulties or trauma.

The actions required for each of these four types of learners are very different. Children who can behave but choose not to will respond to a no excuses policy with clear rules and routines, and a carefully tailored reward and sanction system within a framework that emphasises choice and pupil voice.

The second group, children who lack fundamental social and emotional skills, are unlikely to respond to a standard behaviour management system in the long term. You can't punish (or reward) a child into doing something they don't know how to do. If a child cannot read, we teach them to read; if they cannot work with others or manage their emotions, we similarly need to take on the task of teaching them. These children – and they are a large group – need help to learn how to recognise, discuss and handle emotions (self-awareness, managing feelings), how to put themselves in others' shoes and 'feel for and with them' (empathy), how to make and keep friends and work with others (social skills), and how to set themselves goals and work towards them even when the going gets tough. The needs of this group will be discussed in the next chapter.

The third group, children who have the underlying social and emotional skills they need, but struggle to maintain them at difficult times, need responsive pastoral systems that recognise when they are under stress. These children should be provided with opportunities to check in for a quiet chat at the start of the day, a listening ear, and a place in school they can take themselves to when things get too much. Action may well need to be taken to try and sort the family stressors or events that are troubling them.

The last group are those children who tax behaviour systems the most, and all too often end up 'managed out' of their school through exclusion or other means. Many will never have felt loved or learned to regulate emotions through early interaction with a warm responsive adult. They may also have experienced significant trauma, so their nervous systems are in permanent trip-wire state; they don't feel safe so we need to help them feel safe in school, and get them some specialist help.

Let us look in more detail at possible responses for each group.

The children who can behave but choose not to

Simple steps like tight rules can work for this group. In the secondary age group we can be firm on not allowing banter; we can decide on who sits next to whom; we should insist on homework completion, as homework does improve attainment in secondary pupils (EEF, 2018) and failure to complete it is a significant factor in the attainment gap between disadvantaged pupils and their peers.

Behaviours for the 'can but choose not to' pupils help them obtain something desirable or escape something undesirable. A first step in tackling classroom behaviour difficulties will be to check whether the pupil is able to do the work that has been set. An interesting study (Johnson et al., 2019) found that 20% of the time misbehaviour could be attributed to academic problems: either students didn't understand the work or the assignment was too difficult.

At St Ives secondary in Cornwall, staff and leaders understand that poor behaviour is often a symptom of an underlying issue. Where behaviour is troublesome, pupils' reading age will be reviewed, and they may be assessed for possible dyslexia, or speech, language and communication difficulties.

From some point in KS2 children's allegiances shift from adults to peers, and peer attention becomes a powerful driver of classroom behaviour. In the secondary years, being told off can become a status symbol, a badge of honour amongst the group. Remedies include private rather than public reprimands.

> Teachers who tell off boys publicly and by constantly referring to the troublemakers by name – Jack, stop that messing about. Jack, can you not put your pencil in Amir's ear please. Jack, could you please refrain from sticking post-it notes on Susan's forehead – are simply giving the boys the attention and rebel status they crave. Teachers would do better to reprimand boys privately.
>
> Matt Pinkett and Mark Roberts, 2019. *Boys don't try*

Pinkett and Roberts also suggest that to avoid pupils misbehaving for peer attention, teachers avoid using pupils' names: 'I'm just going to wait while those at the back stop talking.' Other research-based behaviour management techniques that help all pupils, but are likely to be particularly effective with disadvantaged pupils, especially boys, include:

- Being concrete and specific about the behaviours needed for different activities – actively teaching the behaviours using the language of 'we' ('in this classroom we . . .'), noticing and feeding back on examples of appropriate behaviours.
- Setting very specific goals for what students are expected to do and providing frequent feedback on progress: 'Write a paragraph about . . . aim for at least ten lines in the next five minutes . . .,' 'Last year's Y9 got 60% of these quiz questions right – see if you can beat that.'
- Helping students monitor the amount of work they are getting done in a lesson. The teacher can stop the class at a given point and ask them to put a dot in the margin of their work, then again five minutes later. Repeated over a number of lessons, this exercise allows pupils to evaluate their effort and challenge themselves to be more productive.

- Commenting on the behaviour not the pupil: 'That was unkind behaviour and not how we talk to each other in this class' rather than 'You're unkind and unhelpful.'
- Avoiding shouting, sarcasm and 'banter with the boys', as it damages the relationship between pupil and teacher.
- Using the kind of assertive but polite language that tells pupils what behaviour is expected rather than what you don't want them to be doing – 'The behaviour I want to see right now is . . . thank you.'
- Phoning parents to tell them their child has done well with their learning and behaviour.
- Focusing on positive behaviour and tactically ignoring minor misbehaviours.

Many researchers have found that constantly carping on about small issues does not work. One study (Reinke *et al.*, 2016) observed primary teachers' interactions with pupils at the start of the school year, then followed the pupils up later. Children who initially received more negative feedback (for not paying attention or for briefly talking in class, for example) than positive feedback were rated at the end of the year as having a significant increase in problems with emotion regulation, concentration problems, and observed disruptive behaviour, whereas children who received more positive feedback demonstrated significant increases in positive, pro-social behaviours.

Increasing the amount of praise given for positive behaviour, on the other hand, has been consistently found to be effective – though for secondary students the praise, like reprimands, needs to be private. Studies (Caldarella *et al.*, 2020) in which the ratio of praise to reprimands was deliberately increased in classrooms show a linear relationship with pupils' behaviour – the higher the teacher's praise-to-reprimand ratio, the higher the students' on-task behaviour.

The teenage brain is more responsive to rewards than punishments

In a fascinating experiment (Palminteri *et al.*, 2016), volunteers aged 12 to 17, and 18 to 32, completed tasks in which they had to choose between abstract symbols. Each symbol was consistently associated with a fixed chance of a reward, punishment or no outcome. As the trial progressed, participants learnt which symbols were likely to lead to each outcome and adjusted their choices accordingly.

> The results showed that adolescents and adults were equally good at learning to choose symbols associated with reward, but adolescents were less good at avoiding symbols associated with punishment.
>
> The authors suggest that 'a reward-based approach, rather than punishment, is more likely to be effective in adolescent learning.'

The children who can behave but temporarily lose it when life gets too much

Pupils who generally behave well but have days when they seem to go to pieces need good whole school listening systems where someone will pick up on the change in their behaviour and give them 'a good listening to'.

I recommend regular emotional check-ins for all at the start of the day, and perhaps after the lunchbreak, as a way of noticing any child who might be feeling angry, sad or anxious – as well as of helping children learn to be aware of and express their own emotions rather than act them out in unhelpful ways.

In emotional check-ins, primary pupils can attach a laminated photo of themselves to a display, which might be of emojis, *Inside Out* icons, or an emotional barometer labelled with a range of different emotion words.

In secondary schools, tutors can ask pupils to put their thumbs up, down or sideways to show how they are feeling, then talk to a partner about why they chose that gesture (making it clear that they should just talk about what they are comfortable with sharing). Emojis and the well-known 'blob tree' work for older pupils too. Subject teachers can introduce check-ins, asking pupils for example 'What landform/colour/sport resembles your mood right now?'

In one Pupil Referral Unit I saw students attach their names on cards to a poster of a beach with a scurrying crab, a deckchair, a swimmer waving from the sea, a person fishing and a gasping fish, to indicate how they were feeling. Another school asked pupils to choose which of a display of memes (grumpy cat and so on) best matched their mood.

Our Monday mood checks are the most informative, because they tell me what kind of teacher I need to be. When I know dad left mum over the weekend, my job is to comfort and console, to offer a few more calm breaks and time to talk. If I didn't know that, I'd be doing more harm than good.

Year 4 teacher at Billesley Primary School (quoted in Butler, 2020)

Such check-ins need to be followed up. This is easier in primary schools, where the class teacher or a TA can take a child aside for a chat if they are not feeling good. Secondary form tutors might have a quiet word, or simply remind pupils of schoolwide systems they can use, such as drop-in times with a school counsellor or learning mentor. Ideally, the school will have established recognised spaces to which pupils can take themselves voluntarily and for a limited time if they need to calm down – a chillout room, or a corner of a primary classroom equipped with smooth pebbles to handle, intricate patterns to colour in, a lava lamp, lavender-scented cotton balls and a rocking chair.

The wellbeing zone

Magna Carta secondary school in Surrey created a wellbeing zone for pupils, a large area transformed with murals. There are four spaces within it: an anti-bullying pop-in room; a wellbeing pop-in room; 'club chill' (an invitation-only lunchtime room specifically for the most vulnerable to hang out); and a wellbeing centre for private meetings by appointment with adult mentors.

Students can self-refer to the wellbeing centre at lunchtime, or they can be referred by a staff member. The adult wellbeing mentors who staff the centre have training in youth mental health and are experienced in delivering non-directive supportive therapy. They are available to students at all times.

There are also pupils who are appointed as wellbeing ambassadors, and offer a lunchtime listening service. They have had training in active listening skills and focus on empathy rather than giving advice, although they can signpost students to further support if needed.

The children who can't behave because of attachment issues/trauma

Often we think of trauma as a dramatic event like an earthquake, terrorism or an assault. A broader definition encompasses any event, or series of events, that overwhelms a person's capacity to cope and has a long-lasting impact on them. Many disadvantaged pupils have experienced trauma of this kind. So one good approach is to stop asking these pupils the question 'What's *wrong* with you?' and replace it with 'Could you help me understand what's *happened* to you?'

Children who have experienced trauma or not been able to establish secure attachments to reliable, responsive parent figures often lack trust in adults. It is important to build a strong bond with at least one person in school, using some of the strategies described later in this chapter in the section on relationships. If that adult is not in school there should be another key adult the pupil knows well, to whom they can turn when they are upset; these children need 'safe faces' as well as the calming places (safe spaces) we have already touched on.

It can help if we create a personalised workspace somewhere in the school which has their name, a picture of things they like, a go-to box of things that calm them down (a photo, feather for breathing, a smooth stone to touch, a calming bottle of glitter that slowly settles after you shake it) and their personal school timetable on display. For some pupils, we might provide alternatives to the playground/outside areas, perhaps via lunchtime clubs, so as to avoid placing them in social situations they are not for the moment able to navigate.

A sense of belonging

Researchers have found that students who feel confident that they belong in their school and class, and are valued by their teachers and peers, have fewer behaviour problems (Romero, 2018). They also learn better; it has been argued that that when pupils are unsure about whether they belong, they are constantly on the look-out for cues in the environment that signal whether or not they fit in. This hypervigilance uses up cognitive resources that are essential for learning.

This is likely to be a particular issue for any group of pupils who feel that their culture and background is not valued in school - so potentially (though not of course inevitably) pupils from minority ethnic backgrounds, pupils who have a disability, economically disadvantaged pupils and other groups protected by equalities legislation.

There is evidence that on average pupils brought up in persistent poverty do feel less supported by peers; one study of children born at the millennium (Gibb *et al.*, 2016) found that age 11, compared with children with no experience of poverty, they were less likely to have a good friend, less likely to be liked by others, more likely to play alone and less likely to talk to friends about their worries.

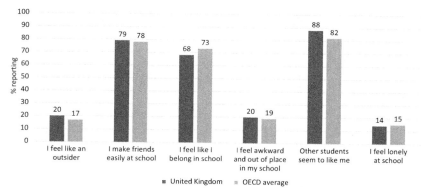

Figure 8.2 Results of international wellbeing survey of secondary school students
Source: Data from Organisation for Economic Co-operation and Development (2017)
PISA 2015 Results Volume 111 : students' well-being.

> A key factor in engaging boys from low-income backgrounds was a strong emphasis on establishing a clear sense of community where everyone felt 'accepted', with something of value to add to the life of the school and the neighbourhood.
>
> Ofsted, 2008. *White boys from low income-backgrounds: good practice in schools*

The sense of belonging in school – or lack of it – seems to be a particular issue in the UK. An international study by the Organisation for Economic Co-operation and Development (2017) found that teenagers with a sense of belonging in school were more likely to perform better academically and be happier with their lives. Students in the UK, however, had a weaker sense of belonging at school than the average for other developed countries (Figure 8.2).

So what can we do to increase pupils' sense of belonging? A team at London's Institute of Education have been undertaking action research in this area:

> A group of schools worked with a university team (Riley *et al.*, 2018) to explore how far students in their schools felt a sense of belonging. The research was undertaken by staff and by the students themselves. The schools then developed initiatives to increase the sense of community

and shared identity. In one all-through school, whose founders' symbol is a star, there was a collective exercise when over a period of some 40 minutes the whole school community came together on the school's playing field to form a star shape – which was filmed with the help of a drone. In another school, sofas were placed in the central atrium and pupils encouraged to use the space to work and hang out together. In one primary school, children created a welcome song and short dramas about how you can go from not belonging to belonging when others let you join their game.

As a first step in promoting belonging, we can deliberately engineer activities which develop bonds in each class or tutor group. Traditional Y7 team-building transition activities are very helpful here, and there is no shortage of ideas available for tutors. The resources for the SEAL themes 'A Place to Learn' and 'Learning to Be Together,' for example, are specifically designed to create bonded and cohesive groups of Y7 students.

Some of my favourites, from a variety of sources, are:

- Having students work in groups to explore how they could create their ideal tutor room, making it feel comfortable and distinct to their class, drawing designs and discussing their ideas.
- Making a tutor group collage of 'my happy place' – photos or drawings of places where pupils feel happy, safe and comfortable.
- Playing 'Just like me' in which students stand up when the teacher makes a statement that applies to them – 'Everyone who is the youngest in their family,' 'Everyone who as a blog or YouTube channel' or 'Everyone who has been to more than two schools' and so on.
- Breaking the class into teams, marking off an area that is wider than all the team members standing side by side then challenging each team to get one member from one side of the area to the other without touching the ground or being carried.

A nice idea for primary pupils of any age is to give each child a paper jigsaw piece, which will interlock with others. They decorate their piece with drawings to represent themselves and their interests, then fit their pieces together on a large display.

At the start of the new school year in one Y6 class the teacher introduced her class to West African Adinkra symbols. Each child chose a
symbol that they felt represented their qualities, beliefs and interests
and printed it on a strip of cloth. Then the cloths were woven together
to create a rope representing the whole class. At the end of the year,
the rope was unpicked and the children took their own strip home.

Another good way to build a sense of belonging at the start of the year is to
develop a classroom charter, which sets out how people will behave towards
each other. Research shows that this will not only build a sense of community,
but will also lead to greater rule-following. In one online survey filled in by
over a thousand students aged 11–19 in different schools, findings showed that
if students follow rules because they accept them as their own, they are less
likely to misbehave or feel resentful (Aelterman *et al.*, 2019).

One secondary school develops tutor group social contracts, built from
the responses of four essential questions from the teacher. 'How do you
want to be treated by me? How do you want to be treated by each other?
How do you think I want to be treated by you? And how do you want
to handle violations of the contract?' Students answer those questions
independently, and then share their ideas. One class agreed to handle
violations of the contract in a way that doesn't cause a disturbance
while the teacher is teaching. They agreed to use the thumb sideways
as a cue to say, 'Check yourself and check the contract.' At intervals the
class review how things are going, using a simple three/two/one rating.
'Three, we nailed it. We followed everything in the contract. Two, there
may have been a distraction or two. One, we had major issues.'

As the school year goes on, we can continue to explore the commonalities
there are amongst class members. An inspiring example comes from Springfield Primary in Cheshire, where Y6 pupils watched a Danish TV advertise-
ment called 'TV 2 | All That We Share,' that is easily found on the internet.
In the film, people step forward if they share a common characteristic; many
different characteristics are explored, from 'those who are self-confident' to
'those who have ever been bullied' to 'those who are step-parents.' By the

end it is clear that in any group there will be more we have in common than that which divides us. The Springfield Y6 pupils then made a similar YouTube film featuring themselves; that too can be found on the internet (under the title Y6 All that we share) and is well worth watching, as an example of how to break down differences and create cohesion.

More prosaically, it is useful to structure paired activities over the school year to ensure that everybody has a chance to work with everyone else in the class – randomly assigning children to pairs who work together for a week or so and really get to know each other, before becoming part of another pair.

One teacher I read about uses a very interesting strategy to help ensure that students experience a sense of belonging in his classroom. Because he always has at least one pupil join the class mid-year, he leaves one desk empty for them. Seeing an empty desk when they arrive signals that the class has been waiting for them all year. Other teachers use some of the ideas from the primary SEAL materials to encourage pupils to welcome newcomers, for example having children work in groups to prepare a 'welcome bag' containing everything a new pupil would need to know about their class.

Finally, to increase pupils' sense of belonging we can create structures and situations that encourage pupils to show kindness to one another and include everyone. These can include:

- Buddying systems, such as pairing Y11 with Y7, or Y6 with Reception pupils
- Friendship stops or buddy benches in the playground, where anyone who temporarily has no one to play with can go and know they will be scooped up by peers and invited to join their game
- Systems of awards for those showing kindness to others, and challenges like the 'bucket-fillers' below
- 'Secret friends', in which children draw the name of a peer and have to perform kind actions for them

Secret friends

One teacher set up what he called an 'undercover acts of kindness' project. Children drew a classmate's name from a bowl, keeping it to themselves. Their mission over the next two weeks was to perform acts of kindness to the classmate, if possible without giving away who they were. The kindness had to be big enough for the classmate to notice but not cost any money. At the end of the fortnight the children wrote a 'mission report' about what they did and how it went.

Bucket-fillers

At Highfield School in Sunderland the book 'Have you filled your bucket today?' is read in assemblies. The book tells us that we all carry an invisible bucket around with us that fills and empties throughout the day. Your bucket fills up when someone does something to make you feel good. As your bucket fills up, the happier and better you feel in yourself.

'Bucket filling', 'bucket dipping' and 'bucket lids' can act as metaphors for understanding the effects of our actions and words on the wellbeing of others and ourselves. Dipping is when you dip into someone else's bucket and take stuff out; lids means that if someone tries to take stuff from yours, use your lid and don't dip back.

After hearing the book read to them, every class in school is allocated their own bucket. If a child feels someone has said or done something nice to them, they write it down and put it in the class bucket. The weekly challenge is to see which class are the best bucket-filler.

Teacher-pupil relationships

Closely linked to a sense of belonging in school are the relationships children have with their teachers. Research suggests that these are of great importance. One meta-analysis (Quin, 2016) found that in the 46 included studies, strong teacher–student relationships were associated in both the short and long term with improvements in attendance and behaviour – and in academic attainment. The effects seem to be particularly strong for disadvantaged students (Immordino-Yang *et al.*, 2018).

Many years ago, Professor Michael Rutter (2006) undertook a longitudinal study of children identified as being at risk of poor outcomes because of family factors – poverty, long-term unemployment, alcohol/substance misuse, domestic violence, mental health problems, social isolation and criminal involvement. In adulthood, one-third of these children were doing well in life. They not only survived, but thrived.

A number of factors appeared to have contributed to their resilience, but a key factor was whether a child had at least one strong and enduring relationship with an adult. Often this was a parent or grandparent, but in some cases it was a teacher. In fact, it has been found that favourite teachers who took a personal interest in them were the most frequent such non-family role models for resilient children (Howard *et al.*, 1999).

In the UK ethnographic study we looked at in earlier chapters, in which researchers interviewed white disadvantaged boys who were doing well at school, the students emphasised the powerful effect such teachers can have.

> What makes this school unique is the dedication that a lot of teachers have towards all of us. I mean that in every school, there will be one teacher that you feel cares about you as a person.
>
> King and Welch, 2012. *Successful white boys, of British origin, eligible for free school meals.*

Ben Pollard, Pupil Premium lead at Heathfield secondary school, writes powerfully on similar lines (Pollard, 2020).

> So the next time you're struggling on your way to your next lesson, carrying a pile of books that you can barely see over, rapidly running out of time to visit the loo, feel free to forget about those slightly inconvenient questions from students on the way. Or the next time that you're teaching (again, it will happen!) and that student is trying to hide their smile after you've just said how amazing their response was, feel free to move on to the next thing without too much thought. Just know that the students won't do this. Because these are the little moments that make the difference for disadvantaged students, for all students, in a way that no amount of intervention or catch-up plan ever will.

In the context of behaviour, teachers who have worked hard to build up credit in the 'relationship bank' with a pupil have reserves on which they can draw to work through problems positively when that child's behaviour becomes difficult.

I've seen schools that manage behaviour purely through relationships. They seem to run on love – as at St Mary's primary school, which we met in Chapter 5, where children simply don't want to disappoint their teachers and headteacher. No one has to shout; all the adults have to say is 'You've really upset me, you've let me down, that's not the St Mary's way' and the children in this very disadvantaged community soon change their behaviour.

That's not so easy with teenagers, of course. I've encountered many secondary schools which believe they can create adherence to rules by encouraging pupils to take pride in 'our values'. I'm not sure that this works. In the end, adherence to values is about our relationships with people who care about us. If they do, and the relationship is strong, we will take on their values. So if we want buy-in from those disadvantaged children whose behaviour is troublesome, we need to apply some pretty relentless caring to them.

Good relationships may come naturally – if so, that is a cause for celebration, but if not then teachers and other staff need to plan how they will consciously build them.

This may involve both whole-school structural solutions (such as keeping tutor groups with the same form tutor for several years, and organising activities which allow teachers and pupils to spend time together outside the classroom), and strategies which home in on individuals.

Relationships in a secondary school

Great Torrington Secondary has been a regional winner in the Pupil Premium Awards. Data from the EEF families of schools show they do better for pupils eligible for FSM than similar schools. Influenced by John Hattie's rankings of effective approaches to raising attainment, the school has developed a range of strategies based on building strong teacher–pupil relationships. A July transition week for the new Year 6 includes two-and-a-half days spent with their primary school teachers and secondary staff, surfing, dangling off ropes and camping in the summer rain. It is the start of building those relationships that will be key for the next five years.

Tutor groups are vertical, and in general pupils have the same tutor for five years. Each of the four school houses has a Pupil Coach with a solely pastoral role. When disciplinary systems have been used, the coaches will work with students to get them back into lessons, mediating the re-integration process. They help students explore barriers to their learning (this year, undertaking 360 degree reviews with those eligible for the Pupil Premium) and develop goals and plans.

Adults offer weekly enrichment activities in school time, involving things they are passionate about – surfing, programming robots, fishing, hair and make-up, community involvement projects and volunteering. Children take part in mixed-age groups.

Initially Y11 did not take part in the Thursday afternoon activities, but this changed when the school's data showed that these sessions helped pupils make more progress than the more traditional mentoring/coaching approaches.

More recently, the school noticed a palpable reduction in the standard of behaviour of the Year 7s when they were unable to run the usual transition programme and enrichment activities because of the pandemic; staff felt they were struggling to establish strong relationships with many of the pupils, even by Christmas. This has confirmed to the senior leadership team that the focus on building strong relationships is the right one.

Spending time together in informal settings is a particularly effective way of building relationships. Inclusion expert Daniel Sobel (2020) tells a story about one secondary school where a group of boys were not doing well in maths and hated the subject. Instead of putting in a maths intervention programme (more of what they hated), staff arranged for the boys to go on a five-day camping trip with their maths teachers. Their attitudes and progress were transformed as a result. Another headteacher used £30k of his Pupil Premium allocation to take all Y8 to Butlins in Skegness along with 35 staff, and describes it as a turning point for the school.

'Homing in' on individual pupils who don't have strong relationships with teachers can take a number of forms. One is identifying a small number of named pupils to whom *all* staff, from the office staff to senior leaders to lunchtime supervisors, will make an effort to say a word or two individually.

One primary school keeps what it calls a 'vulnerable pupil register' to target in this way. The list is not the usual names of children with SEND or eligible for the Pupil Premium. It includes any child who might be going through a difficult time, from parents separating to a pet dying.

At St Ives secondary school, which we met in Chapter 7, staff have created a set of criteria indicating that a pupil might need additional support – a recent bereavement, a parent in prison, this being the second or third secondary school the pupil has attended, and so on. Pupils are assessed on these criteria and information regularly updated. Where a pupil meets a threshold number of criteria, staff will explore whether support might be needed and what form it might take, from one-to-one time with a member of the pastoral staff to referral to outside agencies.

Other strategies include:

- Trying to make time for one-to-one conversations between teachers and pupils they are not getting on with – perhaps just asking about their weekend or how their football team is doing. One good idea is the 'Two by ten strategy' (Wlodkowski, 1983), in which teachers focus on their most difficult student. For two minutes each day, ten days in a row, they have a conversation with the student about an interest they have. This reliably improves the behaviour of the target student and often of the whole class – perhaps because the personal connection makes an ally of a student whose behaviour has previously had a negative influence on others.
- Asking their opinion – on how the class could learn better or work together better, on how lunchtimes or playtimes are organised and so on.
- Taking extra care to greet the child and say goodbye every day. Research with 11–14-year-olds (Cook *et al.*, 2018) suggests that greeting students personally and positively at the classroom door has a high yield in terms of improving pupil behaviour. Where teachers also used the greetings to remind students of expected behaviours, praise those who have kept to them, and provide guidance and encouragement to students who struggled with behaviour the previous day, the greeting increased academic engagement by 20 percentage points, and decreased disruptive behaviour by nine percentage points – adding as much as an additional hour of learning over the course of a five-hour teaching day.
- Always suggesting a 'fresh start' by saying 'OK I know we had a bad day yesterday, and I'm sorry about that. No hard feelings – let's just start again and do better today.'
- Making an effort to notice small successes and strengths: 'I've noticed you have a real talent for solving problems in maths. What did you do that made you able to learn this?'
- Making sure the pupil feels 'seen' as an individual: getting them to create personal blogs or films that show something about their interests, or

about people and events that have influenced their lives or dreams for the future.

- Listening to them without giving advice or opinions, and showing that we understand how they feel: 'That must have made you very angry/ frustrated . . .'
- Not being afraid to tell the child we like them and that what happens to them matters to us: 'You really matter to me and it's important to me that you do well this year.'

Chris Kilkenny grew up in poverty. His mum was a heroin addict. He was the main carer for his younger brothers and sisters. He has succeeded in life and now speaks and writes about what made a difference for him. The main thing he needed at school, he says, was 'just someone who took the time to ask me, every day, how I was doing' (Kilkenny, 2018). One could add to that – and waited for the answer.

As a primary teacher you can also have lunch with the child from time to time, try to involve them in a lunchtime or after school club you run, invite them to help you with daily tasks or invite them to have a cup of tea with you – sending a proper invitation, making clear they can bring a friend if they want to, and making the occasion special: one teacher always brings out a lace cloth, a china teapot and sugar tongs for her 'guests'.

Attendance and mobility

A recent investigation (Claymore, 2019) examined the relationship between the KS4 outcomes achieved by disadvantaged pupils and a broad range of pupil and school background factors (individual pupil gender, prior attainment, ethnicity, SEND status, absence, moving school, exclusions and geography). It found that the strongest association with Progress 8 outcomes was absence from school, with mobility also important. Fifty-five per cent of the gap between disadvantaged pupils and their more affluent peers could be explained by the between-group differences in absence, exclusion and KS4 movement rates during secondary school, at both pupil and cohort level.

There is, however, remarkably little hard evidence on what works in improving attendance or reducing pupil mobility. There is some on what doesn't reliably work – such as fining parents. Research on parental sanctions (Apter and Whitney, 2017) suggests that they only work to improve long-term attendance with a small proportion of families whose value system is inherently 'pro-social'.

An interesting, randomised study in the United States (Lasky-Fink *et al.*, 2020) looked at the effect of sending parents two different kinds of truancy notifications. One group received standard, legalistic, punitively worded warning letters. The other received messages that used simplified language, highlighted the negative incremental effects of missing school, and aimed to build parents' self-efficacy – their belief in their ability to help their child attend school. These letters began, for example, with the words 'We need your help' and ended with 'Please remember that every absence matters and just a couple of days each month can add up. You are key to improving Jason's attendance.' The redesign led to an approximate 40% improvement in attendance over the estimated impact of the standard letter.

Rewarding pupils for good attendance is another strategy used in almost all schools, for which the evidence is not good. In one study (Robinson *et al.*, 2019) over 15,000 secondary students were randomly assigned to one of three groups. In the first group students were told that they would be eligible for a special attendance award if they had no absences in the next month. In the second group, students with perfect attendance for a previous month were given an award, but were not told in advance that they might receive one. The third group received no awards. Contrary to expectation, telling students beforehand that they could earn an award for perfect attendance had no overall effect on the number of days they missed school. The awards did have a small positive effect for the youngest students in the study, aged 12, but as students got older, the benefits reduced.

The biggest surprise was what happened after the awards were given out. Absences actually increased in the following month, especially among students with poor school performance. The researchers suggest that may have been because the awards diminished students' own internal motivation, signalling that their performance had exceeded expectations and giving them license to take a break. Alternatively, peer-group influences may have been at work, with students trying to reclaim their image as someone who did not care much about education.

The likely impact of awards, then, has to be understood in relation to the psychology of individuals – what they think, what they feel, their self-perceptions. This seems to be true to when we look at the limited evidence there is on what *does* work in improving attendance. A report from the American Institutes for Research (Chang *et al.*, 2019) describes four school characteristics that promote attendance – physical and emotional health and safety; belonging, connectedness and support; academic challenge and engagement; and adult and pupil social and emotional competence. It suggests that persistent poor attendance should be seen as a symptom, and used to diagnose weaknesses in the conditions for learning that the school provides. Research has found, for example, that pupils in the lowest socio-economic quartile often did not attend school because of their teachers' low expectations for their success and for the fear of humiliation in class (Whitehead, 2007).

Solutions to poor attendance, then, may lie in school climates that promote high expectations, strong relationships, belonging and social and emotional learning. *Engagement* with school and what it has to offer is what matters. An important study (Jackson *et al.*, 2020) found fewer absences (as well as more students graduating from school and going on to college) in schools where pupils reported greater sense of belonging and better peer relationships, and where teachers helped them develop social and emotional skills (resilience, growth mindset, self-regulation). The difference was greatest for the student populations who struggled the most in school.

At Scalby secondary school, staff work hard to build relationships with pupils who have poor attendance and their families, rather than 'throw the book at them.' There is a full-time attendance officer who works within a very strong pastoral team. This includes a non-teaching Head of Year in each year group who is able to get to know pupils well. The school has as a result seen reductions in persistent absence in its disadvantaged pupils' cohort from 40% five years ago, to under 20% now.

Engagement with school is seen as vital. Each year after Christmas a group of Y11 students (mostly boys, at risk of switching off from learning) are taken on a 12-week college course for one day a week, experiencing a carousel of trades like bricklaying and plumbing. This has been very successful in maintaining their engagement right through to their GCSEs.

Extra-curricular activities can support engagement; research has found that sponsored extra-curricular activities motivated students in economically disadvantaged high schools to stay in school rather than dropping out (Killgo, 2012).

Lateness is a common issue and one school decided to provide a whole-some breakfast at 8 a.m. – this increased punctuality and morning school engagement manifold.

Another school tried this and it failed miserably, there was no uptake. After speaking with the students they found out that providing something like kick-boxing or karate would get them to school for 8 a.m. and they did that with great success.

Daniel Sobel, 2015. *Creative uses of the Pupil Premium*

Engagement and relationships, in this case with parents as well as pupils, may also be key to reducing some aspects of pupil mobility. Many schools are familiar with the scenario where parents serially move their child from one school to another in the local area, usually when they have fallen out with staff, or fear their child will be excluded. The schools where this is less common are those which have made heroic efforts to build trusting relationships with families, like those we will look at in Chapter 10.

There are of course many other reasons for pupil mobility. Disadvantaged children are almost twice as likely as those who are better off to move from one school to another outside of normal transition points – because a parent loses a job, or parents split up, or have to move to another area to find affordable housing (Rodda *et al.*, 2013).

Apart from avoiding 'managed moves' and subtle suggestions to parents that their child might be better off elsewhere, there is not always a lot that schools can do to prevent such school moves. What they can do, however, is ensure that social and emotional learning in school includes helping children develop empathy for newcomers and adopt welcoming behaviours towards them, along with the strategies which focus on the sense of belonging in one's class and school that we looked at earlier in this chapter.

Key take-aways

- Conduct and emotional problems are more common in disadvantaged groups of pupils, because of the stressors linked to family poverty, but can be prevented by protective factors such as having an adult to turn to for support and having good quality friendships.

- Research evidence suggests that 'no excuses' policies are less effective overall in reducing behaviour problems in schools than restorative practices and approaches which build social and emotional skills.
- Some pupils (those who can behave but are choosing not to) will respond well to straightforward, consistent rewards and sanctions approaches. Others (those who lack underpinning social and emotional skills, are under temporary stress, or have had early attachment difficulties or trauma) require a more nuanced approach.
- If pupils have a sense of belonging and being valued in school they are more likely to adopt its norms and values, behave well and learn effectively; a sense of community and strong teacher-pupil relationships can be fostered in a planned way.
- Such efforts are more likely to work in tackling poor attendance than attendance awards or punitive approaches.

9 The importance of social and emotional learning

In Chapter 8 we suggested that one explanation for poor behaviour and attendance lies in some children's need for support in developing the social and emotional capabilities they need to thrive in school. Social and emotional learning (SEL) is the process of acquiring these capabilities – the ability to recognise and manage emotions, develop caring and concern for others, establish positive relationships, make responsible decisions and handle challenging situations. A large body of research suggests that students' social and emotional capabilities not only predict their school success, but also their employability, physical health, and overall mental health and wellbeing (Greenberg *et al.*, 2003; Weissberg *et al.*, 2015).

Much social and emotional learning takes place at home, but schools can also contribute. Extensive research has shown that children's skills can be improved purposefully through school-based SEL programmes, and that such programmes not only impact on behaviour, but also on learning. The EEF (van Poortvliet *et al.*, 2019) find that on average the impact of SEL is equivalent to four additional months' academic progress. The effects are long-lasting. One meta-analysis (Taylor *et al.*, 2017) examined 82 SEL interventions involving more than 97,000 students aged 5-18. Three-and-a-half years after the last intervention, the academic performance of students exposed to SEL programs was an average 13 percentile points higher than their non-SEL peers. Conduct problems, emotional distress, and drug use were all significantly lower for students in the SEL groups.

Social and emotional learning at Haytor Primary

Every Monday morning at Haytor View Community Primary School in Devon starts with an assembly on one of the themes from the SEAL

DOI: 10.4324/9781003176442-10

social and emotional learning programme (themes like 'Getting on and Falling Out', 'Going for Goals' or 'Changes'), led by Scott Hampton, Leader of Learning and Development. Children then go to their classrooms to work on their social and emotional learning – rather than the more usual English or maths – until morning break.

This is in a school where 55% of the children are eligible for free school meals, and where academic standards used to be low. Now, they are much improved: in 2019 61% of children reached the expected standard in reading, writing and maths, compared to the England average of 53%.

The school decided in 2005 to introduce a comprehensive social and emotional learning programme during the period when results were not good, a time when many schools would have hesitated to take any time 'away' from the academic basics. SEAL straight away seemed a very good fit.

How staff manage their Monday morning SEAL-related work is up to them. The only 'given' is 15 minutes of relationship-building activities between pairs of children. Each week, children work with a different partner, so that over time they work with all the children in their class.

For the rest of the Monday morning time staff draw on the SEAL resources but personalise the learning to the current needs of their class. So does Scott, in relation to the needs of the school community. Recently, for example, he had observed that children were finding it difficult to notice what was good about themselves, so he planned a highly interactive assembly that got children, parents and adults talking about how easy it is to recognise others' gifts and talents, and why it might be harder to do the same for your own.

Scott also draws on his own experiences in his assemblies. For the 'Changes' theme, for example, he will tell stories about his own life – how it felt to go to university as a mature student, how it felt later for him and his family to move area and house, how difficult and uncomfortable that was. He does not tell children what they should do in order to cope with change, but helps them recognise that these experiences are common to all. By sharing their thoughts and perspectives, the children learn to find the solutions within themselves.

Another example of this approach is how is how the school has incorporated the requirement to teach British Values. At Haytor you will not see displays with Union Jacks on them, but you will see children learning about the similarities and differences between people, and that these are to be celebrated. Many of the children are exposed to different values at home; when these are reflected as behaviours in school, the approach taken is not to simply attack this as wrong, but to help the children feel for others, explore different perspectives, and think for themselves.

In Friday assemblies, children and their parents/carers are celebrated for showing progress in social and emotional learning. They might be nominated for an award for listening to others' points of view, recognising and valuing differences, understanding how to be a friend, being happy not being perfect, or showing empathy.

Social and emotional learning and disadvantage

Social and emotional capabilities fall into three broad groups (Figure 9.1) and include:

- Self-awareness: the ability to recognise our emotions and thoughts, and understand how they influence our behaviour
- Self-management: the ability to regulate our emotions, focus on a task, control impulses, persist, bounce back after failure
- Social awareness: the ability to show empathy
- Relationship skills: the ability to interact positively with peers and adults and effectively manage social situations
- Responsible decision making: the ability to set and achieve goals, solve interpersonal problems and make constructive choices

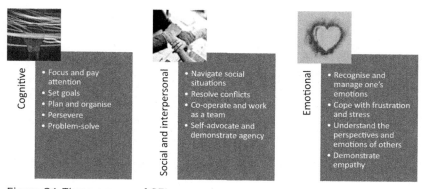

Figure 9.1 Three groups of SEL competences
Source: Adapted from National Commission on Social, Emotional and Academic Development (2019) *Nation at Risk to a Nation at Hope*. Aspen Institute

It is not difficult to see why skills like these might be particularly important in narrowing the disadvantage gap. We know, for example, disadvantaged children on average have fewer opportunities to talk about feelings. Research for the Joseph Rowntree Foundation (Gibb *et al.*, 2016) shows that children who live in persistent poverty are just as likely as other children to say they are happy with their families, but are less likely to talk to someone at home about their worries than those never in poverty; they are also less likely to talk to their friends about their worries.

As ever, the disadvantage gap starts early. The International Early Learning and Child Well-being Study (Kettlewell *et al.*, 2020) asked a nationally representative sample of children in England to respond to story-based scenarios about a set of cartoon characters; they had to identify an emotion using emoticons (emotion identification) and decide on the reasons for the characters' emotional states (emotion attribution). Children eligible for free school meals (FSM) had significantly lower development than their peers, with the difference equivalent to approximately five months in both emotion identification and emotion attribution. There were also large gender differences across the whole sample, with girls five months ahead of boys in emotion identification and seven months ahead in emotion attribution, but no significant differences related to ethnicity.

There is evidence that disadvantaged children can show stronger benefits from SEL than their more advantaged peers. In an interesting study (Rozek *et al.*, 2019), students took part in a ten-minute exercise just before a test, in which they were encouraged to see stress as 'a beneficial and energising force.' They learned that small amounts of stress can help us to focus and remember things by increasing the flow of oxygen into the brain. Students were then asked to write short answers to two questions: 'How do people sometimes feel in important situations?' and 'How can the way a person feels in important situations help them do well in those situations?' This exercise allowed the students to reinterpret their response to the prospect of the test and regulate their emotions. They went on to perform better on their high school science exams. The number of students failing their science course reduced by half – but it was the low-income students who saw the biggest benefits.

Does this link between SEL and disadvantage mean we should target SEL work *only* at disadvantaged children, or those visibly struggling with emotions or behaviour? In fact, the evidence suggests that SEL should be offered universally, to all students, rather than simply targeting one group. There are several reasons why this is important. The first is about minimising the numbers of children who need extra help. It relates to the familiar three-level approach (Figure 9.2).

At the base of the triangle is quality first teaching of social and emotional skills to all pupils. The better this is, the fewer children there will be who need additional help at the next level (small group work or support from a non-specialist). The better this is, the fewer children there will be who need help at the top of the triangle – more specialised support, for example from a mental health professional.

The second reason for adopting a universal approach is about creating the kind of classroom environments and cultures where children with social, emotional and behavioural difficulties will be supported by their peers. For this to happen, classmates need to have developed their own skills of empathy, being a good friend, handling conflict, and being resilient in the face of difficulties.

Finally, a universal approach involving everyone in a school allows for whole-school systems which give pupils the chance to apply the learning from any extra, targeted help they have, in a wider context. If we teach them

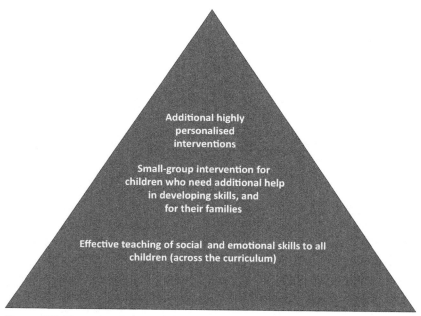

Figure 9.2 Three levels in social and emotional learning

to communicate their feelings, they need adults out there in their everyday lessons who are prepared to listen to and respect those feelings. If we teach them not to lose control when they are angry, they need to see adults around them doing the same in school. If we teach them ways of resolving conflict, they need adults in the playground who can help them use their new skills. All these are components of a whole-school approach – as is switching our usual school reward systems (whether praise, merits, certificates) to occasions when pupils demonstrate social and emotional capabilities rather than 'good behaviour' (and even better, having a system in which pupils can nominate each other for awards).

A whole-school approach at Billesley Primary

Billesley Primary in Birmingham is part of the EEF's Research Schools network and has described its work on social and emotional learning in network blogs.

The school serves a disadvantaged area, with nearly half of the pupils eligible for free school meals. It is devoting 'much more time' to SEL than it did five years ago. One of its initiatives has been to create safe spaces – designated areas where children can choose to go to calm down and take time to process events and emotions. It is seen as a positive behaviour choice if they move themselves to the safe spaces when they need to.

Mentors are available to talk with children in the safe spaces and can provide de-escalation strategies. Children choose to use the safe space to self-regulate and then return to class.

Pupils are actively involved in the safe spaces initiative. Representatives from Y4-6 act as ambassadors for the Student Well Being and Awareness Group (SWAG) to support positive mental health across school, with one of those responsibilities being to look after the safe space and promote its use.

The school also has an explicit SEL curriculum taught in short, dedicated sessions, within timetabled PSHE and in Philosophy for Children lessons. All staff have access to a 'Social Emotional Toolbox,' a digital compendium of teaching and learning resources which link to a progression framework of social and emotional skills.

The explicit teaching is supported by everyday practices – not just the safe spaces but also:

- Regular emotional check ins, using mood meters, differentiated to ensure progression across year groups
- Regular practice of calming tools such as deep breathing
- Self-regulation strategy posters and 'calm down kits'
- Teachers modelling strategies for identifying feelings and managing uncomfortable emotions
- Using stories to examine characters' feelings through reflective questioning
- Using consistent approaches to solving problems and setting goals, which teachers practice with children outside of crisis moments, and help them use when problems arise

On top of a whole-school approach we can layer targeted support for those who struggle with particular SEL capabilities, in the form of small-group work. This is where, for example, anger management programmes in secondary schools fit. But as with interventions for literacy, maths and so on, pupils will benefit most from targeted approaches when they link to whole-class learning and build on skills already taught to all. This was the principle used in the national SEAL programme. It provided resources for KS1, KS2 and KS3 small group interventions, focusing for example on conflict resolution, working together, problem-solving and becoming independent. One suite of small-group activities is about encouraging children to take responsibility for their learning and develop goal-directed behaviour. They are designed for children who appear unmotivated, lacking interest in schoolwork.

All the small-group sessions in SEAL link to a theme that children will be learning about in class through the universal lesson resources, and to ideas for developing that theme across the curriculum and through assemblies and whole-school systems. The resources, including a progression in social and emotional learning objectives from nursery to Y8, are all still available free to download at www.sealcommunity.org.

Targeted primary SEAL has been subject to evaluation by randomised controlled trial and found to be effective (Humphrey *et al.*, 2008). The universal resources do not qualify as an evidence-based programme using rigorous standards of evidence. Primary SEAL has had no randomised controlled trials. Secondary SEAL had one quasi-experimental study which did not show impact, after a relatively short period of implementation which varied in quality from school to school.

Nevertheless SEAL is certainly 'evidence-informed', drawing on the best ideas from evidence-based US programmes but translated into what is likely to work in a UK context. For those seeking SEL programmes that do have evidence of impact from randomised controlled trials, a list can be found on the website of the Early Intervention Foundation. It currently includes PATHS, Positive Action, the Penn Resilience Programme, Zippy's Friends, Learning Together, the '.be' mindfulness programme, MindUp, Bounce Forward, RULER, the Kindness Curriculum and Incredible Years. It should be noted, however, that trials of some of these programmes in the UK have often failed to replicate the effects seen in the US and other countries. Not all of them seem to travel well.

UK schools on the whole tend to steer clear of set programmes in favour of flexible teaching strategies that draw on multiple sources. Usefully, the EEF (van Poortvliet *et al.*, 2019) have drawn out from a number of evidence-based programmes the commonly recurring practices they share. Building on this work, I have developed an additional resource for readers of this book, to illustrate how social and emotional skills can be taught as part of PSHE programmes, how work in wider subject areas can reinforce the learning, and the classroom and whole school environments that support generalisation of skills. Table 9.1 shows an extract; you can find the full resource (*Teaching social and emotional skills and helping pupils apply their learning*) under this book's Support Materials on the Routledge website: www.routledge.com/9781032009322.

Let us now look at some of the specific SEL capabilities that are especially relevant to the challenges that can be faced by disadvantaged children, and boys in particular.

Self-regulation

Self-regulation – children's ability to manage their own behaviour, emotions and aspects of their learning – is emerging as a key social and emotional skill, described by EEF as consistently linked with academic success; they note that strategies that seek to improve learning by increasing self-regulation have an average impact of five additional months' progress (EEF, 2018). There is, however, some confusion about what self-regulation means and how it relates to other concepts such as executive function and self-regulated learning. Table 9.2 explains the relationship between these constructs.

Specific evidence-based programmes are available to develop self-regulation. One that I think we should be trialling in the UK is *Tools of the Mind*. In this early years programme, techniques for teaching and scaffolding executive functions are interwoven in classroom activities across all areas of learning.

Table 9.1 Teaching self-awareness and helping pupils apply their learning

Primary schools

Examples of explicit PSHE teaching	Examples of teaching through other subjects	How teachers can reinforce the skills in the everyday classroom	How the learning can be reinforced through whole-school activities and environment
Show children photocards of different emotions and ask them to identify what emotion might be shown. Have them act out different emotions and discuss what the body/face/voice looks like/sounds like for each. Pairs of children choose an emotion word from a vocabulary display, then make a video demonstrating or explaining what it means. Children are given words that describe the same emotion but at different intensity (for example annoyed, cross, angry, furious, livid). They have to arrange the words on cards in order of intensity and describe a situation in which they experienced one of the feelings.	When teaching about characters in history, science and geography ask children to identify protagonists' emotions and their consequences. In English, have them map the changing intensity of a character's feelings over the course of a narrative using a feelings graph. Provide sentence stems 'I can tell they felt . . . because. . .,' 'That character felt . . . and I have felt like that too when. . .' Use 'hot seating,' in which one child plays a character in a text and the rest of the class ask them questions about their feelings and how those feelings influence the choices they make	Provide a model by talking about your own feelings: 'I'm feeling a bit xxx today because. . .' Help children identify their feelings about events in school: 'How did that make you feel?' or 'I'm wondering if you are feeling a bit scared about tomorrow?' Place a 'worry box' in the classroom, in which children can post a note about a worry they have When a child has behaved inappropriately, sit down with them later to help them chart how they felt and how others felt during the period leading to the problem behaviour, how that affected their actions, and what different choices could have been made	Whole-school systems (praise in assemblies, notes to parents, peer nominations) are used to celebrate children who have been able to articulate their feelings rather than display problematic behaviour in emotionally charged situations Adults regularly refer to displays of emotion words, and scaffold children's use of the words 'in the moment', for example in the playground There are designated places in the playground where conflicts can be discussed. Each child says how they feel, and why. They must listen to each other and 'say it back' ('So you're saying you felt left out?') before coming up with possible solutions to the conflict that would make everyone feel OK Children know that an adult will be available if they need to talk about how they are feeling. There is a special box where they can post their name if they want to talk

(Continued)

Table 9.1 (Continued)

Secondary schools

Examples of explicit PSHE teaching	Examples of teaching through other subjects	How tutors can reinforce the taught skills	How the learning can be reinforced through whole-school activities and environment
Students are introduced to Yale University's free Mood Meter app, which allows them to plot their feelings using an extensive vocabulary of emotion words Pupils learn about how stress manifests itself in the brain and body. They learn about the relationship between feeling stressed/anxious and performance, where a little stress make us perform better but too much makes us perform worse. Finally they create their personal lists of stress indicators for low, medium and high levels of stress Pupils explore optimism and pessimism, and play 'Two sides of the moon' in pairs – taking it in turns to give a bright side and a dark side perspective on scenarios like starting a new Saturday club or winning the lottery. They practise ways of switching negative statements to positive ones	Ask children to identify protagonists' emotions and their consequences when teaching about historical events, scientific research and current affairs In art, students can explore ways in which artists use colour to convey moods and emotions, and use different media (photography, paint, pastels) to represent a mood of their choice In English, pairs of pupils can act as interviewer and a character in class novel. The interviewer explores the emotions that the character experienced and how that influenced the choices they made	Provide a model by being prepared on occasion to talk about your own feelings: 'Just to let you know, I'm on a bit of a short fuse today for various personal reasons. Sorry about that. I'd appreciate your help in keeping the noise down' 'Name it to tame it' – encourage students to talk briefly about how they are feeling when they are frustrated by a piece of work or when someone annoys them When a pupil has behaved inappropriately, sit down with them later to help them chart how they felt and how others felt during the period leading to the problem behaviour, how that affected their actions, and what different choices could have been made	Whole-school systems (merits, notes to parents/carers, peer nominations) are used to notice pupils who have been able to articulate their feelings rather than display problematic behaviour in emotionally charged situations There are designated places in school where conflicts can be discussed. Each child says how they feel, and why. They must listen to each other and 'say it back' before coming up with possible solutions to the conflict that would make everyone feel OK Students know that an adult will be available if they need to talk about how they are feeling. There is a drop-in time or system for posting a request if they want to talk

Table 9.2 The relationship between self-regulation, executive function and self-regulated learning

---

Executive function
The brain's air traffic control system – enables us to plan, focus attention, remember instructions, and juggle multiple tasks successfully. Consists of a skill set of three elements:
- Inhibitory control /self -control (resisting habits, temptations and distractions)
- Working memory (the ability to retain and manipulate distinct pieces of information over short periods of time)
- Mental flexibility (the ability to sustain or shift attention in response to different demands, or to apply different rules in different settings)

Performance on executive function (rather than general intelligence) predicts how well children do in early maths and reading by the end of their first year in school (Blair and Diamond, 2008)

Self-regulation
The ability to think before acting, persist at an activity, manage strong emotions, remain calm, and control impulses – underpins aspects of self-regulated learning, and overlaps with the inhibitory control/self-control element of executive function

Cognitive self-regulation/control	**Affective (emotional) self-regulation/ control**
The 'thinking' part of self-regulation – for example, controlling thoughts and monitoring how we are getting on with tasks	The ability to manage one's emotions

Self-regulated learning
The application of both cognitive and affective aspects of self-regulation to learning, plus the use of metacognitive strategies – thinking about and managing your own learning

---

Role-play and making 'play plans' play an important role. The programme has a significant impact on attainment in high-poverty areas (Blair et al., 2014), particularly in maths (Baron et al., 2017), and for children with initially high levels of hyperactivity and inattention.

Even without a formal programme, early years staff can encourage children to use planning boards, to set goals for their self-directed activities and review afterwards how the activity went and what they'd like to achieve next. They can use questions like:

- What are you trying to do?
- What will you need?
- What are you going to do first? Then what?
- How will you know when you've finished?
- Oh, a bit of your model broke – how will you keep going?
- How did you know you had finished?
- What were you pleased with?
- Was there anything you would change?

Teaching impulse control

Y9 pupils are asked to consider whether they are the type of person who usually acts on impulse or likes to think first and act later. They are each given a marshmallow and told they can eat it now if they wish, or if they are able to wait until the end of the lesson they will be given another one. Their teacher then asks them to rate themselves according to how easy they would find it to hold on to their marshmallow, and to come up with ideas they could suggest to a younger pupil, to help them resist the temptation and wait. They watch a video of the original marshmallow experiment, in which four-year-olds were given the same offer of one marshmallow now or two if they waited. The teacher asks the students to choose one of several scenarios when they think they might find it hard to delay gratification, such as doing homework when friends are playing online, or saving up for something special rather than spending money now. They then work in groups with others who have chosen the same scenario and discuss what they have tried or could try to help them hold back the impulse. At the end of the lesson the teacher shares the findings from the original marshmallow experiment – that those with the ability to wait had better wellbeing and scored higher on attainment tests when they were followed up many years later.

A useful way of developing affective self-regulation at any age is introducing children to the idea of 'zones of regulation', for which many teaching resources are available via an internet search. There are three 'zones': blue, green, yellow/amber and red. When we are in the red zone we are in a state of intense emotion, such as rage or panic. In the yellow zone we are in a heightened state of alertness but still in control, experiencing stress, frustration, anxiety, irritation, excitement or nervousness. When teachers describe children as 'silly' or wriggly they are often in the yellow zone. Green means a calm state of alertness, when we are feeling focused and content. In the blue zone we are low in alertness and experiencing 'down' feelings; we feel sad, tired or just listless and bored.

The zones can be compared to traffic lights. When in the green zone, we are ready to go, ready to learn. Yellow or amber means we need to take care, whilst red means 'stop'. The aim of the zones approach is to help children recognise their zone based on the environment and its demands; in the playground, heightened states of silliness and excitement might be OK, but not in assembly. Children can then learn how to take action when necessary to either 'up-regulate' or 'down-regulate', especially when they are on the point of entering the red zone and 'losing it'.

To 'up-regulate', children can undertake a physical activity like doing star jumps, or listen to upbeat music. Techniques for 'down regulating' are described in the additional resource for readers, *Teaching social and emotional skills and helping pupils apply their learning.*

Goal setting and getting, persistence, resilience

In Chapter 3 we looked at evidence showing that interventions to raise pupils' aspirations, although popular in schools, appear to be ineffective. It may be that they would be if they also taught students *how* to go about setting themselves goals – and achieving them in the face of obstacles. The need for this was noted by pupils interviewed for King and Welch's (2012) study of successful white British boys. They valued what their schools had done to give them in-depth advice, not just about further or higher education, but to help them 'set five and ten year goals with a series of manageable steps mapped out towards achieving them.'

Perseverance can be a key issue for disadvantaged learners. An international report (OECD, 2016), for example, found that 15-year-old disadvantaged students were less likely to persevere in the face of challenge than their more advantaged peers, and that the gap between the perseverance of high and low academic performers in the UK was greater than the OECD average.

It is possible to increase pupils' ability to set goals and persist in achieving them through a combination of direct teaching and whole-school approaches. The SEAL programme, for example, has a complete set of materials for both primary (the 'Going for Goals' theme resources) and secondary (the 'Keep on Learning' theme). There are assemblies (such as one about a boy who has a huge task to do and succeeds by telling himself 'keep going, keep going'), follow-up PSHE lessons, ideas for work in other curriculum subjects, ideas for generalising the learning across the school day, small-group activities for pupils needing additional help, and in the primary materials, also take-home family activities.

We often ask pupils to set themselves goals in school. Much less often, however, do we teach them *how* to set realistic goals and work towards them over time. The process can involve:

- Pupils setting a goal then discussing it with a partner, who questions them about how they will feel when they reach their goal, who else will know when they have met their goal, and how those people will feel.

- Breaking down their goal into small steps along the way and recording them, for example, as a track, ladder or stepping stones.
- Adding the name of a 'coach' (a friend, or a trusted adult) who will help them achieve the goal, checking in with them on the way and providing encouragement.
- Thinking about and recording how they will celebrate or treat themselves when the goal is achieved.

To help pupils learn to break goals down into steps they can use scaling, where they plot their current position in relation to the goal on a scale of 1–10, where 10 means reaching the goal. They can decide what it would look like if they were one point further up on the scale, and what they could do to get there, repeating the scaling at given intervals.

To practise goal-setting they might be asked to work with a partner on a goal that interests them both and could be achieved in the next few days (such as running times, juggling, video game score, skateboarding). Each child uses a proforma which specifies their goal, the time period in which they will achieve it, how the goal will be achieved (in at least two steps), and the name of their buddy. At the end of the proforma is an evaluation section in which children reflect on whether they met their goal, what helped or hindered them, what their buddy did that helped them, whether they needed to change the plan as they went along, how their plan might be improved and what they could do next.

Pupils will need opportunities to generalise their learning. Ideas include:

- Providing merits, praise, notes home or certificates for working towards goals with determination
- Subject teachers providing opportunities for pupils to set goals, time targets and success criteria for their work
- Having children take on extended pieces of work and plan how to break a task down into manageable steps
- Developing class goals for behaviour, attendance and punctuality
- Combining work on goal setting with curriculum challenges (such as working up to deliver a five-minute TED Talk to the class), and wider challenges such as raising money for a charity or tackling a community issue

A useful addition to teaching goal-setting is the idea of mental contrasting. Here, pupils are asked to follow four steps:

Step 1 Write down or think about several positive aspects associated with completing your goal. For example, if you are trying to eat healthily those positive aspects could be: being able to run faster, stopping your mum nagging you, feeling livelier and so on.

Step 2 Home in the most positive aspects. This could be one especially large benefit, or a few smaller ones. Then take a few moments to visualise those benefits – the more detail, the better.

Step 3 Write down or think about several obstacles in the way of you completing your goal. For example, if you're trying to eat healthily, those obstacles could be being tempted by snacks or being offered fizzy drinks.

Step 4 Home in the largest obstacles. Then take a few moments to visualise those obstacles and you overcoming them. Picture how you will do this.

Research has shown that this technique is effective. Angela Duckworth and her colleagues (2013) found a significant impact on the academic performance of an experimental group of ten-year-olds taught mental contrasting, compared to a control group which received typical 'Believe it and you can achieve it' messaging.

The strategy only works if children set goals that they believe are achievable. If they have low expectations of success at the start, they may actually do worse academically than pupils not using mental contrasting – perhaps because the technique reminds them of the impossibility of their task and serves to reduce their confidence and motivation.

When working towards a goal they have set, pupils can be asked to identify strategies to use to overcome barriers and perhaps make up catch phrases for each of them, for example:

Foil Frustration – relaxation, distraction, having a break, doing something completely different for a short while

Beat Boredom – setting themselves a shorter term target and giving themselves a reward like a break or a drink, taking time to draw what it will look like when they reach their goal

When they are on the point of giving up, strategies might include talking to their coach, asking for feedback from others, breaking down the task and setting a time challenge for each bit, and using a repeated mantra like 'keep on keeping on.'

Similarly, pupils can be asked to do a fairly tedious task in class (like making paper chains in groups, competing with other groups to see who can make the longest), discussing ways they helped themselves persist. Pupils can make a class display of what we can do to keep going and share with other classes and people at home. Alternatively, they might work in threes and take the role of a learner who is trying to complete a long and difficult piece of work, the Gremlin who throws in the thoughts, feelings and distractions that stop the learner from getting on, and the angel who challenges the Gremlin's contributions.

To practise resisting distractions, a volunteer can be asked to complete a simple copying task while the rest of the class try to distract them in whatever ways they can (within reason); after a while the volunteer is asked to explain some of the strategies they used to maintain concentration.

Epic fails, graffiti walls and the flat-pack challenge at Woldingham School, Surrey

At Woldingham School in Surrey there is a planned programme to help students develop the ability to work towards goals and persist in the face of challenge.

Year 7s were presented with mystery challenges in boxes, ranging from sampling a food they had never eaten before to agreeing to run a year meeting the following week. Then tutors gathered pupils' ideas about how we can be inspired by others, and how to break up difficult tasks or skills into small steps. At the end of the morning, everyone signed up to a 30-day challenge to try something new.

Year 8s thought about failure, contributing to a graffiti wall of things they said to themselves when they thought they had failed – words like 'Loser' and 'You're hopeless.' They then watched a video clip of a young American boy, running in a race. The boy has cerebral palsy but wanted to run even though he could have chosen not to. He comes last by many minutes but his classmates cheer him over the line.

This led to a discussion on what it means to fail. Students came up with some amazing definitions, including: 'Failure is when you don't even try, because you are afraid of not achieving your goal.'

They were given a seven-day 'Epic Fails' diary, and asked to record a failure a day, how they felt at the time (drawing on a vocabulary list of words for emotions), and how they could bounce back from the failure.

Staff development activities focused on persistence and reactions to difficulty. Teams of staff took part in a flat-pack challenge, in which they had to build furniture, with some instructions missing.

Subject teachers developed the ideas in their lessons. A religious studies teacher deliberately gave students the wrong task to do, then led a discussion on why we find it difficult to get things wrong and just cross work out and start again. In maths, students were encouraged to self-assess how willing they had been to persist with problems, and there were displays of 'work in progress' and interesting errors rather than the finished product.

The work has made a significant difference to pupils' attitudes. Inspectors visiting the school noted that students 'react positively to challenges and occasional setbacks, and thus develop excellent confidence and strong resilience, which enables them to respond successfully to the choices open to them at the different key stages of their educational development.'

Adapted from an article in the *Times Educational Supplement* (Haythorne, 2019)

YouTube is awash with films about people bouncing back after difficulties, such as the 'Freedom to fail forwards' films, and almost any subject from PE to geography offers examples of figures who persisted and overcame obstacles in order to achieve goals. In English, pupils can explore Arthurian legends and Greek myths about quests and tasks, creating storyboards with thought bubbles showing what a protagonist was thinking and feeling at each stage. In PSHE lessons they can match famous people with the obstacles they faced – like Elvis Presley who was fired after one performance (the boss said 'You ain't going nowhere, son. You ought to go back to driving a truck'), and Alexander Graham Bell, who was told after meeting with the President to demonstrate his new invention, the telephone, 'That's an amazing invention, but who would want to use one of them?' Pupils also enjoy watching the reactions of unsuccessful participants in TV reality programmes and coming up with ideas about how they manage to bounce back after failure.

Peer pressure

Another important SEL skill we should seek to develop is how to resist peer pressure. A strand running through many research studies (Francis *et al.*, 2010) is that teenage boys in general often feel stuck between their own desire to succeed in school and the norms of their friendship groups. These divided loyalties seem particularly acute if they are disadvantaged (Evans, 2006).

If you are working class and successful, you have got to abandon your mates and your community, because our system requires you to move on and be different. It is a big cultural ask for some youngsters at that very tense teenage point.

Denis Mongon, giving evidence in Parliament (House of Commons Education Committee, 2014)

Learning about peer pressure (both helpful and unhelpful) can be part of the PSHE curriculum. Pupils can reflect on whether they want to 'be a lemming' and follow the crowd, and develop the assertiveness skills they will need in order to resist peer pressure. Here are some examples:

In a Y4 class children form an outer and an inner circle of equal numbers – the outer circle facing inwards and the inner circle facing outwards. The outer circle moves clockwise at a given signal and the inner circle moves anticlockwise. When the adult says 'Stop,' the children from the inner and outer circle who are facing each other form a pair. Each pair has to discuss how they would handle a situation described by the teacher ('Your friend always wants to sit next to you but sometimes you like to sit next to someone else,' 'You are fed up with your friend helping herself to your crisps and saying that friends share'). They have to come up with a way to say no, or disagree, without hurting the friend's feelings.

A Y5 teacher has written the words aggressive, passive and assertive on the whiteboard. She explains that there are basically three ways of approaching a difficult situation, argument or conflict:

Aggressive: sounding angry, trying to 'win' or get your own way by force or because you are bigger or stronger, without thinking about the other person;

Passive: giving in or running away from the situation, so that the person left gets their way, or wins because you don't want to say anything;

Assertive: trying to come up with a solution or result that everyone feels OK about.

She asks half the class to adopt aggressive poses. The other children's role is to observe and describe their body language. They do the same for passive and assertive. Children then sort cards ('You're just an idiot,' 'OK – let's talk about it,' 'I wanted to ask you . . . Oh, don't worry – it doesn't matter,' 'That's making me feel really annoyed; I'd like you to stop, please') into piles of aggressive, assertive and passive types of language. In the next lesson, a week later, they look at different scenarios and come up with sentence starters ('talk moves') they can use in situations when they feel they are being pushed by other children into doing something they really don't want to do.

Y9 pupils are given a sheet with a continuum with 'me' at one end and 'them' at the other. They consider examples like 'I'm tired and want to go home to bed – so I go home even though my friends tell me I'm spoiling their night out,' and 'I'm tired and want to go to bed. I tell my friends that I'm going but they tell me not to be a spoiler and pressure me to stay. I stay.'

For each scenario they put a cross near either the 'me' (I go home) or 'them' (I stay) end of the continuum. The teacher takes a tally of what students think they would do in each situation and asks pupils to come up with ideas about when they should decide to follow peer pressure and when not, and with things they can say to their friends when their choice is not to conform.

Key take-aways

- Social and emotional capabilities play an important role in the disadvantage gap – particularly those relating to self-regulation, goal-setting, persistence and resisting peer pressure.
- There is good evidence that social and emotional capabilities can be developed by explicit teaching within a supportive whole-school context, and that this is likely to have a positive and long-lasting impact on attainment.

10 Secrets of successfully engaging all parents

All school leaders want parents to support their child's learning, and nine out of ten see lack of parental engagement as a barrier to improving the attainment of disadvantaged pupils (National Audit Office, 2015). Yet far fewer – just over half – say that they have interventions in place to address the issue.

EEF surveys (van Poortvliet *et al.*, 2018) find that fewer than 10% of teachers have received training on how to engage parents. Only a quarter of schools in this survey had systems in place to monitor parental engagement, through simple measures like investigating whether particular groups of parents find communications from school helpful, whether they attend meetings with teachers, or feel they have a say in school decision-making processes.

Yet if we can implement strategies to engage parents, the prize can be great. John Hattie (2008) estimates that the effect of parental engagement is equivalent to two to three additional years of learning over a pupil's school career. Figure 10.1 shows that this engagement is more predictive of attainment in Y11 than disadvantage per se, and much more predictive than the effectiveness of the school pupils attend.

The data in the figure comes from a longitudinal study of young people in England (Lessof *et al.*, 2019). Parental engagement was calculated on the basis of pupils' answers to three questions: how frequently their parents discussed school reports with them, whether they attended parents' evenings, and how much their parents talked with them about their future plans for studying. After adjusting for the effect of the other types of disadvantage, the proportion of young people with parents showing less engagement who achieved good passes in English and maths was 24 percentage points lower than among pupils whose parents were more engaged.

Another set of questions looked at the quality of the relationship between the parent and pupil, based on how often the parents reported arguing with the young person. After controlling for other factors, the educational penalty

DOI: 10.4324/9781003176442-11

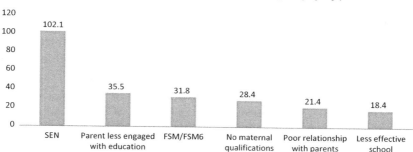

Figure 10.1 The individual attainment penalty associated with each of six disadvantages (from multivariate regression)

Source: Data from Lessof et al., 2019. *Multiple disadvantage and KS4 attainment: evidence from LSYPE2*

associated having a poor relationship with parents was the equivalent of around three-and-a-half GCSE grades.

The well-rehearsed negative correlation between socio-economic disadvantage and parental support for learning has been thrown into sharp relief by the COVID pandemic, with studies showing that children from higher income families spent 30% more time on home learning than those from poorer families (Marmot *et al.*, 2020).

These overall lower levels of engagement in disadvantaged families do not, however, mean that every disadvantaged family will struggle to support their child's learning. There are many families who buck the trend. In parenting it is what you *do* not what you earn that counts, as this example shows:

> A teacher came up to me at a conference to tell me about her own experiences. She came from a family where money was tight and where education had not been valued. Her Nan thought that school was a waste of time. Her mother, however, was different.
>
> When she was small, she took her daughter to a 'stay-and-play' session in a local park, where staff talked about the importance of sharing books and modelled reading *The very Hungry Caterpillar* aloud. The mother was impressed by this, borrowed the book but also went out and bought pipe-cleaners to make a caterpillar to thread in and out of the holes in the book, while she read the story.
>
> This mother may have been poor, but she knew what to do, or was ready to learn. Her daughter, the teacher, went on to tell me 'I was the first person in my family to go to university.'

What can we do to promote parental engagement?

There are two reasons, I think, for the mismatch between schools' concerns about parental engagement and the lack of focus it seems to have in their plans to close the disadvantage gap. One is that it is often hard, uphill work. The second is that there is little evidence, in fact, in support of specific interventions to involve parents (van Poortvliet *et al.*, 2018).

In my view this is because successfully engaging parents involves a long-haul approach to building relationships and trust. It is about developing the right school climate, one that promotes parents' confidence and self-efficacy, rather than about a set of interventions that can be tested in randomised trials.

So this chapter is less about research and more about examples of great practice in schools. I will describe schools that have gone the extra mile, and have strategies in place to reach out to parents whose own experience of education may make them anxious or angry when coming into school, parents who themselves may have low literacy or numeracy levels which make it difficult for them to help their child, parents who perhaps have simply got tired of hearing yet another teacher tell them their child has problem.

From these examples I have pulled out nine shared features – the secrets of successfully engaging all parents.

Let us begin with the story of two schools we have met previously.

Broken Cross Primary School

Parents of children at Broken Cross tend to be anxious about education and afraid of being judged. Staff have worked successfully to build trust and break down barriers, often by providing practical support for families. 'If they need an emergency dental appointment, we'll book it,' says headteacher Donna Lewis. 'Once you can win over those first few families and they trust you, then the message gets out.'

Support for families starts early. The local Children's Centre closed and the nearest is now a 40-minute walk away, so the school has tried to replicate some of the former provision – training staff in the Triple P parenting programme, for example. The school's nursery is open from 7.30 in the morning till six in the evening and takes children from the age of two.

Donna and her husband run a 7.30 a.m. school breakfast club daily. There is an after-school club that families pay for, but if a parent is having a difficult time Donna will often say 'Do you want to pop them in for a couple of nights this week and we won't charge you?' Staff are always willing to go the extra mile for children, for example taking children to speech and language therapy appointments if parents have not managed to get them there.

The school puts a lot of effort into how it communicates with families. Staff take care to 'speak the language of our parents'; an example is 'book and butty time' when parents get a bacon butty in the school hall when they come in to share a book with their child.

There are clear messages about home learning expectations, which aim to reduce anxiety: 'It is our job to do the teaching; you don't need to worry about that. What you can do is give your child a love of learning.' Staff have produced 'one-minute guides' on topics such as 'How to talk to your child about a book.' Homework tasks involve families in talk, for example when children asked their parents about favourite toys they had as children, as preparation for making a book for a history topic on games and toys.

Haytor View Community Primary School

Staff at Haytor View 'properly listen' to parents, and with respect. They treat them as equals and make it clear that Haytor is 'their' school. Parents are always welcome in the building, which is open and transparent - there are (by design) no corridors (so getting to one class means going through another) and no offices for the senior leaders, just bookable meeting rooms.

A great deal of effort goes into building relationships. Leaders make sure they are always out in the playground at the start and end of the day, just to say hello, to ask 'How was your weekend?' and 'to remember what happened the previous weekend - and ask about it,' says Scott Hampton, Leader of Learning and Development.

Scott talks about the importance of trust, and that trust is based on predictability. 'If a parent knows that school leaders will be outside every day, not just when they have time, they come to say more than hello to us.' Trust is hard to gain and easy to lose, he notes – especially in relationships with those living lives where trust has often been abused or absent.

The process of developing trust starts when families first apply for a place in the nursery. Sarah Butler, the Foundation Stage leader, phones every parent and invites them in with the child for an hour-long chat. She puts out play materials and talks to the parent about how wonderfully well their child is doing, describing every bit of learning she can see in the child's play. Parents are then invited to stay-and-play sessions in school.

Parents choose how they want the next stage, when their child starts to attend the nursery, to be managed. Some choose to stay with them for an hour or a whole session, for a few weeks or longer, getting to know staff as they do so.

Right through the Foundation Stage all parents come in and play with their child at the start of the day. Staff meet six families every week on a Friday after school, to talk and share details of each child's learning.

The school took part in an EEF-funded trial of the PEEP Learning Together programme, involving 20 weekly one-hour sessions in the nursery. Every Tuesday a group of parents came in with their children – babies and toddlers as well as the older children. They had coffee, biscuits and a chat before sitting on a rug to talk together about a topic – from why they had chosen their child's name, to how language develops or how to support early reading. This was followed by an activity and a story. Two years on, the parents in that group still engage very actively with all the school has to offer.

Haytor View operates a flexible start to the school day, with doors opening at 8.35 and the register taken at 8.50. In KS1 and 2 this provides a window when children and parents can be in classrooms together, working on 'time to think' activities that everyone can undertake and succeed in. Seeing the classroom full of other parents makes those who are less confident feel safe to come in. Some parents come to Monday SEAL assemblies, and many more to the Friday assemblies where pupils and parents are celebrated for their achievements.

The school has also run 'Time to think' trips, taking children on free visits to interesting places, and inviting parents to come along. One trip was up Haytor, the prominent hill which gives the school its name. Some parents had never been there, despite looking at it every day.

The school moved away from traditional parents' evenings and made a commitment to meet every parent in or after school at a time of their choice, instead. Some parents missed the old format so now the school runs both.

Communications with families are carefully monitored for tone and language – warm, friendly, easy to read. Staff volunteer to read things to parents if it would be useful, rather than wait for them to ask for help.

The first secret: Walk a mile in their footsteps

There is a Native American saying that goes 'Never judge a man until you have walked a mile in his moccasins.' I've learned the truth of this over many years of jumping to conclusions about people and finding myself wrong.

It is easy to interpret the research on disadvantage and parental support for learning as indicators of inadequacies in parenting. It can be easy to judge. But it is important not to, for many reasons.

I remember a radio programme about poverty in isolated rural areas, in which a group of women spoke about the nearby Cornish beaches to which they never go. One said 'The beach isn't for us, it's for the tourists' – implicitly, those with mobility and money. Another said 'Well it's not easy . . . you have to get a bus . . . we did go once but we didn't stay because when we got there, there was nothing to do.'

She had never been taken to a beach as a child, never learned to just mess about with sand and water. People know about trips and reading to children and having conversations with them only to the extent that they have experienced them. The way children are brought up transmits itself from generation to generation, and settles in communities. There is no point in blame.

When parents don't turn up for meetings, we often assume they don't care about their children, or can't be bothered. But all sorts of reasons may prevent them from coming . . . working a second job, having no one else to look after the children, lack of the bus fare, lack of confidence or actual fear. When parents did not do well at school themselves, their children's school is a scary place.

Inspirational teacher and trainer Martin Illingsworth (2018) reminds us of this when he describes what life is like for a boy born in a former fishing and mining area, where there are few jobs.

> Your school is brand new . . . when it was opened someone came to cut the ribbon. . . . You wanted to go but your mum wouldn't take you. The idea of school still makes her nervous. She doesn't like to go into them even though she left ten years ago. Over the next few years she is not going to come to any of your parents' evenings. This is probably just as well because you haven't been doing very well. To be honest, your mum never mentions school other than to tell you you have to go.

In order to work effectively with parents, we need first to put ourselves in their shoes. We need to understand that there is little point talking to a parent about improving a child's attendance unless we are willing to provide some practical help in getting a broken washing machine fixed so the child has clean clothes to wear. We need to understand that our role is to make less confident parents feel safe when they interact with us. I have never forgotten the story told by a headteacher of a Cheshire school serving a disadvantaged area; she spoke of an initiative called Talking Boxes, in which children and their parents were invited to decorate a sturdy wooden box which they then filled with objects that were special to the child. The school found this a good way of getting parents to come into school. 'We would never have got them in for literacy or numeracy,' the headteacher said. 'But decorating a box – everyone felt they could do that. That was safe.'

The second secret: ask what you can do for them before what they can do for you

I once saw this on a school's website:

> Parental engagement is required in two ways. Firstly to ensure that students' attendance, dress, attitudes for learning and preparation are of a high standard. Secondly, taking an active role in supporting students' learning and their choices of learning pathways.

The school also expects parents to take an active role in the life of the school, contributing to activities and events as appropriate to the time and skills that they are able to offer.

I looked in vain for any parallel information on what parents could expect from the school in return; this clearly wasn't a two-way street. Yet we will not succeed in engaging parents whose days are a struggle unless we provide concrete demonstrations that we care about them, that we will do what we can to help them tackle the pressing issues in their lives.

Benjamin Adlard Primary in Lincolnshire does this. The school offers a breakfast club, uniform banks, a food bank, adult learning projects and support with children's behaviour. It is working on setting up a community hub at the school, where families can access debt counselling and housing support.

Netherfield Primary in Nottinghamshire offers the 'Switch On' reading programme to parents who have literacy problems, as well as to children. A father of a Y5 boy went to see the headteacher to explain that he had two older boys in prison, and didn't want the youngest to go the same way. 'Teach me to read,' he said. The school did, and the boy came into school one day and said 'My Dad can read now. He read me a bedtime story.'

Netherfield also worked with a local college to bring basic skills and employability courses to the school site, and found a local charity willing to use a room in the school for confidential support with domestic violence.

What the most effective schools do, I have observed, is *ask* families what they need from the school, then try to provide it – like a workshop on how to write a good personal statement/job application, a session with a speaker on how to cope with children's sleep problems or tantrums, or one on how to keep children safe online. It need not be hard to build in 'educational' messages, such as the importance of bedtime stories in a session on sleep.

Every teacher can make a difference

Abigail Hawkins, secondary teacher and blogger, was used to sending invitations to parents' evenings and finding no one turned up. But one year, when she found herself with a few free periods in a row she decided to start a regular two-hour coffee morning for parents, with bacon butties provided. For one session she invited a local company to come and talk about disability benefits; another was about how to set up an e-mail account. The first week, 16 parents representing 11 students turned up; numbers rose and at one point 25 students had a parent come in. Parents began to support each other, filling in forms, going with each other to hospital appointments, helping with childcare. They also became much more willing to attend regular parents' evenings, once relationships had been built and barriers broken down.

Adapted from Matt Pinkett and Mark Roberts' book *Boys don't try*, 2019

Cradle-to-career provision: The Reach Children's Hub

Feltham is a community in outer London with very high levels of disadvantage and poor access to services. Parents often need to take two buses to get to the job centre, council offices and other services they need. Since Reach Academy Feltham, an all-through school, opened there in 2012, it has worked hard to bring accessible support to local children and families, from the time a child is born through to the time when they are moving into further education, training or work.

In 2017 Ed Vainker, the Academy's visionary executive headteacher, took the school's existing family support a step further and initiated a consultation to identify what the community might need. From this emerged the Reach Children's Hub.

The Hub has its own dedicated building, with an open-to-all, community-facing entrance. Young people and parents can be referred in to Hub programmes, such as a Girls' Group and parenting courses. Increasingly, local people also access resources, such as a Community Farm, on a structured walk-in basis.

Two Family Support Workers based in the Hub have a case-load of families that they work with over a term, dealing with issues such as housing, benefits, substance abuse and domestic violence. The Hub team also deliver Family Links parenting courses and provide outreach to other schools and early years settings in the area.

A partnership with the local authority has brought adult education programmes to the Hub – from English Language, through Numeracy to Teaching Assistant training.

Since 2018 the Hub has been partnering with Save the Children on its national Early Learning Communities initiatives. New schemes have been introduced which focus on the home learning environment, such as the PEEP Learning Together programme and Families Connect, a programme for four- to six-year-old pupils and their parents that gives parents the tools and confidence to support their child's education at home.

Another programme is the National Childbirth Trust's 'Birth and Beyond' project, which provides support to new parents, particularly those who are isolated. Local mothers have completed a 20-hour OCN accredited training programme to become Birth and Beyond Community Supporters, offering peer support to families around Feltham.

The third secret: build trust over time

Winning the trust of vulnerable families can be hard. It is easier for schools with relatively low turnover of staff and students, but not impossible for others.

St Mary's Primary

Amanda McGarrigle, headteacher at St Mary's Primary in Kent, stresses that building relationships with families takes time. Her own deep knowledge of the community (she has been headteacher at the school for 14 years) is important. Another factor is the way the school 'grows its own' staff, funding long-standing teaching assistants to go on to train as teachers. They then stay with the school, and 'we don't lose the investment in relationships with families.'

Staff provide practical support, reading paperwork for parents and helping with forms and bills. During the pandemic, the Family Liaison Officer (FLO) worked with a local church and Tesco to make sure every family had food. The school buys into the Magic Breakfast programme; all children have a free breakfast at school, first thing every day, with teachers sitting with them over bagels and cereal.

There is a 'Worry Box' for parents, situated in the entrance to the school. If a parent has a concern about their child (medical, friendships, bullying, or anything else) they can leave a message in the Worry Box and will be contacted privately by phone.

Much effort has been invested in developing relationships with Traveller families. The school had a governor from the Traveller community until very recently. Families from the community call the headteacher Amanda rather than Mrs McGarrigle, part of the staff's understanding that they need to be less formal and 'more human' than might be the case if the school served a different area.

It is accepted that Amanda and the FLO will come round to the house or trailer if a child is not attending school. She and her staff have won families' trust. Amanda tells the story of how one mother handed over her baby to her to look after while she attended a school event – a real example of the strength and informality of the home-school relationship.

Some schools with less long-standing relationships than St Mary's have found ways of working with volunteers from the community, who act as ambassadors or champions, reaching out to other parents to encourage them to take part in school activities or helping them develop their own child's language or literacy skills at home. Another idea is to welcome parents whose child is new to the school by assigning them a 'buddy family' with a child in the same year group.

Other schools employ or share a paid worker (often someone known and trusted by the community) whose role is to bridge the gap between home and school, engaging with parents on a personal level and providing practical support as a first step towards building trust.

Relationships are also built by reliably listening to parents and valuing their opinion. Sadly, too many parents would agree with one who told me 'Whenever I go to school, they want to TELL me what to do at home. They never ask me what I think. They never ask me anything.'

Meetings with parents (conversations in which both partners are often anxious) need not be like this, if we think about seating (always at an angle, never opposite the teacher) and use starters that open up dialogue, like the ones in Table 10.1.

Building the relationship with fathers is worth special effort, as their involvement is strongly linked to children's success at school, particularly for boys and disadvantaged pupils (Blanden, 2006). The involvement is as important for fathers who do not live with the child as it is for those who do (Asmussen and Weizel, 2010).

Table 10.1 Examples of positive ways of opening up dialogue

☐ Has there been anything he's specially enjoyed at school lately?
☐ How is she feeling about school and her work this term?
☐ Tell me what he is interested in and likes doing outside school.
☐ I'm having some trouble getting Jason interested in reading, and I'm wondering if you could help me? I know you feel you don't know much about how we teach reading, but you do know Jason. . .
☐ What have you noticed is the best way to get him enthusiastic about learning?/Do you think that there is anything getting in the way of him making progress?/What might help?/What's worked for him in the past with his other teachers?/What was it about that which worked well for him?
☐ From what you say, it sounds as though things are really tough for you just now . . . but you're still managing to cope. Is there something we could be doing in school to help?
☐ Maybe a good target to work at would be for him to . . . What do you think?
☐ Are there things I could be doing differently, so he could get on better, do you think?

Consumer research suggests that events billed as for parents attract only mothers, so the most successful schools target programmes and activities explicitly at fathers or other male relatives – like the 'Big Lads and Little Lads' project at Pipers Grove Primary in Barnsley, where boys and their chosen adult worked together over six weeks, using the school's computers, to write a book about dangerous sports. Events can draw on particular interests: one school ran a camping night out where fathers and their children built dens, made a fire, cooked sausages and gathered round the fire to read stories. Another school opened its grounds every Saturday morning for fathers to play sports with their children.

We should make clear the purpose of any organised event and how it is linked to improved educational outcomes, since research suggests this is particularly important for fathers. It can also help to build in an element of challenge, like the early years setting which posted messages saying '80% of dads say they haven't got time to read a bedtime story to their child – that can't be true *here*, can it?' They followed this up by sending home story sacks and a disposable camera for the family to take a picture of Dad reading, to send in to the setting for a display.

The fourth secret: build parents' own self-efficacy

In Chapter 7 we explored the idea that disadvantaged children may benefit particularly from explicit efforts to build their sense of agency. It seems that this is important in work with parents, too. One fascinating study found that holding other factors constant (including family background, mother's education and children's own locus of control/self-efficacy), children whose pregnant mothers ranked in the top 25% of the internal locus of control scale tended to obtain total GCSE scores around 17% higher than children whose mothers ranked in the bottom 25% (Lekfuangfu *et al.*, 2018).

The first step in building parents' own self-efficacy is to make sure they feel competent. In relation to homework, for example, we can make it clear that what is important is not that they help with the content, but rather that they let young people know they place value on the work being done. When asking parents to help their child learn to read, we can make it clear that it is not their job to *teach* the child, but just to give them lots of practice to build fluency. We can also send home specific tasks which everyone will be able to succeed with – as in Reading Recovery, where every day the child takes home a sentence they have written in school, cut up into separate words or phrases, to re-assemble with an adult.

For maths, every parent will be comfortable with playing games with their child: a good source is the free Maths At Home section of the Mathematics Shed website, and a paid-for Games@Home KS1 pack available from Every Child Counts at Edge Hill University. I am also really impressed with the Family Maths Toolkit from National Numeracy, and 'Maths with Parents,' run by the innovative charity Learning with Parents (along with a developing 'English with Parents' programme). The scheme targets children aged 4–11, and particularly those who are disadvantaged, through an online platform with videos (such as a child explaining how to carry out a certain mathematical operation) and activities that use objects easily found around the house. Parents access the ideas on their phones and can upload photos; children are rewarded for taking part by progressively accessorising a character they have chosen, and schools receive termly data reports about the number of activities undertaken by FSM-eligible pupils compared to those not eligible.

Wroxall Primary School, on the Isle of Wight, is situated in one of the 40% most deprived neighbourhoods in England. It has been involved in a parental engagement project run by the charity National Numeracy. This recognised that parents may have negative attitudes to maths and focused on showing that it can be fun. Homework tasks included cooking and measuring, or using hands to measure the height of family members then finding out how many hands' difference there was between them.

It is also helpful in building self-efficacy to foster supportive connections between parents as well as between parents and the school, and to let parents know how *well* they are doing. There is much to learn from the kind of parenting programmes that are called 'strengths-based'. Here parents might for example watch a video of themselves interacting with their child alongside a worker who points out the moments when the interaction is going well, and helps the parent to identify what they were doing in that moment. Other approaches encourage adults to remember a time when they felt proud as a parent, giving them a positive place to start, instead of feeling as if they have failed because they need to take a parenting 'class'.

Finally, we can build parents' self-efficacy by enabling them to make a difference to others – through volunteering in school or in the community, for example. Educational expert Nicola Morgan suggests that schools sign parents up to the Time Credits system run by the charity Tempo, in which people earn credits for anything they do for their community or school. Parents can paint classrooms, help look after the school garden, fundraise for the school, read with children or help out with breakfast and after school clubs. The credits they earn can be exchanged for special events like a day out at an adventure park.

Empowering communities – the case of Netherfield Primary

At Netherfield, an explicit aim is to build pride and self-efficacy in a whole community, to inspire whole groups of people to achieve things they had never dreamed possible. Sharon Gray, former headteacher, describes how it can be done.

'In 2014, twelve children who had received integrity awards for outstanding behaviour went to Italy on a skiing trip. The year before, it was Egypt. This was an incredible opportunity for the twelve children attending. But it was much more than that. Children know that as they reach the latter stages of KS2, these potentially life changing experiences could become available to them. The whole community knows about it – "Our children, from Netherfield, have been skiing in Italy."

Dedicated members of staff give up their time to put on adult reading classes, which has increased parents' chances of getting into employment but perhaps even more importantly to them, allowed them – for the first time – to be able to support their own children with their reading. The school also puts on courses led by tutors from the local FE College, teaching key skills in numeracy, literacy and ICT. Many parents have accessed these courses, building their confidence, restoring their self-belief and often supporting them in finding work.

Parents and carers feel part of their child's education. There is no "them and us." An increasing number are coming in as volunteers, not just for the traditional "hearing readers", but to lead after-school clubs, sharing their skills and expertise with the children attending.

Another key element of what makes Netherfield so special is the "Integrity in the community" scheme. Local shopkeepers, as well as community officers and those who lead youth clubs in Netherfield, have all been given small cards to award when they see children acting with real integrity. Back at school, children are recognised and rewarded for their good choices by being celebrated during a whole school assembly. This has had a clear impact throughout the community, showing that the school cares about the choices children are making wherever they are.'

Empowering communities – the case of Blackpool's parks

In 2015, Blackpool began ambitious work to rebuild several of its parks. Before this the parks were fairly grim spaces with spiralling levels of anti-social behaviour. The general opinion in the community was that they were not places to go to, especially with children.

The parks were redesigned with extensive input from local people, who in some cases have gone on to form active local community groups, creating new community gardens. It was their ideas that led to pirate ships, musical blocks, singing stones, fairy meadows, memory swings, worm farms, mud kitchens and mounds.

Local people have been appointed to paid posts as Early Years Park Rangers. They help families get the most from the parks, by delivering weekly sessions and forest schools all across Blackpool. Two big Father's Day events have been held in one park; joint projects between the Park Rangers, Blackpool Football Club Community Trust and schools provide regular outdoor activity sessions.

The turnaround in use of the parks has been phenomenal. Children and families in the area now have a stake in their local outdoor spaces, and as a result vandalism is a thing of the past.

The parks project is just one of many designed to build the self-efficacy of local people. In another, they are asked if they would like to make a difference to their local area. Funding of up to £1,000 is available to help groups of two or more local people tackle something which really matters to families, taking full control over how the money is spent.

The fifth secret: make it easy and friendly

Schools that succeed in engaging all parents take account of work patterns when planning events. They attend to detail – like checking when the last bus leaves the bus stop outside the school, when scheduling parents' evenings, or helping to arrange carpools and lifts for families without a car. Many have gone a step further and replaced traditional parents' evenings with one-to-one bookable slots throughout the year covering the whole day from 8 a.m. to 7 p.m., or with online meetings. If neither of these works, they are happy to meet in a place where parents feel comfortable – like a coffee shop or leisure centre, or by hiring a room in the local shopping centre.

They may also offer to meet in the parents' home, whilst taking care not to visit only once, or parents may feel they are being checked up on.

Events where parents and children undertake activities together seem to have a particularly friendly feel for families, like those at Exminster Primary.

Pop-up events at Exminster Primary School

Each year, staff at Exminster Primary run a series of five weekly Family SEAL sessions for new Reception class parents. The format is an adult session immediately followed by time for adults and children to undertake activities together.

Parents are told 'over the next few weeks we will be investigating what happens in our children's brains as they grow.' One session focused on attachment, with activities that involved eye contact between parent and child. Children and adults made pipe cleaner spectacles, drew around each other and had a competition to see who could make the tallest tower.

The next session looked at children's brains and what happens to them when they are upset or angry. There was discussion about how we can help our children when this happens. Activities were based on mirroring and trying to relate to children's mood.

Another week was about relaxation and massage. Everyone learned a simple massage with a story attached, which allows gentle touch. Later children and their parents tried different ways to relax such as hand massage, colouring and reading.

Then the school had the idea of running one-off sessions for other year groups. One was a 'pop up' session towards the end of Y6 that enabled children to spend time with their parents reflecting on their time in primary and their aspirations for the future. The children helped design the afternoon activities. There were blindfolded trust games, designing and making cards, dressing up and a photo booth, photo frames for memory photos, listening to stories the children had heard when they were younger and making worry dolls.

Food is a great way of breaking down barriers. At the former Candleby Lane Primary school, which serves a former mining area, teachers used to be afraid to go out into the community, and parents were afraid to come into school. In response, the school invited families in for a free bacon cob in the school hall. At first only a handful of parents came, but word soon spread. Now there can be up to a hundred parents, who often stay for workshops on how to help their child with learning.

At Scalby secondary school, staff hold events to share what their children are learning with parents. They get good attendance with strategies like a 'Pie and peas night' with first food, then information about what pupils will be doing to prepare for exams. 'Get them in, feed them, tell them what we do in English, maths and so on . . . and give them some useful resources they can take home' is the guiding strategy.

Finally, making it easy means conveying that there are simple, straightforward things parents can do to support their child's learning and development, which they can build into the day without a huge time commitment. The research suggests that these should focus on four areas where parental engagement seem to make most difference (Social Market Foundation, 2016):

- Talking with children, at all ages
- Reading to children in their first five years
- Showing an interest in schoolwork
- Being in control – feeling able to insist on homework before screens, regular bedtimes and so on

'Chat with your child, and read to them when they are small,' is a simple message, well backed up by research. For example, we know that where parents read to a four-to-five year-old child every day, or almost every day instead of twice a week or less, this will have the same effect on the child's reading skills at age eight to nine as being almost 12 months older (Kalb and van Ours, 2013).

A large international study (Organisation for Economic Co-operation and Development, 2012) found that after controlling for socio-economic background, children whose parents regularly read to them in the first year of primary school score on average 14 points higher in reading tests at age 15. Other important predictors were whether parents talked about things they had done during the day and told stories to their children.

Another study (Organisation for Economic Co-operation and Development, 2017) looked at factors affecting teenagers' wellbeing and found that 'Spending time just talking' was the parental activity most strongly associated with students' life satisfaction. It was also associated with academic success; students whose parents regularly talked with them were one-third of a school year ahead in science, after accounting for socio-economic background.

Messages about talking with your child are all very well, but what parents often say is, 'Yes, but what about?' We need to provide ideas, resources and models, as in these schemes:

- 'Chatterboxes' – boxes that children in the early years take home, such as a nursery-rhyme 'Twinkle Twinkle Little Star' box with the rhyme, a biscuit recipe and a star-shaped cutter, some glow-in-the-dark stars, a star finger puppet and a card star to thread with wool.
- Using the '50 things to do before your child is five' mobile app, which suggests local places for families to visit and fun things to do on their doorstep.
- Talk Homework, where the school posts a topic for the week for families to discuss at home. At Parkside Primary in Bradford, there is large banner on the playground wall that says 'Talk with your child . . . check out the speech bubble below for ideas.' The ideas (such as 'If you were an animal, what would you be?') are changed weekly.

- Bedtime story events, where parents are invited to bring their child in wearing pyjamas, adults model sharing a book and then parent and child read together. The modelling is important; not all parents know that talking together about a book is better for developing language than just reading it aloud. I learned this from one mother who explained to me 'I do read to him, but he keeps on interrupting.' She really wanted her child to be ready for school, and thought that listening passively is what teachers would expect to see.

There are many evidence-based formal 'programmes' which schools can seek out, that aim to get parents talking, playing and reading with their child in the nursery and Reception years. Table 10.2 lists those with evidence of impact on language and literacy outcomes.

Table 10.2 Programmes which support parents in talking, playing and reading with their child

Programme and provider	Description
Parents and Children Together (PACT) University of Manchester- kelly. burgoyne@manchester.ac.uk	For three- and four-year-olds; encourages parents of preschool children to spend 20 minutes a day at home, five times a week over 30 weeks, on shared reading and fun activities. Delivered by nursery staff.
Making it REAL National Children's Bureau	For three-and-a-half- to five-year-olds; includes home visiting and events that bring families together. Usually delivered by teachers.
PEEP	Age-specific curricula delivered by PEEP-trained early years practitioners (including teachers) for 20–33 weeks of group sessions. All sessions include talk time, songs and rhymes, sharing books and stories, and things for families to try at home.
Early Words Together National Literacy Trust	A targeted programme for families with children aged two to five; six, weekly group sessions with families, run by trained peer volunteers. Sessions focus on building talking into everyday activities.
EasyPeasy	App-based parenting programme for families with children between the ages of two to five. The programme aims to improve language and self-regulation.

Table 10.3 describes evidenced programmes for all age groups which help parents feel in control of their child – important since research (Lexmond *et al.*, 2011) shows that positive child outcomes, including resilience and attainment, are linked to parenting styles that are warm but firm (authoritative) rather than domineering and harsh (authoritarian) or permissive (lacking in boundaries).

Table 10.3 Programmes which help parents develop warm, responsive and authoritative parenting skills

Programme and provider	Description	Impact
Families and Schools Together (FAST) Save the Children UK	Eight-week after-school programme for groups of families with children aged three to eight. Families sit at tables and eat together. Parents are coached by trained volunteers on how to give instructions and have the child follow them. Children then go off to play while parents discuss an issue of their choice in groups. At the end there is a 15-minute play session in which each parent plays with their child, coached to follow their child's lead. Delivered by accredited FAST trainers, usually members of school staff.	Reduces teacher-rated emotional and behavioural difficulties and increases 'prosocial' behaviour.
Families Connect Save the Children UK	For families with children aged four to six, in schools in disadvantaged areas; eight group sessions in school. In each session, the first hour is for parents only; the second hour is for parents and children together. The sessions cover social and emotional development, literacy and language development, and numeracy. Delivered by two trained Community Practitioners in each school, usually members of school staff.	Increases teacher-rated prosocial behaviour, learning-related activities at home and parents' self-efficacy.

(Continued)

Table 10.3 (Continued)

Programme and provider	Description	Impact
Incredible Years	Early years and primary programmes for parents who have concerns about their child's behaviour. Parents learn via group discussion, role-play, homework and video vignettes. Delivered by pairs of highly trained mental health practitioners, psychologists, nurses, teachers or social workers.	Reduced behaviour problems and increased reading ability.
Triple P Online	Online programme for preschool up to age 12.	Improved child behaviour.
Resilience Triple P family intervention	Eight-week group programme with sessions for both parents and children between the ages of 6 and 12. Delivered by mental health practitioner, or other school support professional.	Improved child mental health and reduced victimisation.
Group Triple P and Group Teen Triple P	Group parenting programmes for primary and secondary age ranges, delivered by specialist professionals.	Improved child/teen behaviour.
Strengthening Families	For families with children aged between 10 and 14. Can be implemented as a universal programme or targeted at high-risk adolescents. Delivered by trained facilitators.	Reduced anti-social and risky behaviour. Improved academic success (self-report and parent-report).
Empowering Parents, Empowering Communities	For disadvantaged families with children between the ages of two and 11 experiencing behavioural difficulties. Parents attend eight weekly group sessions facilitated by pairs of trained and supervised peer facilitators.	Improved child behaviour.

The sixth secret: attending to the environment

A welcoming reception area will help parents feel confident to come into school. It is worth taking a 'mystery shopper' walk through your school, from the viewpoint of an imaginary disadvantaged parent.

Would such a parent see themselves and their culture reflected in the space? Do they have to cross a large empty space to get to reception? Is there a friendly face there or only an obviously busy person behind a glass screen? Is there any whiff of 'Oh no, not you again' in the greeting they receive? While they wait, does the seating make them feel exposed, as if they are in a goldfish bowl? Is there something engaging they can look at, so as to feel inconspicuous – like one primary school's display of laminated faces, one for every child in the school?

The bright, smart, open spaces emblazoned with awards and cups and vision statements that are so common in schools can be terrifying for less confident parents. They are often about the school's pride in itself, on show for Ofsted and officials, rather than about the needs of the community the school serves.

The schools that are good at engaging parents do things differently. At Watercliffe Meadow in Sheffield, for example, there are copies of 'Hello' magazine on the coffee table in reception, rather than the school prospectus. Local radio, not Mozart, is playing in the background, because that is what is most often listened to at home. There is a buggy park and toys for toddlers.

Another school turned its front reception area into a mini café with colourful throws on chairs and bone china from charity shops. Parents are welcome at any time, to make themselves a tea or coffee, help themselves to a piece of home-made cake and sit down for a chat. Similarly, a secondary school set up a community coffee bar on its premises, run by parents as part of a scheme to help them get into work.

The seventh secret: communicating with parents in ways that fit their lifestyle

The COVID pandemic brought an enormous amount of learning about how to communicate effectively with parents. One has to hope that schools build this into their ongoing practices – not like the headteacher I heard of who said, after children came back to school at the end of the first lockdown, 'When schools are shut again that's how we'll work with parents.'

What we have learned is to go digital, and perhaps scrap for ever the letters sent home in school bags, which all too often never made it out of the bag, or if they did were soon in the bin. Facebook, texting and the ever-growing range of apps like Marvellous Me, Seesaw, Class DoJo and Tapestry are the way to go. I remember Lesley, the parent liaison person at Netherfield Primary, telling me that the school could put messages for parents in letters ten feet high in the hall, but local parents would not look at them. 'It's got to be on their phones,' she said, 'that's where they look.'

The pandemic also taught us that some parents actually prefer remote rather than face-to-face contact. In Blackpool, for example, a 'Dad's Chat' live Facebook event proved very popular, engaging more fathers than had come forward in the past. There is also some research evidence (Hurwitz *et al.*, 2015) that texting can be particularly effective in engaging fathers. And for parents (fathers and mothers alike) who are working a second shift to put food on the table and may not easily be able to talk on the phone or come into school, texting can be a game-changer.

> Using the right vehicle to communicate with parents is essential. At St Ives secondary school, leaders realised that letters home were not reaching or being read by many of its parents. They now make sure that there is an active school Facebook page, and use texts. When the head-teacher texted a link to the regular parent survey the school undertakes, the numbers responding soared.

Parents respond more readily to messages that are personalised, according to research summarised by the EEF. So the apps that allow teachers to post awards and photos of the child's learning or achievements are likely to get looked at – especially if the school uses separate channels for general administrative messages.

Communications do not *always* have to be hi-tech, however. Many schools have had success with simple 'praise postcards'; teachers keep a stock in class and quickly write a personalised message about a child who has done some effective learning or shown good social and emotional skills, to be posted home by the school office. It is especially important in relationship-building to send home positive messages like this for children with behaviour difficulties, so that the parent's first contact with the teacher or tutor is not about what is going wrong. As Reva Klein (2000) puts it, 'Parents don't exist solely as the receptacles of bad news about their children's problem behaviour or poor attainment.'

Another effective low-tech communication strategy is having children go home wearing a sticky label saying 'Today I learned about . . . Ask me about it'. In the early years, staff write the messages, but in the primary years children can write their own labels as part of lesson plenaries.

Finally, perhaps the most effective strategy of all is making positive phone calls home.

> I remember once calling home to speak to the mother of a troubled boy who I'd taught for a couple of weeks. 'What's he done now?' she shouted at me. 'Nothing,' I said, 'I just wanted to tell you how impressed I am with his efforts in English so far.' After apologising, she explained through tears that she'd had enough of the constant stream of calls about fights, detentions and missed homework.
>
> Matt Pinkett and Mark Roberts, 2019. *Boys don't try*

Teacher and blogger Elena Aguilar (2015) has good advice about how to maximise the impact of calling home. When she first meets a class at the start of the year, she gives them a survey where one question is 'Who would you like me to call when I have good news to share about how you're doing in my class?' A few weeks later when it has become clear which pupils might be challenging, she makes it a goal to call their homes with positive news every week. She lets pupils know when she greets them at the door that she will be looking out for 'good news to share with your mum/dad/grandma this evening.' When she makes the calls, she gets the good news in quickly, before the phone gets put down: 'Hello, is this Mrs. _____? I'm calling from school with some good news about _____. Can I tell you about it?' The calls are short (no more than a couple of minutes) but the ripple effects for the child, the class, and the teacher are powerful.

At Maiden Erleigh secondary school in Reading, staff write to the parents of children eligible for the Pupil Premium to explain their child's entitlement and help plan the best ways to use it. If needed, they follow up with a warm, friendly phone call from the child's form tutor, or offer to visit at home.

With a relatively small number of disadvantaged pupils, they get to know most of their parents on a first name basis. Parents are invited to termly 'Tea and Topic' sessions to coach them on how to support their child's learning at home, and many take up the offer.

£100 of each child's Pupil Premium is set aside as a personal budget; a parent can phone up to ask 'Can we spend that money on . . . ?', or a pupil might suggest using it for new school shoes or equipment or revision materials.

The eighth secret: speak their language

I remember seeing a leaflet my grandsons brought home from primary school. It began 'I am the Early Intervention Family Worker connected with your school' and went on to offer help with common issues such as understanding and responding to challenging behaviour. Would parents want 'Early Intervention' (whatever that means), I thought? Would they trust a Worker (whatever that is)?

Too often we speak to families in our own professional language, and imagine we are heard. We use words like 'parenting classes' and 'workshops' that are frankly terrifying for parents. Or we dress them up, like one school who contracted with an organisation providing parenting courses called 'Parent Gym.' Unfortunately, the headteacher told me, this was not understood by a number of mothers, who turned up in leotards – and didn't come back.

Schools that are good at engaging families find non-threatening words – a 'Phonics Party' with balloons and cake rather than a phonics workshop, 'Butties 'n books,' 'Maths and muffins,' 'Lads 'n Dads,' 'Walk-in-Wednesdays' and 'Family Fridays.' They get children to write the invitations to events and use their pester-power to get an adult to come, and always involve a parent in checking that letters, texts, emails and content on the school website are readable and parent-friendly.

'Best seats in the house'

At Parklands Primary in Birmingham, the mission is to make every week's learning exciting, and then celebrate all pupils and their achievements with a 'Best seats in the house' assembly on Friday afternoons. This is regularly attended by over a hundred parents.

The ninth secret: Start with where they are not where you want them to be

Schools that are successful in engaging parents always start where parents are, rather than where they would like them to be. This may mean engaging parents in non-threatening activities to start with, before building up slowly to ones that focus on academic learning and the curriculum.

Activities might range from fitness classes to nail art, from relaxation and stress management to salsa dancing, dressmaking or embroidery – whatever it takes to engage a particular community. Meadowside Primary in Sheffield ran a six-week cooking club, where families made pizza and pasta. Staff at Netherfield Primary worked out that an offer that would be irresistible to parents would be a framed family portrait painted by an artist; while the family sat for the portrait in the school hall, the headteacher worked with them on a family vision for how they wanted their lives to develop in the future.

Free trips work really well as a way into parental engagement. So many times I have heard school staff complain that the children have never visited local landmarks, never been to the beach, even if they live near the sea – so why not arrange a school trip for children together with their parents? In shared outings we can model the ways of exploring and playing and chatting that we assume are automatic, but may not be in all families.

As we saw at the start of this chapter, this is nobody's fault. It is, however, the way that disadvantage gets handed down through generations – and as the schools I have described here show, there is always something we can do to help stop the transmission chain.

Key take-aways

- Engaging disadvantaged parents in their children's learning relies on long-term strategies to build trusting relationships, rather than bolt-on interventions.
- Schools that successfully engage parents understand anxieties based on parents' own negative experiences of schooling, and help parents feel safe in their interactions with staff.
- They provide practical help with day-to-day issues linked to poverty, aim to build the self-efficacy of parents as well as pupils, and choose means of communication carefully to fit parents' lifestyles.

Conclusion

We started this book with Jason's story, and it seems right to return to Jason now. I'd like to think that some of the strategies in this book, in the hands of schools with great leadership, could have helped him escape from the inter-generational cycle of disadvantage and changed the course of his life. I'd like to think that the strategies will be helpful for other children, too.

Every child who experiences disadvantage is different; there can be no single *prescription*, but there are *possibilities*.

The EEF offers us possibilities, in the form of a menu of 'best buys' from which schools can choose. Its toolkit is really helpful, but if used exclusively can lead to a pick-and-mix approach. In this book I've tried to build on the toolkit with a theory of change, positing that the causes of Jason's academic difficulties lie in early language and literacy difficulties, in low self-efficacy and in gaps in his social and emotional learning. From a theory of change come possible solutions.

Schools need to develop their own theory of change for the groups of children whose attainment gives them cause for concern, based on a real understanding of the life course of their at-risk pupils, and of their individual psychology, together with an understanding of the lived experience of their families and community.

From this understanding they will be in a position to choose wisely from the menu of targeted additional intervention programmes – and some will undoubtedly be needed for language, for literacy and for maths, as early in a child's school career as primary–secondary partnerships can engineer. From this understanding they can also, however, put in place much lower cost social-emotional strategies that aim to help students (and families) think and feel differently about themselves and about learning. These strategies involve changing the language we use so as to build self-efficacy, conveying high

DOI: 10.4324/9781003176442-12

expectations and consciously building the teacher–pupil and teacher–parent relationship.

Policy makers have often assumed that structural changes to schools, such as academisation, or introducing more grammar schools, are key to narrowing gaps, and that longer school days or summer schools may be the solution to COVID catch-up. The evidence suggests otherwise. Everyday interactions between teachers and pupils and their families are what matter most.

In the wise words of Marc Rowland (2021), 'It's a thousand little moments that lead to great attainment for disadvantaged pupils rather than those big, shiny interventions.'

For me, then, the secrets of closing the disadvantage gap lie in applying relational rather than structural strategies, basing them on engaging with the subjective experiences and perceptions of underperforming groups of students. We need to understand what is going on for individual children. We can learn more about how they experience school, for example, if we track them over a school day. We can ask their parents about their strengths, as well as talk about their difficulties. To tailor our teaching, we can listen to children to find out what makes them tick, what they are thinking and feeling. Often, we will find that they feel helpless, with little control over their experiences, and that we need to take steps to make them more powerful in their own lives, and in their own learning.

If we want them to succeed, we must walk a mile in their moccasins.

REFERENCES

Aaronovitch, D. (2020) Poor lives matter whatever their colour. *The Times*, Thursday 25 June

Adani, S., and Cepanec, M. (2019) Sex differences in early communication development: behavioral and neurobiological indicators of more vulnerable communication system development in boys. *Croatian Medical Journal*, 60:2, 141–149

Aelterman, N., Vansteenkiste, M., and Haerens, L. (2019) Correlates of students' internalization and defiance of classroom rules. *British Journal of Educational Psychology*, 89, 22–40

Aguilar, E. (2015) *The Power of the Positive Phone Call Home* www.edutopia.org/blog/power-positive-phone-call-home-elena-aguilar

Ampaw-Farr, J. (2018) A message to my teachers. In Gilbert, I. (ed.) *The Working Class*. Carmarthen: Independent Thinking Press

Apter, B., and Whitney, B. (2017) School attendance, exclusion and persistent absence. *British Psychological Society*, published online 9 June

Arfe, B., Festa, F., Ronconi, L. *et al*. (2021) Oral sentence generation training to improve fifth and tenth graders' writing. *Reading and Writing* https://doi.org/10.1007/s11145-020-10114

Asmussen, K., Law, J., Charlton, J. *et al*. (2018) *Key Competencies in Early Cognitive Development: Things, People, Numbers and Words*. London: Early Intervention Foundation

Asmussen, K., and Weizel, K. (2010) *Evaluating the Evidence. Fathers, Families and Children*. London: National Academy for Parenting Research

Atherton, G., and Mazhari, T. (2019) *Working Class Heroes – Understanding Access to Higher Education for White Students from Lower Socio-Economic Backgrounds*. London: National Education Opportunities Network

Barbu, S., Nardy, A., Chevrot, J. *et al*. (2015) Sex differences in language across early childhood: family socioeconomic status does not impact boys and girls equally. *Frontiers in Psychology*, 6, 1874

Barnes, L. (2021) Written evidence to the Education Select committee, January 2021 https://committees.parliament.uk/writtenevidence/21644/html/

Baron, T., Evangelou, M., Malmberg, L. *et al*. (2017) The tools of the mind curriculum for improving self-regulation in early childhood: a systematic review. *Campbell Systematic Review*, 2017:10

Barton, G. (2011) Word-rich rule the world. *Times Educational Supplement*, 16 September

Barton, G. (2017) The dispossessed in our system. *SecEd*, 20 September

Bates, A. (2020) *Routines and Boundaries and Behaviour –A Myth Buster* https://adelebateseducation.co.uk/routines-and-boundaries-and-behaviour-a-myth-buster/

Bauckham, I. (2020) *Character and Curriculum* https://parentsandteachers.org.uk/character-and curriculum/

Baumeister, R., Campbell, J., Krueger, J. *et al.* (2003) Does high self-esteem cause better performance, interpersonal success, happiness, or healthier lifestyles? *Psychological Science in the Public Interest*, 4:1, 1–44

Beck, I., McKeown, M., and Kucan, L. (2002) Choosing words to teach. In *Bringing Words to Life: Robust Vocabulary Instruction*, 15–30. New York: Guilford Press

Berger, J., and Karabenick, S. (2011) Motivation and students' use of learning strategies: evidence of unidirectional effects in mathematics classrooms. *Learning and Instruction*, 21:3, 416–428

Betthaeuser, B., Bourne, M., and Bukodi, E. (2020) Understanding the mobility chances of children from working-class backgrounds in Britain: how important are cognitive ability and locus of control? *British Journal of Sociology*, 71:8

Bijnens, E., Derom, C., Thiery, E. *et al.* (2020) Residential green space and child intelligence and behavior across urban, suburban, and rural areas in Belgium: a longitudinal birth cohort study of twins. *PLoS Medicine*, 17:8

Blair, C., and Diamond, A. (2008) Biological processes in prevention and intervention: the promotion of self-regulation as a means of preventing school failure. *Development and Psychopathology*, 20:3, 899–911

Blair, C., and Raver, C. (2014) Closing the achievement gap through modification of neurocognitive and neuroendocrine function: results from a cluster randomized controlled trial of an innovative approach to the education of children in kindergarten. *PLoS One*, 9:11

Blanden, J. (2006) *Bucking the Trend: What Enables Those Who Are Disadvantaged in Childhood to Succeed Later in Life?* London: Department for Work and Pensions

Blatchford, P., Bassett, P., Brown, P. *et al.* (2009) *Deployment and Impact of Support Staff Project. Research Brief RB-148.* London: DCSF

Blatchford, R. (ed.) (2020) *The Forgotten Third*. Suffolk: John Catt Educational

Boaler, J. (2019) *Limitless Mind: Learn, Lead, and Live Without Barriers*. San Francisco: Harper One

Boccanfuso, C., and Kuhfeld, M. (2011) *Multiple Responses, Promising Results: Evidence-Based, Nonpunitive Alternatives to Zero Tolerance*. Child Trends https://www.childtrends.org/publications/multiple-responses-promising-results-evidence-based-nonpunitive-alternatives-to-zero-tolerance

Bonell, C., Allen, E., Warren, E. *et al.* (2019) Modifying the secondary school environment to reduce bullying and aggression: the INCLUSIVE cluster RCT. *Public Health Research*, 7:18

Braithwaite, E., Pickles, A., Wright, N. *et al.* (2020) Sex differences in foetal origins of child emotional symptoms: a test of evolutionary hypotheses in a large, general population cohort. *Journal of Child Psychology and Psychiatry*, 61:11, 1194–1202

Bukodi, E., and Goldthorpe, J. (2020) *Social Mobility and Education in Britain: Research, Politics and Policy*. Cambridge: Cambridge University Press

Burroughs-Lange, S., and Douëtil, J. (2007) Literacy progress of young children from poor urban settings. *Literacy Teaching and Learning*, 12:1, 19–46

Butler, L. (2020) *Practical Strategies for Embedding High-Quality Social and Emotional Learning Skills* https://educationendowmentfoundation.org.uk/news/guest-blog-practical-strategies-for-embedding-high-quality-social-and-emotional-learning-skills/

Caldarella, P., Larsen, R., Williams, L. *et al.* (2020) Effects of teachers' praise-to-reprimand ratios on elementary students' on-task behaviour. *Educational Psychology*, 40:10, 1306–1132

Campbell, T. (2015) Stereotyped at seven? Biases in teacher judgement of pupils' ability and attainment. *Journal of Social Policy*, 44:3, 517–547

Carroll, C., Hurry, J., Grima, G. *et al.* (2020) Evaluation of bug club: a randomised control trial of a whole school primary aged reading programme. *Curriculum Journal*, 31:4, 605–626.

Carroll, J., and Breadmore, H. (2017) *Morphological Processing in Children with Phonological Difficulties*. Briefing Paper October 2017. Coventry University and University of Warwick

Cassano, C., and Schickedanz, J. (2015) An examination of the relations between oral vocabulary and phonological awareness in early childhood. *Literacy Research: Theory, Method, and Practice*, 64, 227–248

Castles, A., Rastle, K., and Nation, K. (2018) Ending the reading wars: reading acquisition from novice to expert. *Psychological Science in the Public Interest*, 19, 5–51

Chang, H., Osher, M., Schanfield, M. *et al.* (2019) *Using Chronic Absence Data to Improve Conditions for Learning*. Attendance Works and American Institutes for Research (AIR)   https://www.vcsedu.org/sites/default/files/department-files/School%20Social%20Services/Using%20Chronic%20Absence%20Data%20to%20Improve%20Conditions%20for%20Learning.pdf#:~:text=partners%20and%20policymakers%20can%20use%20chronic%20absence%20data,to%20fully%20leverage%20increasingly%20available%20chronic%20absence%20data

Chowdry, H., and McBride, T. (2017) *Disadvantage, Behaviour and Cognitive Outcomes: Longitudinal Analysis from Age 5 to 16*. London: Early Intervention Foundation

Clark, A., and Henderson, P. (2020) *Improving Mathematics in the Early Years and Key Stage 1*. London: Education Endowment Foundation

Clarke, P., Truelove, E., Hulme, C. *et al.* (2013) *Developing Reading Comprehension*. Chichester: Wiley

Claymore, Z. (2019) *Being Present: The Power of Attendance and Stability for Disadvantaged Pupils*. Slough: NFER

Clegg, J. (2004) *Language and Behaviour: An Exploratory Study of Pupils in an Exclusion Unit*. Proceedings of the British psychological society developmental section annual conference, Leeds, September

Cook, C., Fiat, A., Larson, M. *et al.* (2018) Positive greetings at the door: evaluation of a low-cost, high-yield proactive classroom management strategy. *Journal of Positive Behavior Interventions*, 20:3, 149–159

Coppola, S. (2014) Building background knowledge. *The Reading Teacher*, 68:2, 145–148

Cornelissen, T., and Dustman, C. (2019) Early school exposure, test scores, and noncognitive outcomes. *American Economic Journal: Economic Policy, American Economic Association*, 11:2, 35–63

Côté, S., Doyle, O., Petitclerc, A. *et al.* (2013) Childcare in infancy and cognitive performance until middle childhood in the millennium cohort study. *Child Development*, 84, 1191–1208

Coughlan, S. (2014) *Why Do White Working Class Pupils Fail in School?* www.bbc.co.uk/news/education-27904204

Cummings, C., Lang, K., Law, J. *et al.* (2012) *Can Changing Aspirations and Attitudes Impact on Educational Attainment? A Review of Interventions*. London: Joseph Rowntree Foundation

Cummings, D. (2013) *Some Thoughts on Education and Political Priorities* www.theguardian.com/politics/interactive/2013/oct/11/dominic-cummings-michael-gove-thoughts-education-pdf

Cummins, J. (2008) BICS and CALP: empirical and theoretical status of the distinction. In Street, B. and Hornberger, N. (eds.) *Encyclopedia of Language and Education, Volume 2: Literacy*, 2nd edn. New York: Springer

Damhuis, C., Segers, E., and Verhoeven, L. (2014) Stimulating breadth and depth of vocabulary via repeated storybook readings or tests. *School Effectiveness and School Improvement*, 26:3

Darling-Hammond, S., Fronius, T., Sutherland, H. *et al.* (2020) Effectiveness of restorative justice in US K-12 schools: a review of quantitative research. *Contemporary School Psychology*, 24, 295–308

de Boer, H., Timmermans, A., and van der Werf, M. (2018) The effects of teacher expectation interventions on teachers' expectations and student achievement: narrative review and meta-analysis. *Educational Research and Evaluation*, 24:3–5, 180–200

Demie, F., and Lewis, K. (2010) White working class achievement: an ethnographic study of barriers to learning in schools. *Educational Studies*, 37:3, 245–264

Department for Education. (2019) *Ethnicity Facts and Figures: Key Stage 4 and Multi-Academy Trust Performance* https://www.ethnicity-facts-figures.service.gov.uk/education-skills-and-training/11-to-16-years-old/a-to-c-in-english-and-maths-gcse-attainment-for-children-aged-14-to-16-key-stage-4/3.0

Department for Education. (2020) *Key Stage 4 Performance, 2019 (Revised)* www.gov.uk/government/statistics/key-stage-4-performance-2019-revised

DfES. (2007) *Letters and Sounds: Principles and Practice of High Quality Phonics*. London: DfES

Dickerson, E. (2014) '*Cos I ain't Got a Pencil* https://twitter.com/joshtdickerson?ref_src=twsrc%5Etfw%7Ctwcamp%5Etweetembed%7Ctwterm%5E963275985654251520%7Ctwgr%5E%7Ctwcon%5Es1_&ref_url=https%3A%2F%2Fau.news.yahoo.com%2Fthe-truth-behind-this-students-viral-i-aint-got-a-pencil-poem-38953919.html

Dimova, S., Ilie, S., Brown, E. *et al.* (2020) *The Nuffield Early Language Intervention Evaluation Report*. London: Education Endowment Foundation

Dix, P. (2018) Are we going on the tube? In Gilbert, I. (ed.) *The Working Class*. Carmarthen: Independent Thinking Press

Dockrell, J., Mathers, S., Law, J. *et al.* (2020) *Empowering Staff to Enhance Oral Language in the Early Years*. Report to steering group, personal communication

Donnelly, M., Lazetic, P., Sandoval-Hernández, A. *et al.* (2019) *An Unequal Playing Field: Extra-Curricular Activities, Soft Skills and Social Mobility*. London: Social Mobility Commission

Dowker, A. (2019) *Individual Differences in Arithmetic*. London: Routledge

Duckworth, A., Kirby, T., Gollwitzer, A. *et al.* (2013) From fantasy to action: mental contrasting with implementation intentions (MCII) improves academic performance in children. *Social Psychological and Personality Science*, 4:6, 745–753

Duckworth, K. (2007) *What Role for the 3 Rs? Progress and Attainment During Primary School*. London: Centre for Research on the Wider Benefits of Learning

Easterbrook, M., and Hadden, I. (2020) Tackling educational inequalities with social psychology: identities, contexts and interventions. *Social Issues and Policy Review*, 15:1, 180–236

Education Endowment Foundation. (2017) *Improving Literacy in Key Stage 2*. London: Education Endowment Foundation

Education Endowment Foundation. (2018) *Sutton Trust-Education Endowment Foundation Teaching and Learning Toolkit*. London: Education Endowment Foundation

Ellefson, M., Zachariou, A., Ng, F. *et al.* (2020) Do executive functions mediate the link between socioeconomic status and numeracy skills? *Journal of Experimental Child Psychology*, 194, Article 104734

Escueta, M., Nickow, A., Oreopoulos, P. *et al.* (2020) Upgrading education with technology: insights from experimental research. *Journal of Economic Literature*, 58:4, 897–996

Etchell, A., Adhikari, A., Weinberg, L. *et al.* (2018) A systematic literature review of sex differences in childhood language and brain development. *Neuropsychologia*, 114, 19–31

Evans, G. (2006) *Educational Failure and Working Class White Children in Britain*. London: Palgrave Macmillan

Feinstein, L. (2000) *The Relative Importance of Academic, Psychological and Behavioural Attributes Developed in Childhood*. London: London School of Economics

Feinstein, L. (2003) Inequality in the early cognitive development of British children in the 1970 cohort. *Economica*, 70:277, 73–97

Finnegan, J., Telfer, C., and Warren, H. (2015) *Ready to Read: Closing the Gap in Early Language Skills*. London: Save the Children

Fivush, R. (1989) Exploring sex differences in the emotional content of mother-child conversations about the past. *Sex Roles*, 20, 675–691

Francis, B. (2018) The impact of setting on social justice. *Times Educational Supplement*, 7 September

Francis, B., Skelton, C., and Read, B. (2010) The simultaneous production of educational achievement and popularity: how do some pupils accomplish it? *British Educational Research Journal*, 36:2, 317–340

Francis, B., Taylor, B., and Tereshchenko, A. (2020) *Reassessing 'Ability' Grouping Improving Practice for Equity and Attainment*. London: Routledge

Gardner, B. (2015) *Raising Standards Through Effective Feedback*. Presentation to Catch Up Conference

Gersten, R., Haymond, K., Newman-Gonchar, R. *et al.* (2020) Meta-analysis of the impact of reading interventions for students in the primary grades. *Journal of Research on Educational Effectiveness*, 13:2, 401–427

Giangreco, M. (2010) One-to-one paraprofessionals for students with disabilities in inclusive classrooms: is conventional wisdom wrong? *Intellectual and Developmental Disabilities*, 48, 1–13

Gibb, J., Rix, K., Wallace, E. *et al.* (2016) *Poverty and Children's Personal and Social Relationships*. London: Joseph Rowntree Foundation

Gibson, J. (2018) *The Interplay Between Linguistics and Social Development*. Presentation at the Public Health England East of England CYP Commissioner Forum, Cambridge, 19 April

Gilbert, I. (ed.) (2018) *The Working Class*. Carmarthen: Independent Thinking Press

Gilmore, C., Gobel, S., and Inglis, M. (2018) *An Introduction to Mathematical Cognition*. London: Routledge

Goodman, A., and Gregg, P. (2010) *Poorer Children's Educational Attainment: How Important Are Attitudes and Behaviour?* London: Joseph Rowntree Foundation

Goodman, A., Joshi, H., Nasim, B. *et al.* (2015) *Social and Emotional Skills in Childhood and Their Long-Term Effects on Adult Life*. London: UCL Institute of Education

Gorard, S., Siddiqui, N., and Huat See, B. (2015) *Philosophy for Children. Evaluation Report and Executive Summary*. London: Education Endowment Foundation/Durham University

Gorard, S., Siddiqui, N., and Huat See, B. (2017) *Children's University. Evaluation Report and Executive Summary*. London: Education Endowment Foundation/Durham University

Goulay, G., and Harmey, S. (2020) A reading recovery comparison study: supporting a new implementation in Scotland. *The Journal of Reading Recovery*, 20:1, 59–70

Gove, M. (2014) *Speech to Education Reform Summit*, 10 July

Greenberg, M., Weissberg, R., O'Brien, M. *et al.* (2003) Enhancing school-based prevention and youth development through coordinated social, emotional, and academic learning. *American Psychologist*, 58:6–7, 466–474

Gregersen, H. (2014) Curiouser and curiouser. *Times Educational Supplement*, 4 April

Griffin, V. (2020) Struggling to get teens reading for fun? I'll guide you through it. *Times Educational Supplement*, 3 July

Gross, J. (2018) *Time to Talk* (2nd edn.) London: Routledge

Gross, J. (2020) *Closing the Word Gap: Learning from Five Areas Who Have Gained Ground* www.eif.org.uk/blog/closing-the-word-gap-learning-from-five-areas-who-have-gained-ground

Gross, J., and Members of the KPMG Education Advisory Team. (2009a) *The Long Term Costs of Literacy Difficulties*. London: Every Child a Chance Trust

Gross, J., and Members of the KPMG Education Advisory Team. (2009b) *The Long Term Costs of Numeracy Difficulties*. London: Every Child a Chance Trust

Gutman, L., Joshi, H., Parsonage, M. *et al*. (2015) *Children of the New Century: Mental Health Findings from the Millennium Cohort Study*. London: UCL Institute of Education

Gutman, L., and Schoon, I. (2013) *The Impact of Non-Cognitive Skills on Outcomes for Young People: Literature Review*. London: Education Endowment Foundation/Cabinet Office

Hadden, I., Easterbrook, M., Nieuwenhuis, M. *et al*. (2019) Self-affirmation reduces the socioeconomic attainment gap in schools in England. *British Journal of Educational Psychology*, 90, 517–536

Hallahan, G. (2021) The national tutoring programme is being rolled out – but how do you get the cash? And who do you select to be tutored? *Times Educational Supplement*, 17 January

Hallam, S., and Parsons, S. (2013) The incidence and make up of ability grouped sets in the UK primary school. *Research Papers in Education*, 28:4, 393–420

Hattie, J. (2008) *Visible Learning*. London and New York: Routledge

Hawke, J., Wadsworth, S., Olson, R. *et al*. (2007) Etiology of reading difficulties as a function of gender and severity. *Reading and Writing*, 20, 13–25

Haythorne, G. (2019) Why growth mindset should be a way of life. *Times Educational Supplement*, 26 April

Hinnant, J., O'Brien, M., and Ghazarian, S. (2009) The longitudinal relations of teacher expectations to achievement in the early school years. *Journal of Educational Psychology*, 101, 662–670

Hirsch, E. (2016) *Why Knowledge Matters: Rescuing Our Children from Failed Educational Theories*. Cambridge: Harvard Educational Press

Hirsch, F. (1996) *The Schools We Need and Why We Don't Have Them*. New York: Doubleday

Hollo, A., Wehby, J., and Oliver, R. (2014) Unidentified language deficits in children with emotional and behavioral disorders: a meta-analysis. *Exceptional Children*, 80:2, 169–186

Horst, J., Parsons, K., and Bryan, N. (2011) Get the story straight: contextual repetition promotes word learning from storybooks. *Frontiers in Psychology*, 2, article 17

House of Commons Education Committee. (2014) *Underachievement in Education by White Working Class Children: First Report of Session 2014-15*. London: The Stationery Office

House of Commons Education Committee. (2021) *The Forgotten: How White Working-Class Pupils Have Been Let Down, and How to Change It: First Report of Session 2021-22*. London: The Stationery Office

Howard, S., Dryden, J., and Johnson, B. (1999) Childhood resilience: review and critique of literature. *Oxford Review of Education*, 25, 307–323

Hulleman, C., and Harackiewicz, J. (2009) Making education relevant: increasing interest and performance in high school science classes. *Science*, 326, 1410–1412

Humphrey, N., Kalambouka, A., Bolton, J. *et al*. (2008) *Primary Social and Emotional Aspects of Learning (SEAL): Evaluation of Small Group Work*. London: DSCF

Hurry, J., and Fridkin, L. (2018) *The Impact of Reading Recovery Ten Years After Intervention*. London: KPMG Foundation

Hurwitz, L., Lauricella, A., Hanson, A. *et al.* (2015) Supporting head start parents: impact of a text message intervention on parent-child activity engagement. *Early Child Development and Care*, 185:9, 1373-1389

Illingsworth, M. (2018) The only fresh air is outside in the yard. In Gilbert, I. (ed.) *The Working Class*. Carmarthen: Independent Thinking Press

Immordino-Yang, M., Darling-Hammond, L., and Krone, C. (2018) *The Brain Basis for Integrated Social, Emotional, and Academic Development: How Emotions and Social Relationships Drive Learning*. Washington, DC: Aspen Institute

Jackson, C., Porter, S., Easton, J. *et al.* (2020) *Who Benefits from Attending Effective Schools? Examining Heterogeneity in High School Impacts*. Working Paper 28194, National Bureau of Economic Research

Jay, T., Willis, B., Thomas, P. *et al.* (2017) *Dialogic Teaching Evaluation Report and Executive Summary*. London: Education Endowment Foundation

Jerrim, J., Perera, N., and Sellen, P. (2017) *English Education: World Class in Primary?* London: Education Policy Institute and UCL Institute of Education

Jerrim, J., and Shure, N. (2016) *Achievement of 15 Year Olds in England: PISA 2015 National Report*. London: DfE

Johnson, Z., Goldman, Z., and Claus, C. (2019) Why do students misbehave? An initial examination of antecedents to student misbehavior. *Communication Quarterly*, 67:1, 1-20

Juel, C. (1988) Learning to read and write: a longitudinal study of 54 children from first through fourth grades. *Journal of Educational Psychology*, 80, 437-447

Kalb, G., and van Ours, J. (2013) *Reading to Children Gives Them a Head-Start in Life*. Melbourne Institute Working Paper No. 17/13

Kelly, G. (2018) I work with educational heroes. In Gilbert, I. (ed.) *The Working Class*. Carmarthen: Independent Thinking Press

Kendall, L., O'Donnell, L., Golden, S. *et al.* (2005) *Excellence in Cities: The National Evaluation of a Policy to Raise Standards in Urban Schools*. London: DfES

Kettlewell, K., Sharp, C., Lucas, M. *et al.* (2020) *International Early Learning and Child Well-Being Study (IELS): National Report for England*. London: DfE

Kilkenny, C. (2018) Down but not out. In Gilbert, I. (ed.) *The Working Class*. Carmarthen: Independent Thinking Press

Killgo, J. (2012) Relationship between success in extracurricular programs and student academic performance in economically disadvantaged high schools. *ProQuest Information and Learning*, 73

King, L., and Welch, T. (2012) *Successful White Boys, of British Origin, Eligible for Free School Meals*. Schools Network https://webcontent.ssatuk.co.uk/wp-content/uploads/2013/01/FSM-report.pdf

Klein, R. (2000) *Defying Disaffection*. Stoke on Trent: Trentham Books

Kokštejn, J., Musálek, M., and Tufano, J. (2017) Are sex differences in fundamental motor skills uniform throughout the entire preschool period? *PLoS One*, 12:4

Kraemer, S. (2000) The fragile male. *British Medical Journal*, 321:7276, 1609-1612

Kutnick, P., Sebba, J., Blatchford, P. *et al.* (2005) *The Effects of Pupil Grouping: Literature Review*. London: DfE

Lasky-Fink, J., Robinson, C., Chang, H. *et al.* (2020) *Using Behavioral Insights to Improve School Administrative Communications: The Case of Truancy Notifications*. EdWorkingPaper: 20-271, Annenberg Institute at Brown University

Latham, R., Meehan, A., Arseneault, L. *et al.* (2019) Development of an individualised risk calculator for poor functioning in young people victimised during childhood: a longitudinal cohort study. *Child Abuse & Neglect*, 98

Lear, J. (2018) Careers education. In Gilbert, I. (ed.) *The Working Class*. Carmarthen: Independent Thinking Press

Lee, J., Lee, H., Song, J. *et al.* (2021) Enhancing children's math motivation with a joint intervention on mindset and gender stereotypes. *Learning and Instruction*, 73, 101416

Lee, W. (2008) *The Communication Cookbook*. London: ICAN

Lekfuangfu, W., Powdthavee, N., Warrinnier, N. *et al.* (2018) Locus of control and its intergenerational implications for early childhood skill formation. *The Economic Journal*, 128:608, 298–329

Lervåg, A., Hulme, C., and Melby-Lervåg, M. (2018) Unpicking the developmental relationship between oral language skills and reading comprehension: it's simple, but complex. *Child Development*, 89:5, 1821–1838

Lessof, C., Ross, A., and Brind-Kantar, R. (2019) *Multiple Disadvantage and KS4 Attainment: Evidence from LSYPE2*. London: DfE

Lexmond, J., Bazalgette, L., and Margo, J. (2011) *The Home Front*. London: Demos.

Lloyd, C., Edovald, T., Kiss, Z. *et al.* (2015a) *Paired Reading Evaluation Report and Executive Summary*. London: Education Endowment Foundation and NatCen Social Research

Lloyd, C., Edovald, T., Morris, S. *et al.* (2015b) *Durham Shared Maths Evaluation Report and Executive Summary*. London: Education Endowment Foundation and NatCen Social Research

Lord, P., Bradshaw, S., Stevens, E. *et al.* (2015) *Perry Beeches Coaching Programme Evaluation Report*. London: Education Endowment Foundation and NatCen Social Research

Marmot, M., Allen, J., Goldblatt, P. *et al.* (2020) *Build Back Fairer: The COVID-19 Marmot Review*. London: UCL Institute of Health Equity

Melhuish, E., and Gardiner, J. (2020) *Study of Early Education and Development (SEED) Impact Study on Early Education Use and Child Outcomes Up to Age Five Years*. London: DfE

Millard, W., and Menzies, L. (2016) *The State of Speaking in Our Schools*. London: Voice 21 and LKMCO

Millward, C. (2021) White students who are left behind: the importance of place. *Office for Students Blogpost*, 26 January

Minero, E. (2019) *Six Elementary Reading Strategies That Really Work* www.edutopia.org/article/6-elementary-reading-strategies-really-work

Mol, S., Bus, A., De Jong, M. *et al.* (2008) Added value of dialogic parent-child book readings: a meta-analysis. *Early Education and Development*, 19:1, 7–26

Mongon, D., and Chapman, C. (2008) *Successful Leadership for Promoting the Achievement of White Working Class Pupils*. Nottingham: National College for School Leaders

Montacute, R. (2018) *Potential for Success: Fulfilling the Promise of Highly Able Students in Secondary Schools*. London: Sutton Trust

Moss, G. (2002) Raising boys' attainment in reading: some principles for intervention. *Reading*, 34:3, 101–106

Moss, G., and Washbrook, L. (2016) *Understanding the Gender Gap in Literacy and Language Development*. Bristol: University of Bristol Graduate School of Education

Mueller, C., and Dweck, C. (1998) Praise for intelligence can undermine children's motivation and performance. *Journal of Personality and Social Psychology*, 75:1, 33–52

Multon, K., Brown, S., and Lent, R. (1991) Relation of self-efficacy beliefs to academic outcomes: a meta-analytic investigation. *Journal of Counselling Psychology*, 38, 30–38

Myhill, D., and Jones, S. (2004) Troublesome boys and compliant girls: gender identity and perceptions of achievement and underachievement. *British Journal of Sociology of Education*, 25:5, 459–474

Myhill, D., and Jones, S. (2006) "She doesn't shout at no girls": pupils' perceptions of gender equity in the classroom. *Cambridge Journal of Education*, 36:1, 99–113

NAHT and Royal College of Speech and Language Therapists. (2020) *Guidance for Education Settings on Commissioning (Buying in) Speech and Language Therapy Services and Training*. London: RCSLT

National Audit Office. (2015) *Funding for Disadvantaged Pupils: Survey Evidence from Pupils, Parents and School Leaders*. London: NAO

National Audit Office. (2020) *Supporting Disadvantaged Families Through Free Early Education and Childcare Entitlements in England*. London: NAO

National Literacy Trust. (2011) *2011 Schools Guide*. London: NLT

National Literacy Trust. (2020) *Annual Literacy Survey* https://literacytrust.org.uk/research-services/research-reports/hildren-and-young-peoples-reading-in-2020-before-and-during-the-covid-19-lockdown/

National Scientific Council on the Developing Child. (2020) *Connecting the Brain to the Rest of the Body: Early Childhood Development and Lifelong Health Are Deeply Intertwined*. Working Paper 15, National Scientific Council on the Developing Child, Cambridge, MA

National Tutoring Programme. (2020) *Best Tutoring Practice: Briefing for Schools*. London: NTP

Neuman, S., and Wright, T. (2014) The magic of words: Teaching vocabulary in the early childhood classroom. *American Educator*, 38:2

Nichols, J. (2020) Presentation at National Pupil Premium Conference, 10 December

Nickow, A., Oreopoulos, P., and Quan, V. (2020) *The Impressive Effects of Tutoring on Pre K-12 Learning: A Systematic Review and Meta-Analysis of the Experimental Evidence*. EdWorkingPaper: 20–267, Annenberg Institute at Brown University

Nunes, T., Malmberg, L., Evans, D. *et al.* (2019) *Onebillion Evaluation Report*. London: Education Endowment Foundation

Nye, P. (2020) *How Pupil Characteristics Interact to Influence Education Outcomes*. FFT Education Datalab, 1 September https://ffteducationdatalab.org.uk/2020/09/how-pupil-characteristics-interact-to-influence-education-outcomes/

Office for National Statistics. (2020a) *Social Capital in the UK: 2020*. London: ONS

Office for National Statistics. (2020b) *Child Poverty and Education Outcomes by Ethnicity*. London: ONS

Ofsted. (2008) *White Boys from Low-Income Backgrounds: Good Practice in Schools*. London: Ofsted

Ofsted. (2013) *Unseen Children: Access and Achievement 20 Years on*. Manchester: Ofsted

Ofsted. (2019) *Education Inspection Framework: Overview of Research*. Manchester: Ofsted

Organisation for Economic Co-operation and Development. (2012) *PISA: Let's Read Them a Story! The Parent Factor in Education*. Paris: OECD

Organisation for Economic Co-operation and Development. (2016) *Low-Performing Students: Country Note (UK) Why They Fall Behind and How to Help Them Succeed*. Paris: OECD

Organisation for Economic Co-operation and Development. (2017) *PISA 2015 Results Volume 111: Students' Well-Being*. Paris: OECD

Palmer, J., and Invernizzi, M. (2015) *No More Phonics and Spelling Worksheets*. Portsmouth, NH: Heinemann

Palminteri, S., Kilford, E., Coricelli, G. *et al.* (2016) The computational development of reinforcement learning during adolescence. *PLoS Computational Biology*, 12:6

Parr, C. (2019) Social inequality. *Times Educational Supplement*, 8 November

Parsons, S., and Branagan, A. (2013) *Word Aware: Teaching Vocabulary Across the Day, Across the Curriculum*. London: Routledge

Parsons, S., and Branagan, A. (2016) *Word Aware 2: Teaching Vocabulary in the Early Years*. London: Routledge

Parsons, S., and Bynner, J. (2002) *Basic Skills and Social Exclusion*. London: The Basic Skills Agency

Pascal, C., and Bertram, T. (2016) *High Achieving White Working Class (HAWWC) Boys Project: Final Report*. London: Centre for Research in Early Childhood

Patall, E., Cooper, H., and Robinson, J. (2008) Parent involvement in homework: a research synthesis. *Review of Educational Research*, 78:4, 1039–1101

Pearman, F., Springer, M., Lipsey, M. et al. (2020) Teachers, schools, and pre-K effect persistence: an examination of the sustaining environment hypothesis. *Journal of Research on Educational Effectiveness*, 13:4, 547–573

Perry, L., Prince, E., Valtierra, A. et al. (2018) A year in words: the dynamics and consequences of language experiences in an intervention classroom. *PloS One*, 13:7

Petronzi, D. (2016) *The Development of the Numeracy Apprehension Scale for Children Aged 4-7 Years*. University of Derby: Ph.D. Thesis

Picton, I., Clark, C., O'Keefe, S. et al. (2019) *Improving the Literacy Skills of Disadvantaged Teenage Boys Through the Use of Technology*. London: National Literacy Trust

Pinkett, M., and Roberts, M. (2019) *Boys Don't Try*. London: Routledge

Pollard, B. (2020) Reflections: the impact of school closures on disadvantaged students and the attainment gap. *Heathfield Teach Share Blog*, 6 November

Quigley, A. (2018) *Closing the Vocabulary Gap*. London: Routledge

Quigley, A., and Coleman, R. (2019) *Improving Literacy in Secondary Schools*. London: Education Endowment Foundation

Quin, D. (2016) Longitudinal and contextual associations between teacher-student relationships and student engagement: a systematic review. *Review of Educational Research*, 87:2

Quinn, J., and Wagner, R. (2013) Gender differences in reading impairment and in the identification of impaired readers: results from a large-scale study of at-risk readers. *Journal of Learning Disabilities*, 48:10

Rattan, A., Good, C., and Dweck, C. (2012) "It's OK - Not everyone can be good at math": instructors with an entity theory comfort (and demotivate) students. *Journal of Experimental Social Psychology*, 48, 731–737

Read, K., Furay, E., and Zylstra, D. (2019). Using strategic pauses during shared reading with preschoolers: Time for prediction is better than time for reflection when learning new words. *First Language*, 39:5, 508–526

Reinke, W., Herman, K., and Newcomer, L. (2016) The brief student-teacher classroom interaction observation. *Assessment for Effective Intervention*, 42:1, 32–42

Riley, R., Coates, M., and Perez Martinez, S. (2018) *Place and Belonging in Schools: Unlocking Possibilities*. London: UCL Institute of Education

Robinson, C., Gallus, J., Lee, M. et al. (2019) The demotivating effect (and unintended message) of awards. *Organizational Behavior and Human Decision Processes*, 163, 51-64

Rodda, M., Hallgarten, J., and Freeman, J. (2013) *Between the Cracks: Exploring In-Year Admissions in Schools in England*. London: RSA

Romero, C. (2018) What we know about belonging from scientific research. *Mindset Scholars Network* https://mindsetscholarsnetwork.org/wp-content/uploads/2015/09/What-We-Know-About-Belonging.pdf

Rowland, C., and Noble, C. (2016) *How Does Shared Book Reading Help Boost Child Language Development in the Early Years?* LuCiD Evidence Briefing 3, LuCiD, Liverpool

Rowland, M. (2021) *Podcast Hosted by Sandringham Research School*. Episode 1: Pupil Premium with Marc Rowland https://researchschool.org.uk/sandringham/podcasts

Roy, P., Rutt, S., Easton, C. *et al.* (2019) *Stop and Think: Learning Counterintuitive Concepts Evaluation Report*. London: Education Endowment Foundation

Rozek, C., Ramirez, G., Fine, R. *et al.* (2019) Reducing socioeconomic disparities in the STEM pipeline through student emotion regulation. *Proceedings of the National Academy of Sciences*, 116:5, 1553-1558

Rubie-Davies, C., Hattie, J., and Hamilton, R. (2006) Expecting the best for students: teacher expectations and academic outcomes. *British Journal of Educational Psychology*, 76, 429-444

Rubie-Davies, C., Peterson, E., Sibley, C. *et al.* (2015) A teacher expectation intervention: modelling the practices of high expectation teachers. *Contemporary Educational Psychology*, 40, 72-85

Rutter, M. (2006) Implications of resilience concepts for scientific understanding. *Annals of the New York Academy of Science*, 1094, 1-12

Salmin, D., Bell, J., and Rowland, M. (2019) *Improving Outcomes for Disadvantaged Learners in Disadvantaged Areas: Oldham and Derby*. London: Rosendale Research School

Sargent, C. (2021) How to lead whole-class guided reading in schools. *Times Educational Supplement*, 15 January

Savage, M. (2015) *Social Class in the 21st Century*. London: Pelican Books

Save the Children. (2013) *Too Young to Fail: Giving All Children a Fair Start in Life*. London: Save the Children

Save the Children. (2015) *Early Language Development and Children's Primary School Attainment in English and Maths*. London: Save the Children

Scarborough, H. (2001) Connecting early language and literacy to later reading (dis)abilities: evidence, theory, and practice. In Neuman, S. and Dickinson, D. (eds.) *Handbook for Research in Early Literacy*. New York: Guilford Press

Schunk, D. (1981) Modeling and attributional effects on children's achievement: a self-efficacy analysis. *Journal of Educational Psychology*, 73:1, 93-105

Schunk, D., Hanson, A., and Cox, P. (1987) Peer-model attributes and children's achievement behaviors. *Journal of Educational Psychology*, 79, 54-61

Sealey, C. (2019) Three ways to teach vocabulary so it sticks. *Times Educational Supplement*, 17 February

Sharples, J., Slavin, R., Chambers, B. *et al.* (2011) *Effective Classroom Strategies for Closing the Gap in Educational Achievement for Children Living in Poverty, Including White Working-Class Boys*. London: C4EO

Sharples, J., Webster, R., and Blatchford, P. (2019) *Making Best Use of Teaching Assistants: Guidance Report*. London: Education Endowment Foundation

Sinclair, D., and Murray, L. (1998) Effects of postnatal depression on children's adjustment to school. *British Journal of Psychiatry*, 172, 58-63

Siraj-Blatchford, I., Sylva, K., Muttock, S. *et al.* (2002) *Researching Effective Pedagogy in the Early Years*. London: DfE

Sisk, V., Burgoyne, A., Sun, J. *et al.* (2018) To what extent and under which circumstances are growth mind-sets important to academic achievement? *Psychological Science*, 29

Smith, R., Purdon, S., Schneider, V. *et al.* (2009) *Early Education Pilot for Two Year Old Children Evaluation*. London: DfE

Snowling, M., Hayiou-Thomas, M., Nash, H. *et al.* (2020), Dyslexia and developmental language disorder: comorbid disorders with distinct effects on reading comprehension. *Journal of Child Psychology and Psychiatry*, 61, 672-680

Snowling, M., and Melby-Lervåg, M. (2016) Oral language deficits in familial dyslexia: a meta-analysis and review. *Psychological Bulletin*, 142:5, 498-545

Snowling, M., Nash, H., Gooch, D. *et al.* (2019) Developmental outcomes for children at high risk of dyslexia and children with developmental language disorder. *Child Development*, 90:5, 548-564

Sobel, D. (2015) Creative uses of the Pupil Premium. *Headteacher Update*, 10 June

Sobel, D. (2020) Presentation to National Pupil Premium Conference, 10 December

Social Market Foundation. (2016) *Family Matters: The Role of Parents in Children's Educational Attainment*. London: Social Market Foundation

Spencer, S., Clegg, J., Stackhouse, J. et al. (2017) Contribution of spoken language and socio-economic background to adolescents' educational achievement at age 16 years. *International Journal of Language and Communication Disorders*, 52:2

Strand, S. (2014) Ethnicity, gender, social class and achievement gaps at age 16: intersectionality and 'getting it' for the white working class. *Research Papers in Education*, 29:2, 131–171

Styles, B., and Bradshaw, S. (2015) *Talk for Literacy: Evaluation Report and Executive Summary*. London: Education Endowment Foundation

Sutton, R. (2018) *Pupil Premium Accountability: How to Embed Positive Discrimination* https://my.optimus-education.com/pupil-premium-accountability-how-embed-positive-discrimination

Sutton Trust. (2011) *Improving the Impact of Teachers on Pupil Achievement in the UK*. London: Sutton Trust

Sylva, K., Melhuish, E., Sammons, P. et al. (eds.) (2010) *Early Childhood Matters: Evidence from the Effective Pre-School and Primary Education Project*. London: Routledge

Sylva, K., Stein, A., Leach, P. et al. (2011) Effects of early child-care on cognition, language, and task-related behaviours at 18 months: an English study. *British Journal of Developmental Psychology*, 29:1, 18–45

Tall, S. (2019) *Ten Key Lessons Learned in the EEF's First 7 Years*. London: Education Endowment Foundation

Tanner, E., Brown, A., Day, N. et al. (2011) *Evaluation of Every Child a Reader*. London: DfE

Tassoni, P. (2016) *Reducing Educational Disadvantage*. London: Bloomsbury

Taylor, R., Oberle, E., Durlak, J. et al. (2017) Promoting positive youth development through school-based social and emotional learning interventions: a meta-analysis of follow-up effects. *Child Development*, 88:4, 1156–1171

Teach First. (2019) *GCSE Subjects Reveal Stark Unfairness Faced by Disadvantaged Pupils* www.teachfirst.org.uk/press-release/New-investigation-into-GCSE-subjects-reveals-the-stark-extent-that-disadvantaged-pupils-are-being-left-behind

Tenenbaum, H., Winstone, N., Leman, P. et al. (2019) How effective is peer interaction in facilitating learning? A meta-analysis. *Journal of Educational Psychology* https://doi.org/10.1037/edu0000436

Thomson, D. (2020) The GCSE Attainment of black Caribbean pupils is falling. *FFT Education Datalab* https://ffteducationdatalab.org.uk/2020/10/the-gcse-attainment-of-black-caribbean-pupils-is-falling/

Tomova, B., von Dawans, B., Heinrichs, M. et al. (2014) Is stress affecting our ability to tune into others? Evidence for gender differences in the effects of stress on self-other distinction. *Psychoneuroendocrinology*, 43, 95–104

Torgerson, C., Bell, K., Coleman, E. (2018) *Tutor Trust: Affordable Primary Tuition. Evaluation Report and Executive Summary*. London: Education Endowment Foundation

Torgerson, C., Torgerson, D., Ainsworth, H. et al. (2018) *Calderdale Excellence Partnership: IPEELL Evaluation*. London: Education Endowment Foundation

Torgerson, D., Torgerson, C., Ainsworth, H. et al. (2014) *Improving Writing Quality: Evaluation Report and Executive Summary*. London: Educational Endowment Foundation

Tyner, A., and Kabourek, S. (2020) *Social Studies Instruction and Reading Comprehension: Evidence from the Early Childhood Longitudinal Study*. Washington, DC: Thomas B. Fordham Institute

Travers, M. (2017a) *White Working-Class Boys: Teachers Matter*. London: Trentham Books

Travers, M. (2017b) Streaming dampens the aspirations of white working-class boys. *Schools Week*, 2 July

Trundley, R., Wreghitt, C., Edginton, H. *et al.* (2017) *Supporting Children to Be Active and Influential Participants in Mathematics Lessons Through Effective Use of Assigning Competence and Pre-Teaching*. Devon: Babcock LDP

Vallotton, C., and Ayoub, C. (2011) Use your words: the role of language in the development of toddlers' self-regulation. *Early Childhood Research Quarterly*, 26:2, 169–181

van Poortvliet, M., Axford, N., and Lloyd, J. (2018) *Working with Parents to Support Children's Learning*. London: Education Endowment Foundation

van Poortvliet, M., Clarke, A., and Gross, J. (2019) *Improving Social and Emotional Learning in Primary Schools*. London: Education Endowment Foundation

Vilenius-Tuohimaa, P., Aunola, K., and Nurmi, J. (2008) The association between mathematical word problems and reading comprehension. *Educational Psychology*, 28:4, 409–426

Waldfogel, J., and Washbrook, E. (2010) *Low Income and Early Cognitive Development in the UK*. London: Sutton Trust

Watson, S. (2018) Educating the working class. In Gilbert, I. (ed.) *The Working Class*. Carmarthen: Independent Thinking Press

Webster, R. (2020) Beware the intervention trap. *Times Educational Supplement*, 11 September

Weissberg, R., Durlak, J., Domitrovich, C. *et al.* (2015) Social and emotional learning: past, present, and future. In Durlak, J. Domitrovich, C. Weissberg, R. *et al.* (eds.) *Handbook of Social and Emotional Learning: Research and Practice*. New York: The Guilford Press

Westbrook, J., Sutherland, J., Oakhill, J. *et al.* (2019) 'Just reading': the impact of a faster pace of reading narratives on the comprehension of poorer adolescent readers in English classrooms. *Literacy*, 53:2

Wheldall, K., and Limbrick, L. (2010) Do more boys than girls have reading problems? *Journal of Learning Disabilities*, 43, 418–429

Whitehead, U. (2007) African-American students' perceptions of teacher attitudes on academic achievement and discipline sanctions. *ProQuest Information and Learning*, 68

Whiteside, K., Gooch, D., and Norbury, C. (2016) English language proficiency and early school attainment among children learning English as an additional language. *Child Development*. doi:10.1111/cdev.12615

Whybra, L., Warner, G., Bjornstad, G. *et al.* (2018) The effectiveness of Chance UK's mentoring programme in improving behavioural and emotional outcomes in primary school children with behavioural difficulties. *BMC Psychology*, 6:9

Williams, P. (2008) *Independent Review of Mathematics Teaching in Early Years Settings and Primary Schools*. London: DCSF

Wilson, R., Shenhav, A., Straccia, M. *et al.* (2019) The eighty five percent rule for optimal learning. *Nat Commun.*, 10, 4646

Wlodkowski, R. (1983) *Motivational Opportunities for Successful Teaching*. Phoenix, AZ: Universal Dimensions

Yeager, D., Hanselman, P., Walton, G. *et al.* (2019) A national experiment reveals where a growth mindset improves achievement. *Nature*, 573, 364–369

Zimmerman, B. and Kitsantas, A. (1997) Developmental phases in self-regulation: shifting from process goals to outcome goals. *Journal of Educational Psychology*, 89:1, 29–36

INDEX

Page numbers in *italics* indicate a figure and page numbers in **bold** indicate a table on the corresponding page.

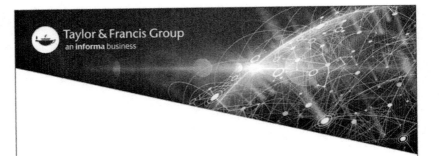

Printed in Great Britain
by Amazon

80987956R00154